T0320808

Accounting for the Fall of Silver

Accounting for the Fall of Silver

Hedging Currency Risk in Long-Distance Trade with Asia, 1870–1913

MICHAEL SCHILTZ

OXFORD
UNIVERSITY PRESS

OXFORD
UNIVERSITY PRESS

Great Clarendon Street, Oxford, OX2 6DP,
United Kingdom

Oxford University Press is a department of the University of Oxford.
It furthers the University's objective of excellence in research, scholarship,
and education by publishing worldwide. Oxford is a registered trade mark of
Oxford University Press in the UK and in certain other countries

Published in the United States of America by Oxford University Press
198 Madison Avenue, New York, NY 10016, United States of America

British Library Cataloguing in Publication Data
Data available

Library of Congress Control Number: 2020937377

ISBN 978-0-19-886502-5

Printed and bound by
CPI Group (UK) Ltd, Croydon, CR0 4YY

This book is dedicated to my son, Yukinari Kaoru, for the jazz and the math ($\sqrt{-1}$), for all our hilarious and profound conversations, and for the many hours of unadulterated friendship.

Preface and Acknowledgements

With the conclusion of the Franco-Prussian War of 1870–1, the world stood, unbeknownst to itself, on the doorstep of a massive monetary revolution. Germany's decision to adopt the gold standard and, in particular, France's determination to obstruct the latter by suspending silver coinage knocked the bottom out of the silver price. Whereas many contemporaries were led to believe this would be a one-off event—after all, the relationship between gold and silver had long turned out to be remarkably stable—nothing was further from the truth. Decisions made in Paris sent ripples of unrest through international capital markets and policy circles. In turn, these led to a series of international conferences desperately seeking to reverse the tide. They were to no avail. The white metal's continuous depression set off a process known as the 'scramble for gold'. At the end of the nineteenth century, the gold standard would become the first international monetary regime in history.

Thousands of kilometers away, in North- and South-East Asia, the consequences were equally profound. Silver instability upset, among others, the established realities of the trade between East and West, not in the least for those in charge of financing trade: the international banks. How some of them coped, and others did not, is the story of this book. Using evidence from contemporary financial journalism, accounting manuals, and the surviving records of the third biggest exchange bank before World War II, we detail the convoluted process that led to innovation in both financial products and bank management. Taken together, they enabled a small club of institutions to cement their position in the region and emerge as formidable players, some of which remain until today.

As I like to think this to be the case of most research projects, this book has not been the result of a predestined trajectory within the field of financial history; it was born out of a curious combination of happenstance on the one hand, and preparation on the other. Happenstance turned out to be a cursory invitation by Marc Flandreau to join him and his colleagues for a semester at the Graduate Institute in Geneva in the autumn of 2014. During a series of discussions, Marc convinced me to work on a book project on the Yokohama Specie Bank (YSB). I took his advice and basically sat down, abandoning my earlier plan to write several journal articles. The end result is, as we will see, not so much a banking history as a history of financial contracts and managerial technologies. Nevertheless, the environment must have been conducive to academic work: in the course of a few months, I had finished more than half of what the reader now has in his or her hands.

Then, for the 'preparation' part. The role of exchange banks (or 'international banks') in Asia had been a longstanding topic of interest of mine. I had become fascinated by their activities in Asia when working on my earlier book project on Japanese money doctoring in the region (2012). I had started collecting histories of these institutions and banking paraphernalia, yet I soon found myself frustrated by the little scholarly information that was out there. Although the likes of HSBC, Standard Chartered, and others have clearly been of overarching importance in linking the nineteeth-century Asian periphery to the money markets of Western Europe, their company-sponsored histories are overwhelmingly dominated by biographical material. Exchange banking *practice* has seldom, if at all, been a topic of attention. In most instances, it is referred to as too technical; in one instance, it is explicitly singled out as too 'dry and dull' to be interesting to the reader (Henry, 1963, p. viii). From the outset, it was clear that accounting procedures, bill workflows, etc., would have to be reconstructed in an almost archeological fashion. First and foremost, I would have to locate the site for my mental excavations.

A professional move to the Institute for Advanced Studies on Asia (IASA) of the University of Tokyo did exactly that. It got me directly involved in the history of exchange banking, in a very personal way. In the aftermath of the bursting of Japan's bubble and consequent mega-bank mergers, the archives of the then defunct Yokohama Specie Bank, the third biggest exchange bank before World War II, had been moved to the University of Tokyo, where they were (and still are) kept at the Resources and Historical Collections Office or *shiryōshitsu* 資料室 of the Library of the Faculty of Economics. After a few talks with its then curator, Professor Takeda Haruhito 武田晴人, it was agreed that I could play a part in the microfilming of the archives.

This encounter was instrumental. As banking historians will know, the archives of exchange banks are remarkably difficult to come by. In several cases, their archives were destroyed at the time of their liquidation (the Oriental Bank Corporation, the Comptoir d'Escompte de Paris, etc.). Others suffered during wartime (large swaths of the archives of HSBC are believed to have been destroyed at the time of the Japanese occupation of Shanghai in World War II). And yet, here were the mostly unscathed archives of a major exchange bank. Not only were its accounting data surprisingly complete; from correspondence and grey literature, it was possible to extract valuable clues concerning the relationship between head office and branches, foreign exchange dealings, exchange positions, and so on.

Hereafter, happenstance and preparation stubbornly appeared in an intertwined fashion. Much-thanked flexibility on the side of the executive agency of the European Research Council (ERC) allowed me to use 'Starting Grant' money for microfilming (ERC grant 240854). Proverbial Japanese generosity and hospitality did the rest. Dr Kojima Hiroyuki 小島浩之 and the outstanding staff of the *shiryōshitsu* (Yano Masataka 矢野正隆, Moriwaki Yūki 森脇優紀, Uchida Marina 内田麻里奈) granted me exclusive access to the—massive— primary materials (the archives themselves have been closed to the general public in view of their preservation) in the cosy and convenient reading room (*etsuranshitsu* 閲覧室). This, in turn, greatly aided the completion of my database of the bank's balance sheets and flow data. Seen in hindsight, the task I had set for myself was rather enormous, and, what was more, I was at the time still unaware of the gems I was to discover. The many hours used for hammering away data in spreadsheets were, thanks to *shiryōshitsu* personnel, neither wasted nor spent uncomfortably. If anything, it reminds one to remain humble when presenting what is, ultimately, only and literally the 'end-product' of one's research.

I am inclined to think that, at the general academic level too, the project has profited from something that can only be regarded as 'luck'. This certainly transcends the micro-level of personal interaction, and the all too human-centered sphere of niceties and services academics are supposed to do for one another. I fondly remember the many times I discussed with my close friend Fujioka Hiroshi and the students in our 'Mindhacks' seminar, how the arrival of the Internet and a host of digital tools had transformed the many ways I chose to approach the historical material from which springs this book. Nowadays, the python-language and services as plotly[1] (based on the d3js library) do not only make it possible to create graphs and drawings that are both precise and aesthetically pleasing; they also allow portability and transparency through code-sharing. I have found myself an avid user. Other academic trends have had an equally profound impact. Interested readers will find that Fig**Share**[2] has made it possible for them to engage with the data behind my findings in ways that I have not thought of and, more importantly, without having to go through the trouble of entering the data themselves. They are also warmly invited to explore the research logbooks on GitHub.[3]

---

[1] https://plot.ly/plot   [2] https://figshare.com/projects/Yokohama_Specie_Bank___/2173
[3] https://github.com/michaelschiltz/even-keel

Recent advances in network theory and the development of corollary software packages have, for obvious reasons, been enormously helpful. The greatly enhanced searchability of several online databases enabled the exploration of a level of granularity that would be very hard to replicate in the setting of the traditional archive. I think in particular of collections contained within the Internet Archive and HathiTrust, *The Economist Historical Archive*; the *Financial Times Historical Archive*; the *North China Herald*; the Kobe University *Historical Newspaper Clippings Collection*;[4] the *Japan Center for Asian Records Database*;[5] and the National Diet Library *Digital Library from the Meiji Era*.[6]

Of course, there have also been people, many people. Without them, this research, or large parts of it, would be unthinkable. The bulk of this research was conducted in Japan. I have profited most from the excellent research facilities at the University of Tokyo. At the IASA, I have learned a lot from Fujioka Hiroshi 藤岡洋 and Yasutomi Ayumu 安冨歩. Nokubo Masatsugu 野久保雅嗣 was so kind as to provide preservation grade photographs of several rare primary materials. The Faculty of Economics hosted and still hosts several outstanding researchers whose remarks have shaped several chapters. I am grateful to emeriti Itō Masanao 伊藤正直, Namikata Shōichi 波形昭一, Sugihara Kaoru 杉原薫, and Takeda Haruhito 武田晴人. As indicated above, the latter deserves extra mention for granting access to the YSB archives. Okazaki Tetsuji 岡崎哲二 and Shiroyama Tomoko 城山智子 were supportive of the project from its very start; equally important, they remain great friends.

At the Bank of Japan, I thank Hatase Mariko 畑瀬真理子 and Ohnuki Mari 大貫摩里. At the risk of forgetting somebody, I stress my indebtedness to: Shizume Masato 鎮目雅人 and Yago Kazuhiko 矢後和彦, both at Waseda University; Saitō Hisahiko 齊藤壽彦 (Chiba University of Commerce); Hisadome Shin'ichi 久留信一 (Tokyo Shinbun); Taira Tomoyuki 平智之, for early conversations on YSB; Petr Matous, for his knowledge of social network analysis. Kobayashi Atsushi 小林篤史 is thanked for his enthusiastic willingness to build on my and his findings and develop a project encompassing all exchange banks. Very special thanks go to Suzuki Toshio 鈴木敏夫, whose research style has always been an enormous inspiration. I felt very honored and humbled when, on a very pleasant evening of *sake*-sampling in December

[4] http://www.lib.kobe-u.ac.jp/sinbun/index.html   [5] http://www.jacar.go.jp/
[6] http://kindai.ndl.go.jp/

2017, he disclosed to me that he thought the findings in this book were compelling, and its reasoning was sound. Of course, the usual disclaimers apply.

In Europe and the United States, a tightly knit network of like-minded financial historians took the project beyond its Asian contours. I thank (in alphabetical order): Olivier Accominotti, Simon Bytheway, Vincent Bignon, Rui Esteves, Juan Flores, Gabriel Geisler Mesevage, Mark Metzler, Ghassan Moazzin, Kim Oosterlinck, Pierre Pénet, Samuel Segura Cobos, Richard Smethurst, and Stefano Ugolini.

I also thank many friends: Rob Leurentop, for the delightful nonsense and the never-ending music; Ju-Ling Lee, Georges Depeyrot, Hans Coppens, Fred Truyen, the always friendly and happy microfilming crew from Nichimy ニチマイ (Hirooka Jun 廣岡潤, Kudō Hajime 工藤元, Endō Yoshiyuki 遠藤 美行), Yves Corpataux, Marc Le Hénanf, Guillaume Pasquier, and several members of the Graduate Institute Department of International History. Thanks to them, it was a pleasure to arrange and document the *Capital Markets of the World* collection.

It is a pleasure also to thank, for their professionalism, the whole Oxford UP team: Adam Swallow, commissioning editor; Sophie Robinson and Jenny Nugee, Assistant Commissioning editors; Sinduja Abirami, Project Manager; and others whose names and functions I do not know but who played a part in making this book what it is.

One last remark concerns the deepest inspiration for the project. As some of my immediate colleagues may know, I have always been very fond of the works of Leslie Presnell, which seem to have been largely forgotten now, and those of Nishimura Shizuya 西村閑也 (not accidentally a student of the former). If anything, the nascent revolution in data science vindicates their embrace of data granularity, and corroborates their stress on the relevance of contemporary problem consciousness, without which the data could hardly make sense. This approach was especially helpful when digging into the early history of the YSB, as some of its early archives were presumably lost in the Great Kantō earthquake of 1923. I hope that, if my work can in one way or another be considered successful, it will manage to renew interest in defining the historian's work as a forensic endeavor, shunning neither quantitative or qualitative evidence. Obviously, it is for the reader to decide whether my approach was helpful in elucidating a long-forgotten episode in the history of global trade.

Contents

Nomenclature, Conventions, and Currency

Table 0.01. YSB branches: Japanese/Chinese originals or transcriptions into Japanese, pronunciation, contemporary rendering, and their current equivalents

Japanese/ Chinese original	Transcription	Contemporary nomenclature	Current
横浜	Yokohama	Yokohama	Yokohama
東京	Tōkyō	Tōkyō	Tōkyō
神戸	Kōbe	Kōbe	Kōbe
大阪	Ōsaka	Ōsaka	Ōsaka
長崎	Nagasaki	Nagasaki	Nagasaki
倫動・[倫敦]	Rondon	London	London
里昂	Riyon	Lyons	Lyon
紐育	Nyūyōku	New York	New York
桑港 (an abbreviation of 桑方西斯哥)	San Furanshisukō	San Francisco	San Francisco
布哇	Hawai	Hawaii	Hawaii
孟買		Bombay	Mumbai
香港		Hong Kong	Hongkong
上海		Shanghai	Shanghai
漢口		Hankow	Hankou
芝罘		Chefoo	Zhifu (Yantai 烟台)
天津		Tientsin	Tianjin
北京		Peking	Beijing
牛莊		Newchwang	Yingkou 营口
大連		Dairen	Dalian
旅順		Ryojun (Port Arthur)	Lüshun
安東		Antung	Dandong (丹东)
遼陽		Liaoyang	Liaoyang
奉天		Mukden	Shenyang 沈阳
鐵嶺		Tie-ling	Tieling
長春		Changchun	Changchun

Source: Table created by the author, after Yokohama Specie Bank mid-term reports (multiple issues)

Table 0.02. List of abbreviations used throughout the text, their Western original, and transcriptions into Chinese and Japanese

Abbreviation	Original	Chinese	Japanese
CEP	Comptoir d'Escompte de Paris	法蘭西銀行	パリ割引銀行
CBIAC	Chartered Bank of India, Australia and China	渣打銀行	チャータード銀行
CMB	Chartered Mercantile Bank of India, London and China	有利銀行	チャータード・マーカンタイル銀行
DAB	Deutsch-Asiatische Bank	徳華銀行	独亜銀行
HSBC	Hongkong and Shanghai Banking Corporation	滙豐銀行	香港上海銀行
IBC	International Banking Corporation	花旗銀行	インターナショナル・バンキング・コーポレーション
OBC	Oriental Bank Corporation	東藩滙理銀行	東洋銀行
RCB	Russo-Chinese Bank (from 1910: Russo-Asiatic Bank)	華俄銀行 (俄亞銀行)	露清銀行
YSB	Yokohama Specie Bank	橫濱正金銀行	橫濱正金銀行

Sources: Table created by the author after Sano (1905) and Ishii (1999)

1. A Note on Sources and Conventions

Some remarks are in order with respect to linguistic conventions. For romanization of Japanese terms, I have used the revised Hepburn system: this mainly means that I have not rendered *n* into *m* before labial consonants, but stuck to *n* instead (thus *Asahi shinbun* rather than *Asahi shimbun*). Names familiar to English-speaking readers are presented 'as known'; so 'Tokyo' is used, rather than the linguistically more correct 'Tōkyō'. Names of Japanese people are given in the Japanese order (family name followed by given name, e.g., Takahashi Korekiyo) unless bibliographic references are being given to works in the English language in which case the name appears in the Western order. Sometimes the readings of Japanese names are various. I chose to include the reading that is most common in Japanese sources. Chinese terms and names are referred to in their nineteenth-century transcription (e.g., Tientsin) as well as in *pinyin*, but with tonal marks omitted (thus: Tianjin). In all cases, however, I again make an exception for bibliographic references to works in the English language in which names appear differently, or when the author himself or herself prefers a different transcription. Hence, we transcribe

松岡孝児 as 'Matsuoka Kôji' (and not as 'Matsuoka Kōji'), as it is the transcription preferred in the case of his work in French.

2. Currencies

This book uses both common symbols and their transcriptions to refer to respective currencies. '$' refers to US dollars, '£' or 'GBP' to the British pound, 'FF' to French francs, and '¥' or 'JPY' to the Japanese yen. The Indian rupee is referred to as '₨'; 'HK$' are Hong Kong dollars, 'CH¥' are Chinese yuan, and 'M¥' are Manchurian yen. In Japanese and Chinese, the latter was expressed as '圓', in order to distinguish it from the 'domestic yen' (円) in the home country or *naichi*.

Under their gold parities:

£1 = $4.8669 = ¥9.763
$1 = £0.2054 = ¥2.006
¥1 = £0.1024= $0.4985

As a rule of thumb and for his or her convenience, the reader may take $1 as equal to ¥2; related, £1 = ¥10 (or $5). Note that the pre-war British pound was not decimal. The pound (£) was divided into 20 shillings (s) and each shilling into 12 pence (d, from the Latin *denario*), making 240 pence to the pound—hence the so-called £-s-d system. Various coin denominations had, and in some cases continue to have, special names—such as *crown* (5/-, i.e., 5 shillings), *farthing* (a quarter of a penny), *sovereign* (£1), and *guinea* (a coin of approximately one-quarter ounce of gold).

The exchange rates of silver currencies were, at least in the period after 1873, highly volatile. For our calculations, we rely on the data of exchange rates for so-called demand drafts (*sanchaku barai* 参着払い, i.e., bills of exchange paid in the foreign currency upon presentation at the place of payment), as recorded in the 'Reference Book of Financial Matters' of the Financial Bureau of the Ministry of Finance (Ōkurashō, 1994), and nowadays maintained online by the Institute for Monetary and Economic Studies of the Bank of Japan.[1]

---

[1] 「歴史統計：日本銀行金融研究所」 n.d. Accessed November 28, 2017. http://www.imes.boj.or.jp/hstat/data/ferdd/index.html

3. The Chinese Monetary System

I am aware that the Chinese monetary system around 1900, an increase in scholarly publications notwithstanding, is still largely a mystery to economic historians. Put simply, the system was largely bimetallic: copper coins were mostly used for smaller retail transactions, whereas silver served other, primarily mercantile, purposes. In the following chapters, all transactions described are in silver currency; as far as I can see, copper coinage did not play a role in the accounts of exchange banks.

Complicating matters, monetary silver in China took the forms of (1) bullion silver (ingots, often differentiated by means of their form) and (2) dollar coins. When the bank ledgers mention *taels* (Ch. *liang* 両), they refer to an asset or liability to be received or paid out in bullion silver, that is, an amount of silver of a designated *weight*, on the one hand, and of a certain *fineness*, on the other. When they mention a dollar unit of account, they expected a certain number of dollar coins, particular to a certain market, to be paid in or paid out.

This being said, the definitions of both *tael* and silver dollar were not standardized, that is, they differed according to region and custom.[2] As a rule of thumb, the silver *tael* weighed around 40 grams (1.3 ozt). However, the most common government measure was the Kuping (庫平; *kuping*; 'treasury standard') *tael*, which weighed 37.5 grams (1.21 ozt). A common commercial weight, the Caoping (漕平; *caoping*; 'canal shipping standard') *tael* weighed 36.7 grams (1.18 ozt) of marginally less pure silver. Exchange bankers had to reckon with local *tael* varieties, which took precedence over any central measure. In typical examples: the Canton *tael* weighed 37.5 grams, the Convention or Shanghai *tael* was 33.9 g (1.09 ozt), and the Haiguan (海關) or 'customs' *tael* 37.8 grams (1.3334 oz; 1.2153 ozt). For readers interested in a comprehensive discussion of types of silver dollars, I refer to the research of François Thierry (2017).[3]

With respect to the way in which foreign banks interacted with indigenous credit institutions through local credit instruments, the research of Nishimura Shizuya remains monumental (Nishimura, 2005).

---

[2] This considerably confused contemporary foreign merchants and observers. Compare, for instance, with Williams (1897).

[3] Contemporary publications with continuing relevance include: Vissering (1877); Edkins (1901); Wagel (1915).

List of Figures and Tables

Figures

Tables

דעלעטלעוו טימ טלעוו אַ ןפֿאַשאַב טאָה טאָג

Got hot bashafn a velt mit veltelekh.

[God created a world full of small worlds]

(Yiddish proverb)

1

Introduction

Liquidity, Hard and Soft Currencies, and Trade Finance

1. Introduction

The findings presented in this book have started out from the intuition that the adoption of certain economic policies, the creation of specific financial institutions and their success are, to a large degree, a function of one's relative position within the fabric of the international system. More precisely, we infer that, if the international system is differentiated along the lines of center and periphery, there should be concrete evidence of the latter in the way countries with a different position choose to cope with sets of more or less identical challenges.[1]

This may seem self-evident to most readers, and we too believe it should be a central element in any formal analysis. This being said, only a limited segment of literature in financial history appears to agree. A casual look at most available analyses demonstrates that most are *not* aimed at understanding institutions within their specific historical and social context. Instead, the crux of the analysis is with measuring the effects of, for instance, a fiscal or monetary policy change, 'all else being equal' (*ceteris paribus*).

Whereas it is far from our intention to criticize the discipline for this predilection, we consider it important to stress this book has had a very different inspiration. In the following, the structure and hierarchy of the world system are taken seriously. Concretely, we will study the disadvantageous position of a group of peripheral currencies in late nineteenth-century Asia; and we document the efforts by (European and Japanese) exchange bankers to boost these currencies' liquidity, in order to guarantee their viability for functioning as vehicles for financing intra-Asian trade in the period. If anything, they proved to be highly inventive. We will witness experiments with financial

---

[1] One may, for instance, think of differences in gold standard management between Great Britain and Argentina in the period before World War I. See Ford (1983).

Accounting for the Fall of Silver: Hedging Currency Risk in Long-Distance Trade with Asia, 1870–1913.
Michael Schiltz, Oxford University Press (2020). © Michael Schiltz.
DOI: 10.1093/oso/9780198865025.001.0001

contracts related to bill finance; the development of a strategy to hedge exchange risk vis-à-vis the hard currencies at the time; and Japanese attempts at creating hard currency status for the yen by aggressively capturing market share for its semi-national exchange bank, the Yokohama Specie Bank (YSB).

This attention to socio-historical contingency has had its methodological ramifications. When possible, but especially in Chapters 3 and 4, the discussion proceeds in an archeological or 'forensic' way. Concretely, this means that data were not to be extracted from their historical and material environments, but have been introduced *as they were gathered, structured, and formulated within their respective historical context.* This goes well beyond the traditional distinction between quantitative and qualitative research and may, possibly ironically, have only reinforced the concern with quantitative information. Due attention to so-called documentary evidence has helped to ensure that the questions being asked were also relevant to the subjects of our inquiry, that is, nineteenth-century exchange bankers and monetary policymakers. We considered their concerns with the geography of the world system at the time as the validation of the 'structuralist' network theoretical intuitions that underlie much of the analyses and conclusions presented here.

2. Center and Periphery in the Literature

Obviously, this book is not the first to draw attention to the asymmetric nature of the global monetary system. Economic historians have repeatedly discovered the unequal opportunities stemming from a world that has been differentiated along the categories center and periphery. Although it would be an enormous, indeed impossible, task to review all related literature, it is nevertheless instructive to highlight several of the most representative ones.

Incidentally or not, two seminal papers appeared in immediate succession at the end of the 1960s. First, there has been Kindleberger's exploration of similarities between international money and world language (Kindleberger, 1967). Factually a reply to international criticism of the post-World War II dollar standard as a nationalist or imperialist device, Kindleberger points out that there is a dimension to the debate that transcends mere political choice. For reasons that are to be explored later,

> International currencies are not all of equal value as units of account, standards of deferred payment, and media of exchange. They stand in relationship

to one another not as full equals, but in a hierarchical arrangement of ascending utility as international money.   (Kindleberger, 1967, p. 4)

Some are more likely to be used as a unit of account and/or medium of exchange, yet the latter is defined by transaction costs, and not political choice or agency.

Currency prestige cannot be willed into being but is largely a function of a currency's degree of circulation. It is, in other words, a function of what we would now refer to as a network effect: the degree to which it is accepted *by others* drives down transaction and information costs, thereby propelling and bolstering its acceptance. Put differently, what is behind the emergence of one or a limited number of key currencies is 'the ordinary search of the world for shortcuts in getting things done' (Kindleberger, 1967, p. 10). Admittedly, Kindleberger's remarks were formulated in the historically narrow context of the dollar standard, but we highlight them because of their theoretical importance. Later in this chapter, we will come back to Kindleberger's analogy, and due attention towards market share—the 'politics of world language' in shaping the pecking order of the international monetary system.

Twelve years later, in 1979, the French historian Fernand Braudel addressed a similar dynamic in the context of the early development of capitalism (Braudel, 1979), a topic much closer to our discussion. Admittedly devoid of the East-West or North-South divide that has become the focus of later literature, Braudel identifies the very structure of early capitalist societies in terms of core vs. periphery. From his description, early capitalism was a club for the happy few that carefully discriminated against those without a membership card. For the members of the club, capital formation was not only possible but significant; outsiders, on the other hand, were completely choked off from the means and technologies that enabled wealth creation. Braudel has picked his metaphors carefully. Capitalism, in his words, can be likened to a cyst (a 'bell jar') within the larger societal organism. In a developmental perspective, we may refer to the co-development of its parts according to different velocities.

Braudel's metaphor has had considerable bearing upon modern development economics. It has, for instance, been reiterated in the work of Hernando de Soto (2000), who dubbed it the 'mystery of capital', and takes it to be symptomatic of today's financial system. Indeed, many countries have tried to tap into the liquidity of the global capital centers, but the results have been mixed. For some, access to international capital has been hampered by plenty of impediments, from high-interest rates to conditionalities attached to loans and so on.

De Soto's take has, in turn, been popularized as the notion of 'original sin' (Eichengreen et al., 2002, 2003, 2007; Hausmann and Panizza, 2003, 2011; Panizza, 2006). Put simply, original sin refers to the difficulty or outright impossibility of certain nations to borrow in their own currency. This spurs the adoption of macroeconomic policies (a peg with a core currency, for instance) that may alleviate problems related to debt servicing (in the above example, by eliminating exchange risk), yet nevertheless entail a considerable cost and therefore enshrine these countries' financial vulnerability. The dynamics of original sin have come to be understood relatively well. However, its authors do not provide the determinants of the latter. What are the drivers behind the differences in financial solidity and prestige?

3. The Geography of the International Monetary System, 1890–1910

The empirical investigation of the monetary geography of modern capitalism has been a much more recent undertaking. In a series of papers, Marc Flandreau and Clemens Jobst do not only attempt (1) to reconstruct monetary relationships around the turn of the twentieth century (2005), but (2) also try to explain *why* it evolved in the ways it did (2009). Here, we are not so much concerned with the description of the monetary geography of the period. As can be expected, there are not that many surprises here. Flandreau and Jobst confirm the existence of a pyramid-like hierarchy of monetary status, with the British pound as the obvious champion, closely followed by the French franc and German Mark. A secondary layer is occupied by the currencies from (mostly) neighboring countries (Belgian franc, Dutch guilder, and so on). Although not as central as the aforementioned key currencies (Lindert, 1969), these are nevertheless highly liquid, which can partially be explained by their proximity to the large European money markets; the United States dollar is the only, albeit an important, exception here. Currencies composing the broad base of the pyramid are from countries that, among themselves, may have very different geographical locations, yet are united in their remoteness from the core currency countries. This basket comprises the currencies from Southern American, African, and Asian countries.

For now, we are mostly interested in their analysis of the determinants behind the formation of this pyramid-like structure. Clearly informed by

Kindleberger's conjectures, they draw heavily on transaction-costs literature (Kiyotaki and Wright, 1993; Matsuyama et al., 1993) to explain the emergence of monetary leadership. The intuition is straightforward: transaction costs are bound to produce network effects and, by extension, persistence. One may think about it in the following way. When economic actors find themselves in a multi-currency world, they have an incentive to choose the currency that will entail the smallest difference between the price at which it can be obtained and the price at which it can be sold (the so-called 'bid-ask spread', a proxy for a currency's liquidity). As argued by Kindleberger, the main determinant of the latter is market size, or, by definition, a function of the choice of others to be willing to hold that same currency. The latter is bound to produce network effects: the utility of a currency will increase with the degree to which it is adopted internationally. This does not need to imply the inevitable evolution towards one currency (although, in Kindleberger's thinking, that is what full efficiency implies),[2] but, empirically at least, it certainly means that 'the number of currencies used internationally is smaller than the number of existing currencies' (Flandreau and Jobst, 2009, p. 645). Put differently, the aforementioned pyramid is the structural expression of currency competition, the outcome of which translates into a crowding-out of lesser-liquid currencies to the advantage of more readily accepted 'vehicle' ones.[3]

Exploring the latter in an empirical way for the late nineteenth century is no sinecure, for the simple reason that bid-ask spread data are mostly unavailable. Flandreau and Jobst know this, yet have found an ingenious roundabout. They notice that the quotation of a currency in a foreign exchange market should be taken as an indication that (1) there is a sizeable or critical demand for that currency in the respective market and (2) that this demand is predicated upon its liquidity only and not some extraneous element as, for instance, the tyranny of distance. The latter is important: when bankers in a certain center did not draw on another center, it was not because they *could* not; it was rather because they *would* not. From this, it follows that the 'variable "quoted/not quoted" is therefore essentially an index of the bid-ask spread, and thus a measure of liquidity' (Flandreau and Jobst, 2005, p. 983). This does, among others, corroborate their mapping of monetary relationships in the period (cf. supra).

It also allows for the construction of a model. On the basis of the specification of both (a) economic *policy performance factors* (concretely, the gold standard

---

[2] In his own words: 'World efficiency is achieved when all countries learn the same second language' (1967, p. 9).

[3] For a game-theoretical exploration of the latter, see Matsuyama et al. (1993).

as a currency regime) and (b) *friction factors* (inventory costs, i.e., costs related to holding liabilities denominated in a currency), Flandreau and Jobst estimate the relationship between the availability of a quote on the one hand and the value it creates for its users, on the other. The findings are pertinent, and confirm the intuition of the transaction cost approach. They report that friction factors, in particular, turn out to perform well (Flandreau and Jobst, 2009, p. 650). Low short-term interest rates in the issuing country are consistently correlated with the probability of a currency being quoted internationally; geographical proximity and the existence of bilateral trade too are relatively reliable predictors of a currency's international circulation. Curiously, macroeconomic policy variables are *not* univocally strong determinants. In many cases, the adoption of the gold standard even turns out to be negatively correlated to monetary leadership. We will return to this issue in a minute.

For now, it is important to remember that liquidity and prestige are related in a way which logicians and graph theoreticians would identify as circular causality. Liquidity (expressed in the form of low short-term interest rates) is a strong determinant of monetary leadership, as historical research preempted long ago:[4] clearly, the fact that a currency can be bought and sold at prices with only a minimal differential makes it an obvious choice for all market participants. But causality also ran and runs the other way: '[i]nterest rates of leading currencies were lower because lots of agents were using them so that their currencies were more likely quoted abroad and this further strengthened their leadership' (Flandreau and Jobst, 2009, p. 653). Note thereby that this circularity is exactly the stickiness or persistence one would expect to be a characteristic of leading currencies. As Flandreau and Jobst do not fail to note, international monetary competition will lead to an equilibrium that *outlasts the equilibrium that would be warranted in case currency competition would be history-* (i.e., observer-) *free.*

Ranald Michie's explanation of the city of London's consistent preeminence as a global money market, including after the demise of Britain's empire, is a variation on this theme (2012). He speaks of centrifugal and centripetal forces that transcended the inner dynamics of the financial center. What made London thrive was mostly the choice of banks from around the world to go through the trouble of setting up branches there, and maintain correspondent

---

[4] This has been a tenet of a research strand set out by Nishimura Shizuya, and followed up by several of his colleagues (Nishimura, 1971). Suzuki Toshio has famously argued that it was the liquidity of the London money market in which Japanese policymakers wanted to tap (Suzuki, 1994, 2002).

relationships with London-based banks. At the end of the day, they begot most of the improvement of borrowing and lending facilities, the expansion of available funds, and ever newer facilities for employing them remuneratively (Michie, 2012, p. 18).[5] London's record was nowhere short of dazzling. Michie estimates that the annual turnover of bills in the City grew from £425 million in 1840 to a whopping £2,000 million in 1913. In that very year, two-thirds of the bills circulating there were on foreign account (Michie, 2012, p. 29).

It will be obvious that the emerging dollar (Eichengreen and Flandreau, 2009) and the city of New York faced considerable impediments when attempting to dethrone the British pound and the city of London from their position of privilege. The greenback carried the burden of its past relative illiquidity and had to gain momentum in order to catch up with and replace a former leading currency. Typically, only the catastrophic event that was World War I tilted the balance to its favor. As in the case of other emerging currencies, the aforementioned circularity thus operates with a time lag: popularity and status typically lag behind what the effective or 'real' liquidity might command at a certain time.[6]

4. The Peripheral Predicament

Our analysis, however, is not so much concerned with upcoming currencies as with those that have been left out as the result of international competition. Does the transaction cost approach, conversely, contain hints with respect to possible remedies for a low international ranking? Is it possible to hack liquidity concerns and boost prestige as an emerging or vehicle currency, or at least alleviate the symptoms of low liquidity, as there are: exchange risk premia, loan conditionality, and so on?

Authors working in the 'original sin' literature have tended to answer the above questions with a tentative 'yes'. The key, they argue, is the adoption of credible institutions. Admittedly, these have a price. The adoption of a peg to a core currency practiced by a wide range of (semi-) peripheral countries these days or its alternative, debt rationing, are second-best options. Defending the peg at the time of an economic downturn amounts to forsaking the possibility to dampen negative domestic effects by adjusting the exchange rate, for

---

[5] I have also benefited from recent research of Sarah Cochrane (2009).

[6] Flandreau and Jobst express this time-lag in terms of the 'liquidity schedule' and 'popularity schedule' that differentiate in the process of currency competition (Flandreau and Jobst, 2009, pp. 656–61).

instance; restrictive measures (the 'cold turkey' approach to foreign capital), on the other hand, can be detrimental to a country's growth, or may even invite outright recession in times of crisis. And yet, both the so-called 'fear-of-floating' and varieties of debt abstinence are believed to be sensible and may be effective. In the case of Chile, the latter has been described as a successful way of insuring against an acute drought of capital inflows in terms of crisis (a 'sudden stop') (Gallego and Hernández, 2003; Caballero et al., 2005; Eichengreen et al., 2007). It is widely, and rather paternalistically, cited as the one country that set itself apart from the Latin-American club of countries with 'weak institutions' (Izquierdo, 2002).

Historically, however, the evidence in favor of 'strong institutions' is much thinner. As already pointed out before, Flandreau and Jobst find that gold standard adoption was mostly negatively related to currency status; in other words, it was not that adopting the gold standard bought instant credibility. This is in tune with earlier findings. Gold standard adoption reportedly also played no significant role in a country's borrowing cost; it was a 'veil', a 'thin film' over other, deeper fundamentals, and its glitter did not suffice to lure the discerning investor (Flandreau and Zumer, 2004; Ferguson and Schularick, 2012).[7] In the Japanese case, country risk briefly jumped after gold standard adoption (1897): the country faced yields for its bond flotations that were *higher* than before the monetary reform effort, that is, when Japan was still on an assumedly less credible silver standard (Mitchener et al., 2010, p. 41). This would seem to lead to a few obvious questions. Why, given this evidence, would peripheral countries choose gold standard adoption in the first place? The answer to that has been hinted to earlier. Fixing the domestic currency to gold was painful, but floating could be deadly, as it most probably meant being choked off from the liquidity of the core capital markets that was prerequisite for the periphery's development.

And yet, this cannot be the whole story. We possess, for instance, evidence of widespread use of 'exchange clauses' that could be added to international bond issues (Flandreau and Sussman, 2005).[8] In principle, at least, this would make it possible for peripheral countries to float their domestic currencies and, at the same time, service their debt at an agreed rate, that is, in order not to alarm the risk-averse foreign investor, as contemporaries liked to describe it. So why would their proliferation go hand-in-hand with the practice of gold

---

[7]   Factually, this is a refutation of the older view that the gold standard functioned as a 'seal of approval' that provided the direly needed credibility (Bordo and Rockoff, 1996).

[8]   Apparently, the use of exchange clauses had originally been probed by the Rothschilds, but quickly proliferated.

pegging in the second half of the nineteenth century? Bordo and Flandreau put it more poignantly:

> Fully comprehending the logic of these gold clauses is a theoretical chal-lenge [...]. It is not clear, for instance, why investors should have preferred a lower exchange rate risk—but with a greater default risk when exchange rate crises occurred—to a higher exchange rate risk but a lower risk of default.
>
> (2005, p. 437)

We believe that the notion of passing on the cost of managing exchange risk to the issuing governments (pegging as a sort of insurance policy, i.e., a cost incurred in order to protect oneself against an uncertain loss)[9] provides potent clues. Although it seems counterintuitive, especially to people from the economics tradition, insurance is thus treated as equivalent to a *regulatory technology*, a way to *induce* risk-reducing behavior rather than the opposite. As has been argued by others (Ben-Shahar and Logue, 2012), the insurer (in this case, the underwriting institution or a proxy of the latter) must in this set-up be thought of as an entity doing the job of collecting and administering information about risk. Put simply, he or she had skin in the game. There existed clear incentives for standard setting and implementing safety regu-lations (e.g., through conditionalities as, in our case, macroeconomic prac-tices) because of competition. Especially for prestigious underwriters, the aim was to bring down borrowing costs for their customers across the board, for example by carefully guarding the nature of their clientele—in a very direct case, by refusing to insure—, differentiating risk premia and so on. Only thus can he or she guarantee the latter constant, and relative low-cost services. The insured, on the other hand, were incentivized against burning down the house, if they were to maintain access to a club of customers with low yielding debt.

Economic historians have realized the information-heavy duties of con-temporary underwriters. Although still overlooked or brushed aside in large swaths of the literature, monetary reform efforts in the periphery—not accidentally all at the end of the nineteenth century—were in many cases engineered or overseen by advisers from core countries. There exist, in other words, (semi-)colonial aspects to the latter (Flandreau, 2003). Late nineteenth- and early twentieth-century observers were aware of this but their analyses

---

[9]   For an analysis of the cost in the context of the adoption of the gold standard by Japan, see Schiltz (2012a).

were forgotten for many decades (Matsuoka, 1936, 1938); then their ideas had to be reinvented.

De Cecco was arguably the first to rediscover that the establishment of a British-led exchange standard in India was factually aimed at bolstering the imperial core (1975).[10] The finding sheds a rather different light on Keynes' dictum that the rupee was a 'gold note printed on silver' (Keynes, 1913, p. 37). Balachandran has argued along similar lines for the interwar period (1996). With regard to US money doctoring around 1900 and the establishment of the U.S. National Monetary Commission (1908), the evidence points to a similar rationale (Mitchell, 1911).[11] When discussing Japan, Metzler and Bytheway have made it very clear that the vision of the gold standard as an imperial device was shared by all the key policy players (Bytheway, 2005; Metzler, 2006; Bytheway and Metzler, 2016). And, recently, Schiltz demonstrated how a similar understanding of the gold standard by Japanese contemporaries was behind frantic attempts to set up yen-based gold exchange standard systems around North- and Southeast Asia (2012b).

Pointing out this imperialist dimension may seem a trivial addition to many, but is nevertheless crucial as it upsets a commonly held misunderstanding with respect to the relationship between gold(-exchange) standard adoption and integration into the world economy: '[F]ixed exchange rate regimes were not in the nineteenth century an instrument for financial integration .... [G]lobalization in the nineteenth century caused the adoption of the gold standard, rather than the other way round' (Bordo and Flandreau, 2003, pp. 424–6). Put yet differently, *the periphery had already been financially integrated,*[12] albeit not perfectly. The late nineteenth-century flurry with exchange rate regime choice and the consequent 'scramble for gold' are a *product* of globalization, an indication of its fostering, rather than the expression of the desire to become part of it.

5. The Bell Jar Revisited

This peculiar and important core-periphery dynamic is of relevance to yet another finding by Flandreau and Jobst, which bears directly upon all the following chapters.

---

[10]   Michie is more reserved: 'India was drawn into an imperial connection that strengthened the position of London as a financial centre' (Michie, 2012, p. 23).

[11]   Emily Rosenberg should be credited for her research into the history and development of dollar diplomacy (1985, 2003).

[12]   For an important example hereof in the Asian context, see Kobayashi (2019).

Their paper identifies the phenomenon as follows:

> [We find the existence of an] Asian subgroup within the periphery, consisting of China, Hong Kong, British India, Japan, and the Strait Settlements (Singapore). Although these countries are clearly peripheral in their relations with the key and the intermediate group, they differ from the other peripheral countries by being connected among themselves. This [...] marks a clear contrast to Latin America, Australasia, or the Balkans, which are exclusively oriented towards Europe.   (2005, p. 997)

Students of Asian history may see a more or less immediate parallel with a notion that is by now more or less accepted in the field. We will call it the Sugihara conjecture, after Sugihara Kaoru's original coining of the term (1985, 1996).[13] It refers to the fact that intra-Asian trade grew considerably in the period between 1800 and 1913 (i.e., long before the 1870s!), allegedly due to an impetus from the Industrial Revolution and the regime of colonial free trade.[14] Sugihara has furthermore noticed the peculiarities of the latter. Whereas African and Southern-American countries were turned into 'enclave-economies' that had linkages with the core yet not among each other, Asia had apparently developed a region-wide division of labor, and rich intra-regional linkages.

In later paragraphs, we will explore what is behind the apparent anomaly of peripheral currencies quoting each other. First, we should clear up the identity of the quoters.

6. The 'International Banks'

Is it possible that Flandreau and Jobst discovered the financial corollary (banks) of Sugihara's intra-Asian trade sphere? There are more than a few reasons to believe so. First and foremost, we know of a category of institutions that, since the early days of Western trade contacts with Northeast and Southeast Asia, were mandated with trade finance. These were the exchange banks, or, as referred to by Baster, the *international banks* (1935). Located in

---

[13] This has given rise to a school of Japanese economic historians looking into the phenomenon of a so-called Asian trade order, in which the role of mostly British capitalism is preeminent. References are too numerous to include.

[14] Due to the labor-intensive nature of production this Europe-Asia nexus caused, several authors have referred to it as an 'industrious revolution'. For a discussion of the history of the term, see Vries (2008, p. 78ff.).

the many port cities (Webster et al., 2015)[15] (Flandreau and Jobst grouped the exchange centers by country, which has the unfortunate effect of obfuscating the maritime location of major exchange centers in Asia), their business was broadly confined to:

- the sale, for local currency, of bank drafts or telegraphic transfers to Asian clients, who needed the latter to make remittances to Western Europe (and, later, the United States)—in the bank's balance sheet, these are so-called bills payable (B/P), booked under liabilities; and
- the purchase of bills from Asian exporters, and drawn on European centers, for instance London. These bills represented Asian exports to Europe, and were to be collected for payment there (B/C (bills for collection), booked under assets)

Although, at the outset, most of the exchange banks were British banks granted a Royal Charter (or the equivalent thereof), British monopoly in exchange banking had eroded by the 1890s (Nishimura, 2012; Kawamura, 2015). Whatever be the incentive or protocol behind their establishment, these institutions set themselves apart by being mostly, if not exclusively, engaged in the business of foreign exchange (Nishimura, 2012),[16] as can be concluded from the description above. For this reason, they were the producers of the very exchange quotations of the kind of which Flandreau and Jobst could draw on for their database (Figure 1.01).

Second, there is a compelling logical argument for the above. After all, given the peripheral nature of the currencies involved, and their implied low liquidity, there does not appear to be an inherent incentive to hold liabilities denominated in them, especially not after the 1870s. Does the latter, especially in the aftermath of the unpredictable 1870s, not lead to the conclusion that quoting institutions had, in one way or another, to be specializing in trade insurance?

This was indeed the case. Just as the European periphery in the late eighteenth century (Flandreau et al., 2009), large swaths of the densely populated regions of Northeast and Southeast Asia saw their economies flooded and dominated by institutions, financial technologies, and products from the liquid European

---

[15] This has led some authors to refer to the region as the 'Asian Mediterranean' (Schottenhammer, 2005, 2008; Gipouloux, 2011).
[16] Nishimura (2012, p. 55):

   [An exchange bank] may engage in ancillary businesses such as retail banking for the residents of a port city [...] or flotation of loans for the governments of the host countries. But the core of its business must be foreign exchanges and the financing of international transactions.

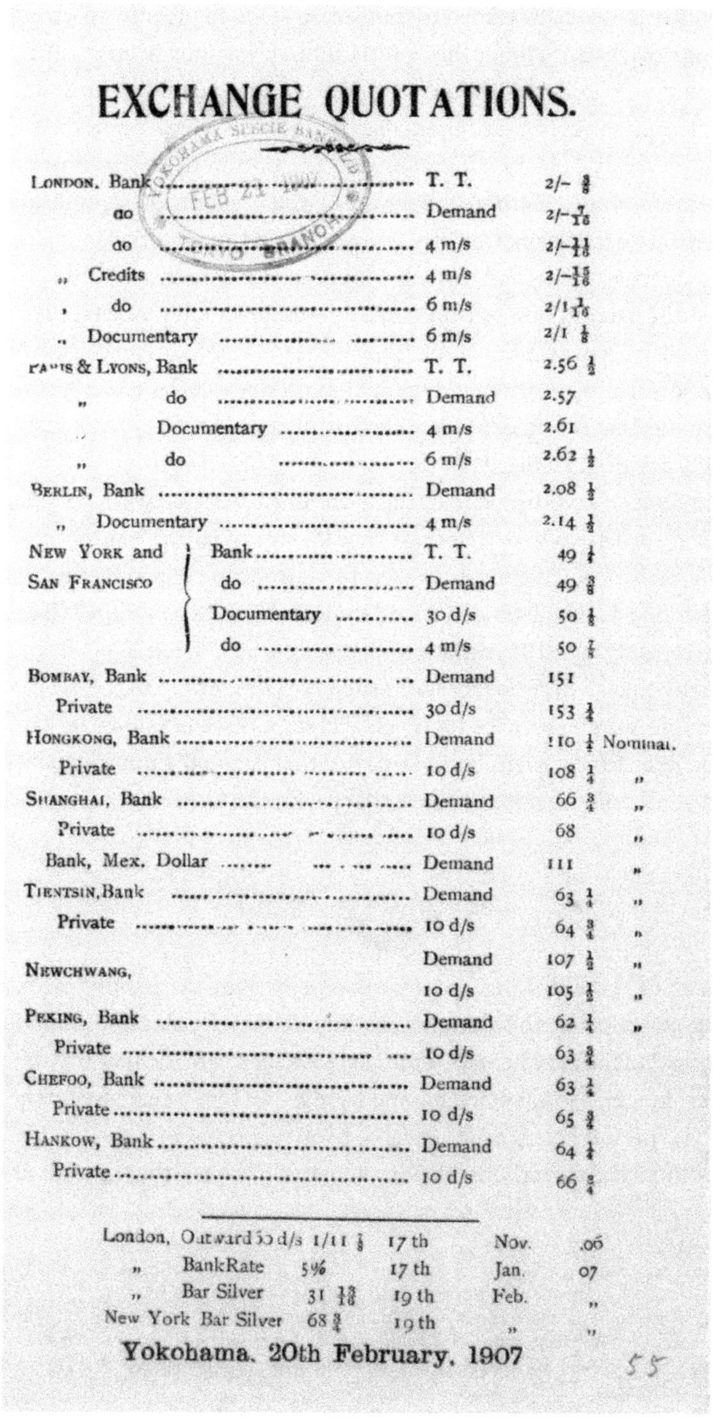

EXCHANGE QUOTATIONS.

London, Bank	T. T.	2/- $\frac{3}{8}$	
do	Demand	2/-$\frac{7}{16}$	
do	4 m/s	2/-$\frac{11}{16}$	
„ Credits	4 m/s	2/-$\frac{15}{16}$	
„ do	6 m/s	2/1$\frac{1}{16}$	
„ Documentary	6 m/s	2/1 $\frac{1}{8}$	
Paris & Lyons, Bank	T. T.	2.56 $\frac{1}{2}$	
„ do	Demand	2.57	
„ Documentary	4 m/s	2.61	
„ do	6 m/s	2.62 $\frac{1}{2}$	
Berlin, Bank	Demand	2.08 $\frac{1}{2}$	
„ Documentary	4 m/s	2.14 $\frac{1}{2}$	
New York and San Francisco — Bank	T. T.	49 $\frac{1}{4}$	
do	Demand	49 $\frac{3}{8}$	
Documentary	30 d/s	50 $\frac{1}{8}$	
do	4 m/s	50 $\frac{7}{8}$	
Bombay, Bank	Demand	151	
Private	30 d/s	153 $\frac{1}{4}$	
Hongkong, Bank	Demand	110 $\frac{1}{2}$	Nominal.
Private	10 d/s	108 $\frac{1}{4}$	„
Shanghai, Bank	Demand	66 $\frac{3}{4}$	„
Private	10 d/s	68	„
Bank, Mex. Dollar	Demand	111	„
Tientsin, Bank	Demand	63 $\frac{1}{4}$	„
Private	10 d/s	64 $\frac{3}{4}$	„
Newchwang,	Demand	107 $\frac{1}{2}$	„
	10 d/s	105 $\frac{1}{2}$	„
Peking, Bank	Demand	62 $\frac{1}{4}$	„
Private	10 d/s	63 $\frac{3}{4}$	
Chefoo, Bank	Demand	63 $\frac{1}{4}$	
Private	10 d/s	65 $\frac{3}{4}$	
Hankow, Bank	Demand	64 $\frac{1}{4}$	
Private	10 d/s	66 $\frac{3}{4}$	

London,	Outward 30 d/s	1/11 $\frac{3}{8}$	17th	Nov.	.06
„	Bank Rate	5%	17th	Jan.	07
„	Bar Silver	31 $\frac{13}{16}$	19th	Feb.	„
New York	Bar Silver	68 $\frac{3}{4}$	19th	„	„

Yokohama, 20th February, 1907

55

Figure 1.01. An example of Yokohama Specie Bank Daily Exchange Quotations, 'Yokohama, 20th February, 1907'

Source: Courtesy of the Rare Materials Reading Room (Faculty of Economics, University of Tokyo).

core countries, especially related to trade finance (or, in other words, short-term financing) (Webster, 2006). The world's money was not so much the British pound, but the 'bill on London'. In a process that started before the 1850s, financial capitalism had imposed itself from above and reinforced a core/periphery ('treaty port' vs. *Hinterland*) distinction in the Asian host country. This was the almost natural follow-up of the creation of trading posts, or 'entrepôts', associated with mostly British free-trade imperialism.[17] The very point is that, as jurisdictionally and economically demarcated units, they did not need the presence of well-organized domestic credit markets, even if they would have existed (we know that they either did not, or lacked the depth of the London market). An already global market for cheap short-term capital was thriving, and it would be up to the periphery's *Hinterland* and institutions to catch up with the latter.[18,19]

These regions and their currencies were in all possible ways outside of the Braudelian bell jar. Or perhaps we should say, given the existence of long-standing mercantile relationships with the European core countries, that they were included as outsiders—'systems are tested on their margins' (Bordo and Flandreau, 2003, p. 419) is a quote that might have been lifted from Niklas Luhmann's theory of modern world society (Luhmann, 2012, 2013). Staying with Braudel's preference for topological metaphors, early financial capitalism could be likened to a Klein bottle: a device that draws the outside to its inside, yet that at all times maintains a boundary with the former.

7. Why This Book?

The focus of the following chapters is mostly with the history of exchange banking practice in the decades leading up to the development of gold (-exchange) standards in Asia, that is, 1850–1910. For China, the time span was even longer, as monetary regime change became a real issue only in the 1930s. The period has to a large degree been neglected by financial historians as transitory. The underlying idea of the latter has been that the 'fall of silver',

---

[17]   Including a comprehensive list of sources would be prohibitive. For the sake of brevity, we refer to the existence of a 'Cain and Hopkins paradigm' (Cain and Hopkins, 1993).

[18]   There are conspicuously few studies on how indigenous institutions dealt with the supra-imposed and evolutionarily superior foreign financial technologies. One seminal example is Nishimura (2005). Kuroda Akinobu's research into complementary currencies appears to hint towards a similar interest, but needs further specification (2008a, 2008b).

[19]   In our view, Bloomfield has been the first to highlight the role of short-term sovereign borrowing through 'finance bills' (Bloomfield, 1963).

spurred by a series of happenings in Western Europe (more specifically, France's decision to ration (1873) and later demonetize (1876) silver in the wake of the Franco-Prussian war) (Flandreau, 1996a), was a cataclysmic event that took the credibility of silver with it.

In this book, we treat that assumption as suspicious. As monetary reform became an issue in the latter half of the 1870s (the so-called Lindsay scheme) (Keynes, 1913, p. 34ff.), and took yet another twenty years to be implemented, we believe that the credibility of silver did not go out with a bang. Rather, as contemporary observers did not have the benefit of hindsight, there are reasons to assume they perceived the aftermath of the Franco-Prussian War as a one-off event, after which the gold par of silver would return to the pre-1870s 'normal'—after all, the gold to silver price ratio had been remarkably stable for a long period, and its stability had never commanded any form of international coordination.

The continued depression of silver throughout the 1870s and 1880s certainly worried contemporary observers but did not cause a massive rush away from holding silver liabilities. Silver's confidence crisis was protracted. Overall, it resulted in the occurrence of premia for silver denominated long-term debt (the rupee bonds issued by the Indian government, for instance), but it did not impede contemporaries to 'go long' on silver when the many international conferences or a unilateral policy initiative as the Sherman silver purchase act (1890) promised the reversal of the white metal's fate.

For institutions specializing in the insurance of trade between the Western gold standard countries and Asia's 'realms of silver' (MacKenzie, 1954), the situation must have been precarious. For one, the intuition is that that one should expect managerial problems for those banks who stuck to the old ways and foresaw the mid- to long-term restabilization of the silver price, possibly at a new par. This is borne out by the historical record. Suzuki Toshio, pointing out that the cadre of the once mighty Oriental Bank Corporation (OBC) had a penchant for bimetallism, has convincingly demonstrated that the bank's failure in 1884 was to a large degree precipitated by the fall of the silver price (yet another reason was the shortening of bill usance, to which we turn in Chapter 3 (Suzuki, 2012)). Although it is difficult to prove that similar reasons were behind the demise of other exchange banks or their retreat from Asia (as in the case of the Comptoir d'Escompte de Paris), because their records were in most cases lost or destroyed, it remains a compelling explanation.

Some banks, notably the HSBC, however, weathered the exchange storm extremely well. This has prompted our second intuition. Given that the track records of several of the most representative exchange banks tended to divert so remarkably, should we not expect to find evidence of furious experimentation with financial products and technologies, including perhaps the elusive harbingers of strategies for hedging exchange risk? Unfortunately, conventional literature on exchange banking has not been very helpful. In many cases company-sponsored studies, they have not delved into the intricacies of nineteenth-century exchange banking practice.[20] Even Frank King's monumental tetralogy on the history of the Hongkong and Shanghai Banking Corporation (HSBC) does not explore the bank's strategy at hedging exchange risk, the title of the first volume notwithstanding (King, 1987). It is nowadays commonplace to assume that nineteenth-century bankers were unaware of hedging technologies (Bordo and Flandreau, 2003, p. 437).[21] It is in this particular respect that this book attempts to fill a gap.

8. Structure of This Book

In order to frame silver's prolonged fall from grace after 1873, it is instructive to review the debate on the credibility of bimetallism (Chapter 1). We argue that recent revisionist interpretations have been correct. Taking account of abortive European schemes at creating a trade dollar for use within the region, we note that these experiments were bolstered by international conferences. Not only were contemporaries convinced that a worldwide gold standard was infeasible, they saw silver as indispensable from the monetary menu. The latter becomes most obvious from discussions on Indian sovereign debt. British policymakers were obviously aware that borrowing in silver demanded a premium, but they seemed confident that the exchange risk associated with a loan in pounds outweighed the former.

Chapter 2 turns to the implications of the above for trade finance. It turns out that experiment with *financial products* started as early as 1876, yet was initially highly disruptive and damaging to banking practice. The drawing of silver denominated bills for British export finance not only distorted the process through which Eastern exchange bankers traditionally recouped their

---

[20]   One notable exception to the latter is Stuart Muirhead's discussion of banking practice in CMBILC (1996, esp. pp. 199–232). This account, however, is largely descriptive, that is, illustrative of individual and non-related instants of aspects of international trade finance; it does not attempt to explore bank management in a systematic, formal way (Muirhead, 1996).

[21]   Compare as well Bonin et al. (2015).

capital, it also left the banker's position unhedged. The shortening of bill usance, driven by the separate development that was the Suez Canal, exacerbated matters. Eventually, however, experimentation led to success. In particular the creation of 'interest bills' in the 1880s, which concerned a deferred exchange transaction, strongly strengthened the exchange banker's chances of gauging the amount of risk he was taking.

From financial products, the discussion moves on to *managerial practice*. In Chapter 3, we demonstrate that several bankers had a keen understanding of hedging exchange risk, by setting off the operations of buying and selling bills against each other. Interest bills and the 'even keel' were complementary aspects of the mindset of conservative banking that characterized the HSBC at the time, and that was adopted by the YSB in the 1890s. Importantly, it also turned out to be a successful recipe; whereas most exchange banks, including the once mighty OBC, floundered or even disappeared, HSBC took over the helm. It is safe to assume that, from the 1890s onwards, *all* surviving exchange banks had developed a hedging strategy of some sort. This chapter also discusses the implications of the 'even keel' for branch network growth.

The latter are addressed in Chapter 5. While tracing the development of the YSB's branch network around the turn of the century, we address the apparent paradox of the bank's development in China and Manchuria *after* gold standard adoption. Although clearly steered by Tokyo's mounting imperialist ambitions in the region, we demonstrate that such expansion also fit within YSB's management system. As a matter of fact, boosting its business within regions that were on a silver unit of account was prerequisite to maintaining the even keel and providing exchange cover for all its operations. The only constraints were the costs associated with raising deposits in liquidity-poor regions. Ultimately, the relatively high interest on deposits was deemed opportune. Before World War I, YSB established itself as a formidable competitor of a club of institutions that were formerly exclusively Western European or American (IBC).

This book's appendices are used to explore several matters of general interest to the discussion. Not in the least, this includes a discussion of the accounting technicalities that had to be considered when constructing the database. Drawing on a range of secondary sources in Japanese, we demonstrate how hedging worked in practice; and we show the peculiar and often misunderstood role of finance bills, especially after 1895.

In conclusion, we hint at venues for further research.

Appendix 1

The Extended East-Asian Mediterranean

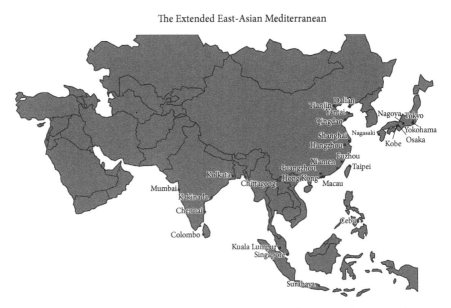

Figure 1.A1. The 'Asian Mediterranean': the maritime location of major exchange centers in the Intra-Asian Trade Network

Source: Map created by the author.

Appendix 2

Table 1.A1. The geographical presence of British and French international banks in Asia in 1870

	Agra Bank	Oriental Bank Corporation (OBC)	Chartered Mercantile Bank of India, London and China (CMBILC)	Chartered Bank of India, Australia and China (CBIAC)	Hongkong and Shanghai Banking Corporation (HSBC)	Comptoir National d'Escompte de Paris (CNEP)
Year of establishment	1833	1842	1854	1858	1865	1848
Royal Charter		x (1851)	x (1857)	x (1853)	x* (1866)	
Europe	**London,** Edinburgh (1861)	**London**	**London,** Edinburgh	**London**	London	**Paris,** Lyon (1868), Marseille (1869), Nantes (1867), London (1867)
India/Ceylon	Calcutta (1837), Bombay (Mumbai) (1845), Madras (1843), Karachi (1860), Agra, Lahore	Calcutta (1842?), Bombay (Mumbai) (1842?), Madras (1846?), Colombo (1842?), Galle (1869), Kandy (1852?)	Calcutta (1855), Bombay (Mumbai) (1853), Madras, Kakinada, Colombo (1854), Galle, Kandy (1854)	Calcutta (1858), Bombay (1858)	Calcutta (1868), Bombay (1869)	Calcutta (1860), Bombay (1862)
China	Hong Kong, Shanghai (1854)	Hong Kong (1845), Shanghai (1847), Foochow (Fuzhou) (1869)	Hong Kong, Shanghai (1854), Fuzhou, Hankow (1855)	Hong Kong (1859), Shanghai (1858), Hankow	**Hong Kong** (1864), Shanghai (1865), Foochow (Fuzhou), Hankow	Hong Kong (1862?), Shanghai (1860)

Continued

Table 1.A1. *Continued*

	Agra Bank	Oriental Bank Corporation (OBC)	Chartered Mercantile Bank of India, London and China (CMBILC)	Chartered Bank of India, Australia and China (CBIAC)	Hongkong and Shanghai Banking Corporation (HSBC)	Comptoir National d'Escompte de Paris (CNEP)
Japan		Yokohama (1864)	Yokohama (1863)		Yokohama (1866)	Yokohama (1867)
Southeast Asia		Singapore (1846)	Singapore (1855), Penang	Singapore (1859), Batavia (1853), Rangoon (1862), Akyab (Sittwe) (1867)	Saigon (1868)	Saigon (1862?)
Australia	Sydney (1862), Melbourne (1864)	Melbourne (1852), Sydney (1852)				
Africa		Mauritius (1852)				Bourbon (Réunion)

Notes: Indication of dates of establishment of branches or offices being granted a royal charter (王室特許状 *ōshitsu tokkyojō*) (or equivalent) and location of the head office (in bold print). Some caution with respect to the exactitude of the presented dates should apply; for some branches, it was impossible to find a reliable date of establishment.

* The HSBC was established under Ordinances No. 2 and No. 5, 1866, of the government of Hong Kong; the latter were equivalent to being granted a royal charter.

Sources: Table created by the author, after Evans et al, 1800–…; Ishii, 1979, 1999; Yokouchi, 1996; Suzuki, 2012.

2

Silver Risk, Silver Exports, and Sovereign Debt in the Nineteenth Century

A Brief Reappraisal

1. Introduction

Arguably the most daunting problem for late nineteenth-century financiers, investors, and economic observers was the chronic fall of silver after 1873 and its erratic volatility after 1886, but especially in the 1890s (see Figure 2.01).

For obvious reasons, the 'silver question' has also been picked up in economic historical literature. Traditionally, it has been discussed as a natural outcome of the flaws of bimetallism (Kindleberger, 1984; Redish, 1995; Meissner, 2013). In this view, bimetallism had to give as soon as its limitations were tested. This happened first, the argument goes, as soon as the 1860s, when the world's silver supply drastically expanded following the discovery of Nevada's Comstock Lode (Smith, 1998). Roughly a decade later, when Germany decided to demonetize silver, bimetallist dreams were shattered for good. With bimetallist fallacies exposed, countries would massively choose to part with silver: it translated into the 'emergence' of the gold standard, not as a concerted international reform effort, but as a spontaneous systemic birth spurred by endogeneity (the fact that, once a critical mass of countries had shifted to one standard, it made sense to do so as well) (Gallarotti, 1995, 2001).

This traditional view has recently been challenged by a revisionist reading of events. Friedman (1990a, 1990b), Oppers (1996), but especially Flandreau (1996a, 2000a, 2004), have argued that bimetallism was if anything, largely *credible* to contemporaries, a conclusion they reach on, among others, the basis of the remarkable resilience and stability of the gold-silver exchange rates before the 1870s. This revisionist strand, therefore, stresses the role of an inherent mechanism of arbitrage, which was recognized by contemporaries and had the effect to dampen exchange rate variability in a multipolar

Accounting for the Fall of Silver: Hedging Currency Risk in Long-Distance Trade with Asia, 1870–1913.
Michael Schiltz, Oxford University Press (2020). © Michael Schiltz.
DOI: 10.1093/oso/9780198865025.001.0001

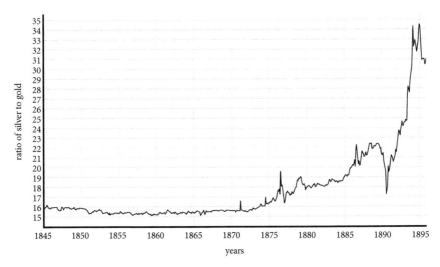

Figure 2.01. The silver price of gold, January 1845 to December 1895
Source: figure created by the author after Laughlin (1896)

monetary world.[1] Put in the most simple terms, it was a textbook version of Gresham's Law. Concretely, a simple comparison of the market price of gold and silver with their legal ratio incentivized especially France to counteract volatility, because it could freely choose to import the cheaper metal: it thus stabilized the latter's price, while releasing stocks of the relatively more expensive one. In the 1860s, it was this mechanism that enabled France to absorb cheaper gold and release large quantities of silver, which were then exported to what observers at the time referred to as 'the East' (Figure 2.02).[2]

Assuming that bimetallism was credible rather than incredible to contemporaries has an important implication for events after 1873. Again in contrast to the traditional view, the demise of bimetallism cannot have been a sudden event: its credibility would, for obvious reasons, have incentivized several people to take long positions on silver at different points of time (later we will see that it indeed did). Flandreau and Oosterlinck therefore stress that its

---

[1] See the following compelling narrative evidence:

[Before 1873], a very great part of the world adhered to the bimetallic system, which made both gold and silver legal tenders, and which established a fixed relationship between them. In consequence, whenever the value of the two metals altered, these countries acted as equalising machines. They took the metal which fell; they sold the metal which rose; and thus the relative value of the two was kept at its old point.

('The American Commission on the Currency.' *The Economist* (London, England), Saturday, Sept. 2, 1876, p. 1025, Issue 1723

[2] For an early appreciation of this arbitrage mechanism and the consequent flows of silver from Europe to Asia, see Laughlin (1896). For evidence in the financial press at the time: 'The Double Standard of Value in France, and Its Effect upon the Drain of Bullion.' *The Economist* (London, England), Saturday, Nov. 10, 1855, p. 1229; Issue 637.

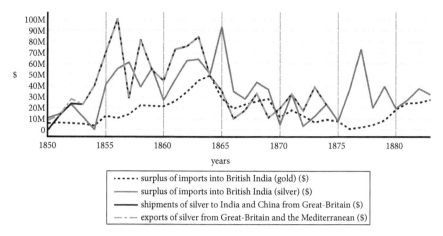

Figure 2.02. Flows of silver to the East
Source: figure created by the author after Laughlin (1896, pp. 252–253)

process was gradual and protracted (2012), an interpretation that will be demonstrated to carry important relevance for the following discussion.

From the very outset, this book aligns closely with the aforementioned revisionist view, in particular where it concerns the expectation dimension. We will seek to relate historical events taking place in East Asia after the 1870s in a meaningful way, and show that these corroborate the notion that bimetallism remained credible until roughly 1890. In its most basic form, I feel one may summarize the problem as a decennia-long exercise in cost-benefit analysis, as said after three-quarters of a century of conspicuous exchange rate stability. Admittedly, volatility had always been the name of the financial game, but in the late nineteenth century, its stakes were invariably higher. We will show that contemporaries were aware of this, and acted accordingly. The questions they faced and the choices they made were far from trivial. Given the long-term uncertainty about the gold value of the white metal, what were the risks and opportunities of holding assets and/or liabilities in one metal rather than the other? Did contemporaries calculate or perceive the (future) returns and losses on these assets/liabilities in one metal in relationship to the other metal? Were such expectations reflected in the spot price of precious metals? And so on.

In the following paragraphs, we briefly review the experience of both core countries and peripheral countries with the fall of the silver price. Core countries, we find, concentrated on efforts to restore the long-term credibility of silver. They attempted to organize the export of silver to the East, with differing records of success. For peripheral countries, the problem was more complicated, because of their financial dependence on the gold countries in the world's center in the short- and mid-term. Mostly on silver and mostly not in the capability of swiftly effectuating an orderly monetary reform, they had to weigh the benefits and costs of floating their debt in silver rather than gold, by monitoring how contemporaries viewed the future ratio of both metals.

2. The Long Bimetallist Swan Song: An East-West Connect

Germany was arguably the first country to grapple with the aforementioned questions. When, in the aftermath of the Franco-Prussian war of 1870-1, it decided to use the French indemnity to go onto the gold standard, it had unwillingly set into motion a series of events that actually created the 'silver problem'. As it experienced soon enough, the decision to move on the gold standard did not only entail a financial problem (accumulate sufficient gold resources before the reform). There also was a considerable, if not enormous, liquidation problem: where did German Thalers, its silver reserves have to go? A major reform effort increased the aggregate demand for gold at the expense of the aggregate demand for silver. In other words, the very decision to demonetize silver would feed back onto the silver price, making it more costly to exchange silver (Thalers) for gold on the world markets, and possibly difficult to implement the reform effort in the first place.

Soon, Germany's decision—or, more accurately, the French choice to suspend silver coinage (Flandreau, 1996a)—would reverberate throughout the whole world, as a wave that grew stronger as it moved from the (Western) core to the world periphery. Realizing the potentially nefarious effects of silver depreciation on the balance of trade between gold and silver standard countries (the latter mostly belonging to the world's periphery),[3] policymakers first tried to reverse the tide, and, realizing that bimetallism had served exchange rate stability quite well in earlier decades, attempted to buffer it.

From its very outset, this took the form of finding new outlets for freshly released silver stocks. Adolf Soetbeers' proposal to create a German trade dollar for use in the Orient was explicitly aimed at creating 'a means of facilitating

---

[3] For an example hereof as early as 1876, see Robert Chapman, then financial secretary to the Government of India:

> India owes, and has to pay, in London, in gold, yearly, the sum of 15 millions sterling. Most of this great yearly charge is permanently fixed. The interest on the sterling debt and on the capital of the Guaranteed Railway and Irrigation Companies (together about 7 million sterling), the pensions and annuities to our officers and their families; as much of the military expenditure as consists of pay and allowances; the pay of the Home establishments; and a large number of other payments, are fixed and cannot be reduced.
>
> (Cited in Bagchi, 1997, p. 26)

the disposal of its surplus silver,[4,5] or, in other words, at gaining a certain degree of control over the silver price. Although Soetbeers' plan was never realized, it is clear that contemporaries were aware of its potential. The creations (and, typically, abortions) of the British Hong Kong dollar (1866-8), the French *piastre de commerce* (1885-95), the Japanese *bōeki gin* (1873-8), and American trade dollar (1873-85)[6] and so on all echo the German plan (Andrew, 1904).[7] Although these moves were uncoordinated and certainly inspired by self-interest, they nevertheless convey an understanding that a global gold standard was not only undesirable but also factually unfeasible (Figure 2.03).[8]

Aggressive European currency tactics in East Asia were echoed on the more gentrified diplomatic battlefield. One is surprised by the long series of monetary conferences (international action, in the parlance of the day) (Willis, 1968 [1901])), convened to tackle the 'monetary question'. A first conference, convened in 1867, ironically at the behest of gold appreciation (cf. supra), had recommended gold becoming the world's monetary standard.

---

[4] Soetbeer (1877, pp. 235–8); see as well Andrew (1901, p. 329). A thorough discussion of attempts to dethrone the Mexican dollar is Ono (1959, 1962, 1963, 2001). For a discussion of the contours of the German debate, and steps taken towards its implementation, see Akagawa (2006).

[5] 'German Silver and the Eastern Absorption.' *The Economist* (London, England) 2 Dec. 1876, p. 1399. Leavens estimates the total sale of demonetized silver by Germany amounted to 114.2 million ounces between 1873 and 1879; the sale of 91.7 million ounces hereof, or approximately 80 per cent, was realized in the three year time window 1876–1879. Afterwards, silver sales petered out and remaining silver was mostly reserved for minting subsidiary coins (Leavens, 1939, p. 354).

[6] Laughlin (1896, p. 103):

> It was not intended to issue a silver dollar which should circulate in the United States, but merely to lend the authority of the Government stamp to silver bullion in order to aid in finding a market for silver in the East, and at the same time to relieve merchants from paying the high premium exacted for the Mexican dollars, sometimes amounting to from 11 to 22 per cent.

[7] Interestingly, the idea of Eastern absorption of surplus silver would continue to draw commentary in the international press: 'German Silver and the Eastern Absorption.' *The Economist*, Dec. 2, 1876, p. 1399. Later observers kept on stressing the importance of Indian silver demand for upholding the price of the metal: 'The Coinage of Silver in India.' *The Economist* 28 May, 1881, p. 662; 'The Statistical Position of Silver.' *The Economist* 14 Aug. 1886, p. 1016; A. Sauerbeck. 'Dr Soetbeer's Memorandum and the Silver Question.' *The Economist* 20 Aug., 1892, pp. 1072–3.

[8] In a similar vein should one see debates about the implementation of fiduciary reserves for national gold currencies around the 1890s. See, for instance, the following appraisal of the Goschen plan:

> Mr. Goschen's main purpose is connected not so much with currency as with banking. He starts from the position, practically conceded to him by all his critics, that our metallic banking reserve is inadequate. Admitting, and indeed insisting, that much may be done by the bankers themselves to remedy this weakness, Mr. Goschen proposes that the State should make a contribution towards the desired end by the formation of a second or relief reserve, to be accessible, under special conditions, in times of special strain.   (Foxwell, 1892, p. 139)

The article explicitly relates Goshen's proposals to the tenets of bimetallism.

Figure 2.03. Silver in East and West

Source: A political cartoon published in the April 25, 1874 issue of Harper's Weekly (p. 353) (out of copyright). Entitled "Rags for Our Working Men—Specie for the Foreigners", the caption for this cartoon reads as follows:

Columbia: 'Dear me, I do think it very wrong that the good nice trade dollar (worth 100 cents) should be sent out of the country for the benefit of the "heathen Chinee," for if these gentlemen are permitted to have their own way, it will take a basket full of greenbacks to buy dinner for my children.'

As is clear from the above cartoon, not all American commoners were convinced that finding an outlet for silver in the East, but remaining on an inconvertible paper currency for the US proper, was a good idea (Table 2.01)

This was in effect a straightforward course of events: with gold pouring all over the world, it made sense to vote the 25 franc gold coin as a global standard. Yet when silver started its decline around 1873, the position of their participants became much more variegated and more difficult to interpret.[9] Indeed, their stances sometimes appear incoherent over time, which in itself is best taken as symptomatic for the actual absence of willingness to cooperate, a danger of which Samuel Montagu, a champion of bimetallist ideas, was acutely aware.[10]

Although a thorough discussion of all viewpoints falls outside the scope of this book, it is nevertheless important to note that none of the financial elites expressed itself in favor of silver's demonetization. Indeed, French authorities

---

[9] For first- and second-hand accounts of some of these conferences, see Coste (1889); Andrews (1893); Reti (1998).

[10] A very good appraisal of the historical importance of these conferences in Japanese can be found in Kumagai (1992); Noguchi (2005, 2006).

Table 2.01 Trade dollars in East Asia, 1865-90

Figure 2.04 The British trade dollar. Weight: 416 grain. Fineness: 900. Pure silver: 347⅗

Wikipedia, The original uploader was Invictus Solis at English. 2007. English: British Trade Dollar B Mint 1900. Self-photographed. https://commons.wikimedia.org/wiki/File:British_Trade_Dollar_Combined_1900.jpg.

Figure 2.05 The Japanese *bōeki gin*. Weight: 420 grain. Fineness: 900. Pure silver: 378

As6673. 2008. English: 1 Yen (Boekigin)-M8-Silver. Own work. https://commons.wikimedia.org/wiki/File:1yen-M8silver.jpg.

Figure 2.06 The American trade dollar. Weight: 420 grain. Fineness: 900. Pure silver: 378.

Bailly, Design and carving attributed to Joseph A. 1873. 1873 United States Trade Dollar. https://commons.wikimedia.org/wiki/File:1873_US_Trade_Dollar.jpg.

Figure 2.07 The French *piastre de commerce*. Weight: 420 grain. Fineness: 900. Pure silver: 378.

Appaches. 2015. English: 'French Indochina Piastre 1885.Png' with Transparent Background. Own work. https://commons.wikimedia.org/wiki/File:French_Indochina_Piastre_1885_without_background.png.

Figure 2.08 The original Mexican dollar. Weight: 417₁₅/₁₇ grain. Fineness: 902₇/₉. Pure silver: 377 ¼. This specimen has so-called chopmarks or *gokuin* 極印, basically certificates added by Chinese merchants or money-changers testifying the coin's purity.

Centpacrr. 2013. English: 1888 Republica Méxicana 8 Reals Silver 'Trade Coin' with Multiple 'Chop' Marks Made by Chinese Merchants to Assure It Authenticity (uploader's private collection). https://commons.wikimedia.org/wiki/File:1888_M%C3%A9xico_8_Reals_Trade_Coin_Silver.jpg

Figure 2.09 The Chinese Dragon dollar. Weight and fineness varied according to region of issuance.

As6022014. 2010. English: China-7sen2hun-1904. Own work. https://commons.wikimedia.org/wiki/File:China-7sen2hun-1904.jpg

Figure 2.10. International Monetary Conferences

Cartoon by Thomas Nast, 'International Monetary Conference in Paris—Silver Currency an Unsound Footing', Harper's Weekly (1881?). Courtesy of the Florida Center for Instructional Technology (ClipArt ETC).

in the 1870s typically only rationed silver coinage, thereby signaling that bimetallism was not doomed.[11] Large market participants, closely monitoring developments with respect to Latin Monetary Union members imposing a quota on the acceptance of foreign silver coin, found it more difficult to hedge their bets. Both in tune with their business interests (e.g., as arbitrageurs of the international monetary order) and/or as a matter of practical concern, everybody preferred the status quo. While rejecting bimetallism as an international orthodoxy, they recommended that bimetal countries remained bimetal.[12] Put yet differently, they supported the continuous monetization of silver if it was based upon the unilateral action of certain governments, but rejected the stabilization of the silver prize through multilateral agreement (Figure 2.10).[13]

---

[11] See, in this respect, the scathing criticism of Andrew directed at Willis' aforementioned interpretation (1968 [1901]). For a compelling story in Japanese, see Saitō (1940).

[12] For a discussion of the Rothschilds' position in particular, see Gutwein (1992).

[13] For a discussion of the implications of this liberalist mindset, see Bagchi (1997).

As we now know, and as is clearly hinted to in the above political cartoon, 'international action' was eventually to no avail: 'uncharacteristic' (Flandreau and Oosterlinck, 2012, p. 653) moves by several countries, such as the US decision to resume convertibility on a gold basis (1873) piled up and cemented each other,[14] thus becoming permanent measures. Yet, whereas the chances for resuscitating silver monetization grew dimmer as consecutive conferences failed, there was at the same time no understanding that gold monometallism was the right thing all the way. As one finds in Reti's diplomatic history, the growth towards gold was a haphazard and cumulative process resulting out of the mercurial nature of a coordination game situation (1998) (Thiemeyer, 2007).[15] Importantly for our discussion, both monetary experiment and political tactics did not cause bimetallism to go with a bang. In the following paragraphs, we, therefore, discuss bimetallism's slow-motion breakdown in a region where silver had been the medium of exchange for centuries: East Asia.

3. Gold, Silver, and the Periphery

Far away from the opportunities of investors and financiers in the world's financial centers, policymakers in the periphery found themselves in a possibly more precarious position. Given their dependency on capital flows from the center, choosing the unit of account for their exports and their long-term obligations vis-à-vis international creditors was no trifling matter. Having the hindsight of the 'scramble for gold' after 1890,[16] a lot of historians have taken the shift towards gold as a natural, obvious matter of course, the reasons for which they feel to be imperfections inherent to bimetallism. Yet, this hindsight was crucially lacking to the nineteenth-century observer. As a matter of fact, the very lack of it, and the uncertainty regarding future monetary regimes

---

[14] The attentive reader will note that a lot of the discussion employs the terminology of criminal law. In this particular case, Friedman refers to the American decision as the 'crime of 1873' (1990b).

[15] An often forgotten factor, including in Reti's study, is the role of the badmouthing of silver, which certainly played a role in the conference's outcomes. Compare, for an early appraisal of the latter:

> Mais on ne peut pas en dire autant de bien des discussions qui se sont engagées dernière- ment dans une partie de la presse anglaise qui ne veut pas admettre la raison d'être du métal blanc en général et de son rôle important dans nos systèmes monétaires. [...] En ce qui concerne les valeurs libellées en argent, leur politique est toute tracée. Ils négligent dans leurs Bulletins de Bourse les mouvements en avant et appuient sur les réactions qui se produisent de temps en temps.   (Haupt, 1890, p. 23)

Economic historical research on the economics of defamation is, unfortunately, scarce. For a hint in the context of pre-1914 France, see Bignon and Flandreau (2011).

[16] Note that we, in contrast to Gallarotti's original use of the term (1995), pin 1890 and not 1870 as the date after which a scramble occurs.

fed back, not only on the convoluted decision-making of that observer's cir-cumscribed present but also on movements in exchange rates.

Scholarly discussions of late nineteenth-century perspectives on the assess-ment of the silver risk, both in the short- and long-term, are conspicuously scarce. Irving Fisher may in effect be credited with discovering the potential of the 'asset-pricing approach', interestingly in the context of nineteenth-century gold- and silver-denominated government securities; yet, he did not expand his theory in an exploration of the credibility of bimetallism (1907). Calomiris was the first to present a survey of the effect of silver risk in the resumption of convertibility of the US dollar (1993). Oppers (2000) and Flandreau have studied the relation between exchange risk and silver (and bimetallic) curren-cies' short-term interest rates. Garber's comparative work on the value of bimetallic versus monometallic (gold) contracts is the first to highlight the long-term aspect (1986), but it compares contracts from very different issuing entities and is therefore forced to conflate silver risk with other risk measures (namely default risk and liquidity risk). As far as we are aware, Flandreau and Oosterlinck (2012) is the only paper to use the asset-pricing approach for understanding movements in exchange rates and price levels of *securities that, apart from the silver (exchange rate) risk, are otherwise perfect substitutes.*[17] In this case, nineteenth-century rupee- and sterling-denominated Indian government securities are the testing ground, for their obvious potential regarding comparative analysis.

As repeatedly hinted at above, contemporaries' expectations with respect to long-term currency shifts are the crux of the analysis. As our approach is arguably ethno-historiographical, we are interested in whether we can find further descriptive evidence of contemporaries' understanding with respect to future exchange rates at the time. Put in the discourse of economics, was there something as an *ex-ante* market-based measure of appreciation/ depreciation (after the century-old discovery of the uncovered interest rate parity) with the silver price of gold as a coordinating price, a 'pure' measure? Concretely, did market participants monitor the gold-silver interest rate dif-ferential when forming expectations of future exchange rates, and did they price assets accordingly? Did, for instance, policymakers assess silver risk when determining the denomination of loans to be issued?

---

[17] Some may object here that Indian securities were also plagued by liquidity risk, but Flandreau and Oosterlinck object (2012, p. 655):

> Rupee bonds were issued in India and thus came from a market whose depth was arguably less than that prevailing at the financial center of the universe (London). However, cross-listing of rupee securities in London and active purchases there and finally substantial holding and trading in Britain must have relieved much of the possible illiquidity.

4. 'Where Ought India to Borrow?'

It turned out that they did. Factually, this is not a surprise. Countries from the periphery and semi-periphery had grown accustomed to a premium being added to their debt issues, and this because of liquidity problems of their currencies. Their experience with this 'original sin' had also taught them that there were possibilities of working around this. Even if a country's domestic market was squeezed, it sufficed to add exchange clauses to the contracts, and in other words float loans on the vast London capital market with a fixed rate to, typically, the pound sterling (Flandreau and Sussman, 2004). Countries with sufficiently mature or sophisticated domestic markets could opt to raise their funding partially domestically and circulate chunks of it in secondary markets (again with an exchange clause, in order to enable the cashing of coupons at low cost in these markets). Importantly, and because of the remarkable stability of the gold-silver ratio until the early 1870s, the yield differentials that resulted from both procedures turned out to be determined irrespective of the metal underlying the currency in which loans had been denominated—what mattered was liquidity, no more, no less (Flandreau and Sussman, 2004, p. 28ff.).

In the 1870s, however, things became more complicated. Especially after 1876, the year in which France ruled out silver coinage, silver-using peripheral countries became aware that the aforementioned liquidity premium on their bonds was now also compounded by an exchange premium ('silver risk') (Flandreau and Oosterlinck, 2012, pp. 662ff.). Its implications appeared immediately on the radar of authorities all over the world. They were certainly behind the establishment of the infamous 'American Commission on the Currency'.[18] In India, the discussion centered on the possibility of emulating the French example. In 1876, it was proposed to suspend silver coinage in India altogether, with the aim of maintaining the value of the rupee by limiting its numbers in circulation, arguably also with problems related to debt servicing in mind.[19]

---

[18] *The Economist* noted the relationship between American borrowing and the choice of metal for its currency from the very beginning:

> to a great borrowing nation like America, it would always be an objection that she would pay in the worse coin of payment, whatever it might be [...] she would possibly have to borrow on terms somewhat less good.
>
> ('The American Commission on the Currency'. *The Economist* (London, England), Saturday, Sept. 2, 1876, p. 1026).

[19] 'The Proposal of the Bengal Chamber of Commerce to Suspend the Coinage of Silver in India'. *The Economist* (London, England), Saturday, Aug. 5, 1876, pp. 909–10, Issue 1719.

What makes the Indian case particularly relevant, however, is that silver coinage was never suspended or even rationed; India maintained the free coinage of silver and the silver-convertibility of rupees until 1894 (Keynes, 1913). The aforementioned 1876 proposal, emanating from the Bengal Chamber of Commerce, was never effectuated, among other reasons, because of the criticism it drew in the financial press. *The Economist*, in particular, was categorical in its rejection. In its view, a

> rupee 'limited'—that is to say, a rupee of which the numbers could not by law be augmented—would do in India what the greenback has done in America. It would be an appreciated artificial currency, instead of a depreciated artificial one.[20]

Although rationing silver coinage may nowadays seem plausible from a monetarist perspective, the historical contingent context gives *The Economist* the benefit of the doubt. Against the background of the great Indian famine (1876–8), the 'debauchery of the currency', as Keynes once put it, might have easily led to another popular uprising against British rule, especially because an appreciated rupee would be detrimental to the Indian export business. It is in this context that one must discuss British unwillingness to establish a gold standard in the colony. Silver was too much part of the fabric of Indian society. Multiple sources point out that hoarding was widespread; the colonial authorities, continually reminded of the 1857 Sepoy mutiny, were wise not to meddle in currency affairs.[21] As a natural consequence, the persistent depreciation of the rupee together with silver was observed but not addressed for almost three decades.

This had its clear implications for considerations of India's finances. Not in the least, the added silver risk eroded the conventional wisdom that the government of India should always turn to London for its loans. At the time of a highly stable gold-silver rate, this had been

> the most natural and easy course, because the English money market was the cheapest and most abundant [...] But in the summer of [1876] there was an understanding that this should be done no longer. The fall in the price of silver and rate of exchange had become so serious that the policy of borrowing in London loans with gold interest seemed very dubious so long as the

---

[20] 'The Proposal of the Bengal Chamber of Commerce to Suspend the Coinage of Silver in India'. *The Economist* (London, England), Saturday, Aug. 5, 1876, p. 909, Issue 1719.
[21] For a strikingly different view: Mitchener and Voth (2011).

Indian revenue was received in silver [...] it was understood that what loans the Indian Government should require should for the present be raised in India only.[22]

At the time of writing, however, the 1876 silver panic fall had temporarily been reversed. And although *The Economist* was in principle sympathetic to raising loans within India proper, it found it wise to adopt a cautious stance for the time being:

In the new state of affairs we believe that the Indian Government should abstain from any irrevocable decision [...] it might issue in London Indian Exchequer bills, or bonds at short dates, which in the present state of Lombard Street could be easily floated on good terms. *If the rate of exchange should keep at its present rate these might [...] be funded hereafter; or if that rate should fall again [...] a loan could be raised in India, and these bills or bonds paid off with the proceeds.*[23]

As we know now, the silver price turned out to be continuously depressed over the following decade. As a consequence, the debate about Indian finance was revisited more than once.[24] Strategies for overcoming the debt repayment mismatch increasingly took into account the desirability for India to borrow domestically, if not for political reasons,[25] then certainly for financial ones. Fair enough, *The Economist* admitted, domestic borrowing often squeezed the domestic credit market, and it had the detrimental effect of driving up interest rates in a country that was traditionally plagued by liquidity

---

[22] 'The Mode in which the Expected Indian Loan Should Be Raised.' *The Economist* (London, England), Saturday, Jan. 20, 1877, p. 57, Issue 1743.

[23] 'The Mode in which the Expected Indian Loan Should Be Raised.' *The Economist* (London, England), Saturday, Jan. 20, 1877, p. 58, Issue 1743 (italics mine).

[24] 'Indian Finance.' Edward Langley. *The Economist* (London, England), Saturday, July 24, 1880, p. 858, Issue 1926; 'The Silver Question.' Edward Langley. *The Economist* (London, England), Saturday, Aug. 28, 1880, p. 1004, Issue 1931; 'The Silver Question.' Edward Langley. *The Economist* (London, England), Saturday, Apr. 16, 1881, p. 479, Issue 1964.

[25] Borrowing domestically would boost India's fiscal self-sufficiency, according to an old adagio of British policy versus the colonies. Compare, for instance:

The calculation of the Indian Government is, that it is cheaper to raise here a sterling loan at 3½ per cent than to pay 4 per cent for a silver loan in India. But there must necessarily be a good deal of speculation in all calculations of this kind; and there are considerations—such, for instance, as the great desirability of inducing the natives of India to acquire a direct pecuniary interest in the railways, and to become themselves the holders of Government stock—which cannot be resolved into a mere arithmetical problem.

('Indian Railways.' *The Economist* (London, England),
Saturday, Aug. 2, 1884, p. 932, Issue 2136)

problems. Yet the Indian government's apparent concern with the limited size of the domestic investor base and, we suspect, a corollary preoccupation with rollover risk related to domestic debt resulted in a case of 'domestic original sin' (Mehl and Reynaud, 2005). Technically speaking, the Indian government could have opted to issue debt domestically with shorter maturities, as issuing short-term debt is typically less expensive than issuing long-term debt. However, the cost of refinancing is higher for short-term debt and frequent refinancing implies a larger risk of financing with higher interest rates. The government thus faced a classic dilemma: on the one hand, there existed an inclination towards cheaper funding costs, which tilted the duration towards short-term maturities yet also induced refinancing risk, which itself tilted the duration towards (safer, but more expensive) longer-term maturities (Broner et al., 2013).

In other words, avoiding the domestic debt dilemma (around 1884, the Indian government's long-term policy was to borrow in London) implied the adoption of a policy that was suboptimal at best. Borrowing in pound sterling was a bet, 'speculation by the Indian Government upon the future price of silver', and this because of the allocation of the risk. In the case of sterling borrowing, the Indian office throws 'on the Government, that is, on the people of India, the risk of loss through a fall in exchange. By borrowing in rupees they have, it is true, to pay for a higher rate, *but the risk of further loss falls on the holder of the loan.*'[26] This mismatch problem and other matters, mostly related to the terms on which the Indian Government had raised the 1885 3 per cent loan, led *The Economist* to question the former's farsightedness and criticize the effort as 'wasteful borrowing'.[27] Taken on the whole, it argued, borrowing in India at a premium might have been a more prudent decision.[28, 29]

---

[26] 'Where Should India Borrow?' *The Economist* (London, England), Saturday, Dec. 13, 1884, p. 1508, Issue 2155 (italics by M. Schiltz).

[27] 'Wasteful Indian Borrowing.' *The Economist* (London, England), Saturday, June 26, 1886, p. 796, Issue 2235.

[28] It is important to be aware of the fact that related debates continued into the 1890s. As this is the time around which one finds growing evidence of upcoming Indian currency reform, the theoretical debate on the merits of borrowing in silver gradually receded. Bimetallists then took on the outstanding silver rupee loan issues, and argued that, in view of US legislation (the Sherman silver purchase act), their associated 'silver risk' price was greatly inflated. If anything, their plans came a day late and a dollar short: the predicted 'negative yield' for silver never was realized, a clear indication that the tide had definitively turned against the white metal (Haupt, 1890). For an exploration of this argument, see Flandreau and Oosterlinck (2012, pp. 656–7).

[29] This section is named after the title of an Op-ed in *The Economist* at the time. See: 'Where Ought India To Borrow?' *The Economist* (London, England), Saturday, Mar. 1, 1884, p. 260, Issue 2114.

5. Chinese Borrowing in the 1890s

Whatever may have been the wiser course of action, silver seemed radically on the out in the 1890s. Or did it not? Although India slowly drifted away from the silver standard, China's defeat in the Sino-Japanese War of 1894-5 appeared to provide yet another opportunity for a silver bet. As a matter of fact, the cost of the war and the enormous amount of the indemnity (200,000,000 taels, or a whopping £32,000,000) made the simultaneous raising of a gold and silver loan seem a necessity. Market conditions, in the meanwhile, were favorable. First of all, China could secure the loans upon the revenue of the Imperial Maritime Customs. It had done so on a regular basis since the late 1870s, and foreign investors had become used to seeing it as 'as a good security',[30] not in the least because the Maritime Customs were firmly in foreigners' hands (for several decades they were headed by an Englishman, Inspector General Sir Robert Hart).[31] China had moreover a record for sound debt servicing; *The Economist* was keen to point out several times that 'the instalments and interest on [former Chinese] loans have always been duly met',[32] and that, for that reason, China 'could have millions of fresh money for the asking'.[33]

Ironically, geopolitical realities were also to the advantage of the Chinese. Knowing that the mythical China market proved tempting for the great powers of the time, China's leadership did what it had done and would do for a long time. It cleverly attempted to play Russia, France, Germany, and Great Britain against each other.[34] To a certain degree, these tactics were successful. When on June 7, 1895, Great Britain's Foreign Office learned of a Chinese-Russian agreement for the floating of a £16,000,000 loan at 4 per cent interest—earlier, much smaller loans had been issued at 6 per cent—it had difficulty hiding its anger. The country's financial press openly rebuked the Chinese choice of the creditor.

It is however much more difficult to judge Chinese success with respect to an earlier silver loan of £1,635,000, raised in November 1894. This issue,[35] underwritten by the Hongkong and Shanghai Banking Corporation (HSBC),

---

[30] 'Chinese Bonds'. *The Economist* (London, England), Saturday, Apr. 27, 1895, p. 544, Issue 2696.
[31] For a digest of the history of this institution, see Brunero (2006); Chang (2012).
[32] 'Chinese Loans'. *The Economist* (London, England), Saturday, Feb. 28, 1885, p. 251, Issue 2166.
[33] 'Some Business Aspects of the Corean Conflict'. *The Economist* (London, England), Saturday, July 28, 1894, p. 917, Issue 2657.
[34] 'Chinese Borrowing'. *The Economist* (London, England), Saturday, July 13, 1895, p. 907, Issue 2707. For a commentary on British diplomatic behaviour in the negotiations, see McLean (1973).
[35] This issue was redeemable in ten equal annual drawings, beginning in 1904.

commanded 7 per cent interest, yet had been negotiated at a time when China's fiscal house was in better order:

> When the silver loan [...] was issued [...] last year, it was stated in the prospectus that the only charge then existing was for the interest and redemption of outstanding loans, amounting to £1,000,000. When, however, in the following February application was made for a new gold loan, it was announced that the amount of the loans then secured upon the Customs [...], was less than £4,000,000, of which, however, about £700,000 would be repaid before June 1st.[36]

More importantly, and telling about the international outlook of silver, foreign go-betweens with the Chinese governments were, after this December 1894 issue, not willing to raise loans on a silver basis, presumably because it was difficult to find investors interested in having exposure to the exchange rate risk embodied in those securities. The Chinese, on the other hand, complained about the mismatch problem they would face if borrowing on a gold basis. In a telling quote from the *North China Herald*: 'They dread loss on the repayment on a gold basis, having once already been bitten and they presume foreigners have the power to raise the value just before their payments fall due.'[37]

The silver risk premium, developed out of recurrent political frustration with international coordination and badmouthing by the 'hard money' proponents in the world center had thus risen to a new level. By the late 1890s, it was high enough for silver-denominated debts to be considered as pure speculation on an all too volatile price (and indeed, as can be concluded from Figure 2.01 in this chapter, the gyrations of the silver price were spectacular around 1895). In effect, this resulted in a new ideological wave in favor of monetary reform, if needed under the cloak of 'foreign assistance'. Japan's Matsukata realized this at an early stage and saved Japan's honor by using the Chinese indemnity to move Japan onto gold, even though that involved a costly trade-off between long-term access to foreign credit and short- to mid-term financial instability (Schiltz, 2012a).

Still, it was the establishment of a currency board for British India that knocked the bottom out of a monetary option that had, only a few decades earlier, been perfectly legitimate. In the United States, arguments against the

---

[36] 'Chinese Borrowing'. *The Economist* (London, England), Saturday, July 13, 1895, p. 907, Issue 2707.

[37] *The North China Herald*, June 14, 1895, 71 (1454), 915, Volume 71, Issue 1454. Compare furthermore: *The North China Herald*, Nov. 2, 1894, Volume 70, Issue 1422; and Nov. 9, 1894, Volume 70, Issue 1423.

Figure 2.11 Republican campaign poster from 1896 attacking free silver:
DUBIOUS ' "What awful poor wages they have in all those free silver countries,
John!" "That's so, wife, but the politicians say it will be different in America."
"I wouldn't take any chances on it, John, It's easy to lower wages and hard to raise
them. Politicians will tell you anything. We know there was good wages when we
had protection. We could never buy clothes for the children on what they given in
free silver countries, could we?" '

deflationary tendencies of the late nineteenth-century gold standard fell on
deaf ears. Its adoption of gold monometallism at once laid the foundations for
the dollar's rise to the world currency par excellence. As if it had decided to
invert Bryan's famous cross of gold speech, the country embarked on a currency crusade in which gold was to play a key role (Conant, 1903, 1909;
United States, 1904; Kemmerer, 1905). Although dollar diplomacy was not
always successful, notably in China, it cemented the interests and political
sway of the 'hard money' proponents. That silver did see a sharp appreciation
in its value between 1897 and 1905, in part because of booming demand for
Chinese industrialization (Kemmerer, 1912),[38] did not matter anymore. The
'inflationary white metal' was, from then on, subject to prohibitively high
premia (Figure 2.11).

[38] Compare, in the context of Chinese modernization and industrialization: 'Silver and Railway
Progress in China'. Orient. *The Economist* (London, England), Saturday, Aug. 21, 1897, p. 1211,
Issue 2817.

3

Trade Finance in the Late Nineteenth Century

Accounting for Silver Risk

For some time after 1874 there was only a certain number of merchants who had become frightened about exchange. It was in 1876 that the great alterations in the method of financing shipments were made, and then a large number of those who traded to the East instead of drawing on London became so frightened about the fall in silver that they drew on Shanghai in taels, or on Hong Kong or on Japan in dollars, as the case might be. The shipper would draw a bill on Shanghai at 60 days, which a bank in London would buy at a rate of exchange they (the banks) fixed themselves, and this saved him from any further risk of a fall in the exchanges.

> (Mr. Provand, a trader with the East, testifying before the Gold and Silver Commission. *Report of the Royal Commission Appointed to Inquire into the Recent Changes in the Relative Values of the Precious Metals; with Minutes of Evidence and Appendices.* 1887–8. London: Eyre and Spottiswoode, p. 160)

1. Introduction

In Chapter 2, we provided further descriptive evidence of Flandreau and Oosterlinck's asset pricing approach with respect to the credibility of the silver price and bimetallism in the field of sovereign debt. That this has received its, admittedly still limited, share of attention in the literature is largely self-evident. Comparing silver- respective to gold-denominated government securities seems the best conceivable proxy for long-term expectations. Yet is it possible to find a corollary of 'silver risk' in other fields of finance, say, for instance, trade finance?

Accounting for the Fall of Silver: Hedging Currency Risk in Long-Distance Trade with Asia, 1870–1913.
Michael Schiltz, Oxford University Press (2020). © Michael Schiltz.
DOI: 10.1093/oso/9780198865025.001.0001

Contrary to what one might object intuitively (as in the 'portfolio approach'), this does not need to imply a shift of attention to short-term capital movements that one can reasonably expect to find as a response (arbitrage) to the short-term variability of the gold-silver exchange rate.[1] Instead, we look at the institution level, and address those institutions that are historically associated with selling trade insurance: exchange banks, or, as they were sometimes referred to, 'international banks' (Baster, 1935). Fully in line with the theoretical search approach outlined in Chapter 1, we point to a demand for *liabilities* rather than assets. Typically, exchange banks must thus be thought of as institutions that are in the business of bearing the cost of holding certain liabilities *in return for the liquidity services the latter will provide.*[2]

The intuition is that these institutions, their very raison d'être being the managers of exchange risk, will reflect their long-term expectations of silver prices in the way they price risk. This may have taken different forms. On the one hand, we may assume that their assessment of the eventual non-credibility of silver led to a (hefty) premium on holding risk denominated in that metal. On the other hand, when silver was still considered credible, one may expect a larger willingness to hold silver-denominated securities and liabilities. Such positions on silver would thus translate into a willingness to carry the exchange risk, rather than shifting it to clients in the silver-using countries.

With all this must come a disclaimer. The following paragraphs build on a—largely Japanese—tradition of business history documenting the evolution of nineteenth-century Asian trade finance with a focus on the London capital market. Highly original in their own right, findings within this tradition have unfortunately remained below the radar of mainstream financial history, be it for linguistic reasons or something else. They were important for this chapter, in that they can all claim to have partially discovered the story behind 'silver risk' in nineteenth-century trade finance.[3]

What follows is necessarily a hybrid account. True to the ethno-historiographical approach adopted in the other chapters, we revisit earlier findings, whether in English or Japanese or other languages, and explore their relationships by means of newly unearthed primary materials, constituting mostly descriptive, that is, 'narrative' evidence. This is in no sense to be

---

[1] For literature on the latter, see the iconic groundbreaking work of Arthur Bloomfield (1963).

[2] Put differently, this explains why exchange banks had a tendency to be 'conservative' in that they avoided looking for immediate returns, for example by drawing on centers in which interest rates and/or discount rates were high.

[3] For a recent, voluminous, and seminal publication wrapping up Japanese research findings in this respect, see Nishimura et al. (2014). For two early, and still relevant papers, see Ishii (1979a, 1979b).

interpreted as a deficiency. In a sense, the narrative evidence is more informative than mere quantitative material, as it touches on the various aspects of bill finance in the nineteenth century. In bookkeeping manuals and treatises of the time I found an unusual yet indispensable companion for reconstructing the accounting workflow characteristic of sterling bills, currency drafts, interest bills, and so on.[4]

The conclusions are pertinent. We find very substantial proof that there existed a form of silver risk in trade finance. The key to our findings is, perhaps surprisingly, financial technology. 'Silver risk' was hard-wired into the contracts used for import and export trade from and to East Asia, either as the underlying mechanisms for pricing risk or as clauses defining who was to bear the risk. Researchers as Nishimura Shizuya, Suzuki Toshio, Kitabayashi Masashi, and others must be credited for explaining how trade finance-related contracts (mostly bills of exchange) evolved considerably in the course of the nineteenth century (cf. infra; Nishimura, 1971; Kojima, 1978; Ishii, 1979a, 1979b; Kitabayashi, 1982, 1987, 1992, 1999, 2001; Nishimura et al., 2012; Suzuki, 2012). Much more intricate than previously thought in the West, nineteenth-century bankers had a very advanced understanding of the issues at stake. Japanese researchers, on the other hand, may be surprised to find how exactly this relates to encompassing stories as the credibility of bimetallism, the emergence of the classical gold standard, etc.

2. The Early Days: London as the Pivot of All International Trade Finance

How did the financing of trade with East Asian countries before the 1870s differ from the that in subsequent decades? As can be gathered from the epigraph, 1876 in particular must be treated as a watershed. This is at least what emerges from Mr Provand's testimony before the Gold and Silver Commission on February 28th, 1887. The testimony is actually doubly relevant: apart from pinpointing a specific date, it also sketches the direct relationship between changes in bill finance and in the silver price. The impact of yet other changes, namely in communication and transportation technology, which certainly

---

[4] For a sample of such sources (in chronological order): Amano (1—); Tsuchiko (1895); Tashiro (1902); Ishikawa (1907); Mizuno (1908); Tamura (1908); Ōtsuki (1909). Most of these publications can be found in full-text form in the digital library collection of Japan's National Diet Library. There also exist a few (very helpful) examples of 'grey literature', that is, as Yokohama Specie Bank (YSB) internal publications: Yokohama Shōkin Ginkō (1923, 1924, 1931).

played their role at the time, are omitted. At the same time, the account contains a certain bias. Mr Provand was, as also succinctly noted in the Report of the Royal Commission, an *exporter* of goods from Great Britain to the East.[5] His points therefore relate to only one side of European trade with East Asia, and one that is probably the more complicated one.

The financing of Eastern exports to Western Europe by means of so-called 'import bills' is arguably more straightforward. The reason therefore is that such finance relates to trade operations that were carried out by traders whose unit of account was silver. The difference is an important one as the latter, by virtue of operating on silver, were also isolated from silver's gyrations after 1874–5. Yet other differences existed, in particular with respect to the *usance* of such bills.[6] It is accepted knowledge among economic historians that Great Britain financed its exports on a long-term credit base, whereas import bills, that is, bills drawn on Great Britain from overseas, were non-renewable short-term credit instruments (Nishimura, 1971, pp. 26ff.). These aspects can, however, be safely left out of the discussion for now. Let us first see what import bills entailed in terms of accounting workflow.[7]

For the exporting house in, say, Shanghai, the operation was actually quite simple. It drew a sterling-denominated bill upon London, which it sold, at the rate of the day, to one of the exchange banks present in the city, or any other Chinese portal trading hub, for that matter. At the same time it sent out its goods ('mostly tea and silk', according to the Report of the Royal Commission). The exchange bank sent the bill on to London, where it was kept until maturity by the London bank. At maturity, the latter collected the payment—in British pounds—from the London importer. If expressed schematically, the transfer of the trade contract, the merchandise and the compensation by the British importer look as presented in Figure 3.01.[8]

---

[5] *Report of the Royal Commission Appointed to Inquire into the Recent Changes in the Relative Values of the Precious Metals; with Minutes of Evidence and Appendices.* 1887–8. London: Eyre and Spottiswoode, p. 159.

[6] Nishimura makes a strong distinction between bills in terms of their usance, and reiterates that bills related to the importation of Asian goods into Great Britain had a particularly short-term character. See in this context as well several articles in *The Economist*, where this is explicitly argued: 'Adverse Exchanges—High Rate of Interest,' *The Economist* (London, England), Saturday, Sept. 3, 1853, p. 985, Issue 523; 'The Economist.' *The Economist* (London, England), Saturday, Oct. 9, 1858, p. 1117, Issue 789.

[7] Descriptive evidence of the activities of the English importer of East Asian merchandise are also contained in the Report of the Royal Commission, but I was not aware of the latter until Suzuki Toshio recently draw attention to it. See, in this respect, for the testimony of Mr John Kenworthy Bythell (Feb. 8, 1887). In *Report of the Royal Commission Appointed to Inquire into the Recent Changes in the Relative Values of the Precious Metals; with Minutes of Evidence and Appendices.* 1887–8. London: Eyre and Spottiswoode, pp. 92–108. Suzuki's discussion can be found in Suzuki (2014).

[8] For inspiration of the figures that follow, see especially: Ishikawa (1907); Andō (1957). The former contains plenty of reproductions of examples of the accounting workflow associated with all kinds

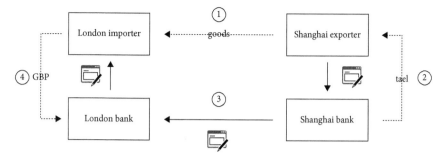

Figure 3.01. The flow of goods, bills, and money (remittances/advances) in the case of the import of Eastern merchandise into Great Britain
Source: illustration created by the author

The accounting workflow corollary to this transaction is illustrated in Figure 3.02. It is clear that, from an exchange banking perspective, this is a clear-cut way of conceiving of a foreign exchange transaction. Upon buying the bill from the Eastern exporter, the exchange bank credited the exporter's account with the amount paid, and booked the acquired bill to its debit (as it had bought a debt) (2). When sending on the bill to the London office of the bank, it debited its 'nostro' account (*tōhō kanjō* 当方勘定) with the latter, and the Shanghai office could treat the bill to its credit under 'bills bought' (*kai kawase tegata* 買為替手形) (3). Conversely, the London office credited the Shanghai office account with itself (referred to as a 'vostro' account (*senpō kanjō* 先方勘定) as it is an account of an entity other than itself in a currency of that entity, yet belonging to the same bank network), and booked the bill to its debit side on the 'bills for collection' (*uketori tegata* 受取手形) account (3'). Upon maturity, the British importer's account with the London office was debited for the amount due, and the bill was booked as a bill collected ('credit') (4).

Rounding up, as can be seen in (5) and (6), the transaction between the Shanghai and London branches of the bank was settled in one and the same currency, namely the British pound. For the London office, the unit of account being GBP, this did not even affect its exchange position. For the Shanghai branch as a unit, on the other hand, it is strictly speaking a settlement in a foreign currency. As the latter keeps its books in the tael unit of account, the transaction resulted in a sterling-denominated credit claim on the London office. In order for the latter to be settled, it had to enter in a reverse transaction, namely one in which its credit claim is matched by a London office claim

of bills. For a full list, see Schiltz (2016c). I used a copy from my personal collection. This bank-internal publication (a training manual?) proved particularly valuable when visualizing the accounting workflow of bill types. I suspect similar examples of 'grey' publications also functioned as the defining influence for several of Kitabayashi's papers referred to above.

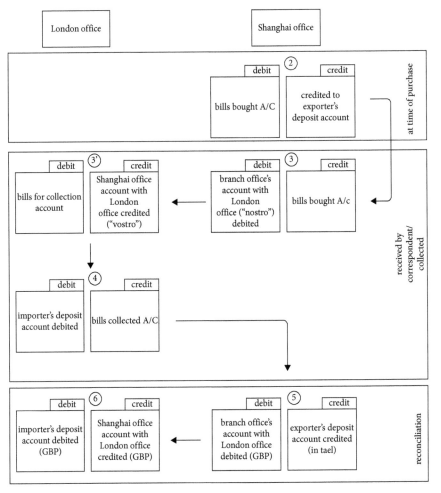

Figure 3.02. Accounting workflow associated with the import of Eastern merchandise into Great Britain, before 1876

Source: illustration created by the author

on Shanghai—in other words, a transaction involving an 'export bill' originating in London, and, importantly, *a consequent remittance of GBP from Shanghai to London*. Returning to the epigraph to this chapter, this is the kind of transactions Mr Provand, the 'trader with the East', was referring to.

As the reader will immediately note, the set of flows related to export bills is not a mirror image of the one relating to import bills (Figure 3.03). This is crucial, as it will explain how fundamentally export finance differed from import finance.

First of all, the London exporting house did not draw on the Shanghai bank, but it, too, *drew on London*. It sent out its goods, for instance, cotton

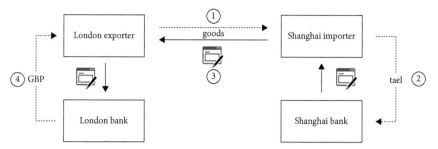

Figure 3.03. The flow of goods, bills, and money (remittances/advances) in the case of the export of merchandise from Great Britain to East Asia, before 1876
Source: illustration created by the author

goods from Manchester, as we are told in the Report of the Royal Commission. Importantly, the goods were sent out on manufacturers' accounts as *adventures*, that is, they were not the consequence of an earlier order from an East Asian importer. As Mr Provand described, this kind of export finance could thrive thanks to the existence of another entity, namely the consignee. Compare the following conversation between our merchant and the members of the Gold and Silver Commission:

'Now, suppose that in the year 1873 […] you sent out a shipment of cotton to Shanghai?'—I bought an invoice of cotton goods in Manchester, and shipped it off. I drew on London for the amount of the invoice at six months, and if the proceeds had not returned from China within the six months, I had the bill renewed for, say, three months. By that time the proceeds of these goods would be back in my possession […] 'In what form?'—In a sterling bill. The consignee of my cotton goods would sell them for taels (if in Shanghai), deliver the goods, get paid his taels, and go to the office of an Eastern bank in Shanghai, say the Oriental Bank or any bank, and buy a draft on London, which he would remit to me. […] 'Your consignee would sell the goods?'—He would sell the goods, receive payment in taels of silver, go to the bank, and buy a draft in sterling on London, which he would remit to me. With the proceeds of that bill, when I received it in London, I would retire the original acceptance, and the transaction would be at an end. […] 'But then you were trading with other people's capital?'—I am describing how 19 invoices out of 20 were treated.[9]

---

[9] *Report of the Royal Commission Appointed to Inquire into the Recent Changes in the Relative Values of the Precious Metals; with Minutes of Evidence and Appendices.* 1887–8. London: Eyre and Spottiswoode, p. 159–60.

As indicated in this short exchange, the original bill the merchant drew on his London bank was never sent out of London; it was, hence, a so-called inland bill (*naikoku kawase tegata* 内国為替手形), *but its purpose was not the financing of domestic trade*, nor did it have a comparable and relatively short usance as ordinary inland bills. Around the 1870s, the usance of inland bills for long-distance foreign trade was typically sixty days sight (equal to eight months' date). It could be renewed several times (in most cases for thirty days per renewal, according to Mr Provand), and it should therefore be treated as a particular type of inland bill, as Nishimura argued long ago.[10]

Note as well the role of the London banker. His role made it possible for the merchant to keep his inland bill with Great Britain, thanks to which that bill can be renewed, as we saw, sometimes several times. In the language of the aforementioned *Report*:

'Then an exporting merchant in England before 1874 used to draw upon his own credit?'—He used to draw it might be on a bank in London or elsewhere, or on a firm, in which case he would pay a commission to them for accepting his draft, or it might be on a house that was doing the business with him on joint account.[11]

The consignee, on the other hand, played an equally important role. Through the purchase of a sterling remittance draft on London (*rondon-ate stāringu sōkin kawase tegata* ロンドン宛スターリング送金為替手形), he or she created the opportunity for the Shanghai bank office to replenish its tael-holdings the latter had paid out when buying bills from Shanghai based exporters (cf. supra). In other words, although the trajectory of export bills is rather different from the one related to import bills, the corollary accounting workflow is perfectly complementary (Figure 3.04).

---

[10] Nishimura (1971, p. 33; italics mine):

Thus, the standard usance of bills could have been different from what could be termed the standard period of transactions. If we take the case of export trade with countries like India, China, Australia […], the time needed for the transportation of the goods and the time needed for sending back the money proceeds could together have been as long […] as eight or nine months till the sixties […]. In spite of this, the export trades to those distant parts were financed by drawing four or six month's bills on London or Liverpool. *Thus, standard usance of bills was in many instances just a fiction to rig up a semblance of respectability by which financing of these long-distance trades was more palatable to the banks which discounted these bills.*

[11] *Report of the Royal Commission Appointed to Inquire into the Recent Changes in the Relative Values of the Precious Metals; with Minutes of Evidence and Appendices.* 1887–8. London: Eyre and Spottiswoode, p. 160.

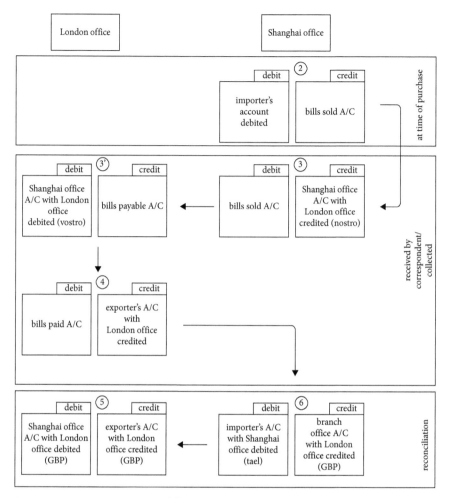

Figure 3.04. Accounting workflow associated with the export of merchandise from Great Britain to East Asia, before 1876; using a sterling draft

Source: illustration created by the author

As the principles of steps (2) to (4) have been explained in Figure 3.02, that needs no repetition here. I only draw attention to the settling of accounts in steps (5) and (6). It is clear that, when compared with Figure 3.02, the accounting workflow implied that, for the London office, the transaction once again does not result in a foreign exchange operation; for the Shanghai office, on the other hand, it does constitute a foreign exchange operation, yet one it needs in order to recoup taels it had paid out when acquiring export bills from domestic exporters. Incoming and outgoing bills could be cleanly offset (*sōsai* 相殺).

3. 1876 and Beyond

The old ways of trade financing eroded after the mid-1870s, however, as argued in our epigraph. A host of factors contributed to the demise of the consignment system, and contrary to what the reader might have come to believe from Mr Provand's testimony, they were not all monetary ones. As a matter of fact, profound changes in the technologies of transportation and telecommunication were equally forceful drivers of change and innovation.

First of all, the opening of the Suez Canal in 1869 allowed ships to travel between Europe and Eastern Asia without navigating around Africa, thereby reducing the sea voyage distance between Europe and India by about 7,000 kilometers, or 4,300 miles.[12] Related to the latter, the introduction of more fuel-efficient ocean steamers made shipping considerably faster (Yoshida, 2014). It also boosted their use, as they were ideally fit to take advantage of the new shipping route. At the same time, this led to the progressive abandonment of sailing vessels for Eastern trade. For them, the canal was not a practical option, as using a tug was difficult and, especially, expensive; this distance saving was not available to them (Jarvis, 1993). To be exact, the distance gained by the Suez Canal and the practicalities involved made that so-called steamers started to replace 'tea clippers' from the early 1870s (MacGregor, 1983).

The telegraph added efficiency to the mix, especially after 1872, when the Eastern Telegraph Company was established (two years earlier, in 1870, the London to Bombay telegraph line had been completed). As argued by Lew and Cater, it reduced, among others, the time ships spent in port; it also allowed ships to travel farther among ports to collect more valuable cargo. This was not all. As the global telegraph network (Figure 3.05)[13] expanded rapidly, it shifted the world economy 'onto real time'. What this meant for international trade practices would soon be obvious: another way in which the telegraph 'enhanced capital saving was in allowing merchants in remote locations to increase their inventory turnover rates' (Lew and Cater, 2006, p. 149)[14] Indeed, telecommunication eventually dealt a deathblow to the practice of 'adventuring' that underlay all pre-1870s bill financing.[15] The

---

[12] Studies on the impact of the Suez Canal on the trade between Europe and (East) Asia are surprisingly scarce. For a representative digest: Fletcher (1958); Adams (1971).

[13] For explorations of the connection between telegraphy and empire, see Kennedy (1971); Winseck and Pike (2007); Wenzlhuemer (2012).

[14] Compare as well: Ejrnæs and Persson (2010).

[15] Compare Nishimura:

A merchant firm relying on mails every four weeks would be inconceivable today, and from this we can get an idea of how different commercial activities were in the middle years of the

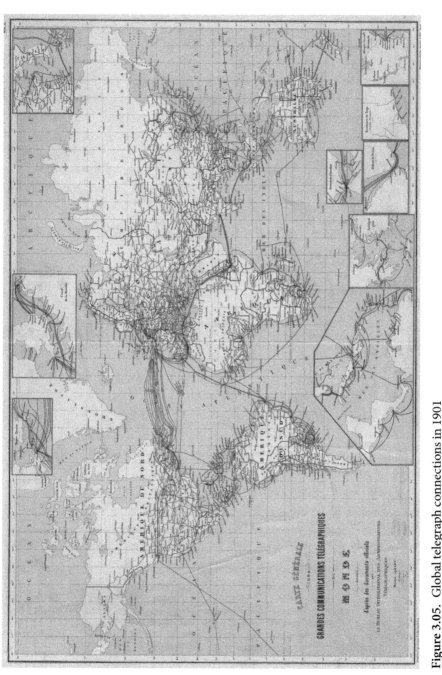

Figure 3.05. Global telegraph connections in 1901

Map reproduction courtesy of the Norman B. Leventhal Map & Education Center at the Boston Public Library.

consequences of its demise for bill financing are important, and will be discussed in later paragraphs.

So how exactly was bill financing affected in the mid-1870s? As already indicated in Mr Provand's testimony, the fall of the silver price added an extra stress-factor to the changes in trade finance that developed in the early 1870s. To put it simply, merchants became unwilling to carry the risk that their exports to East Asia would not find a buyer because of 'adverse exchanges', and, instead, sought to secure a safe return on their shipments rather than engage in speculation. The following is what the Report of the Royal Commission had to say about it:

> '[The merchant house] transferred the risk to the bank?'—It transferred the risk to the bank of a fall in exchange. 'But on the renewal?'—There could be no renewal of such a draft in this country, because this draft went out of the country. It was drawn on the consignee in Shanghai against the goods and in 19 cases out of 20 the bill of lading and the policy of insurance would be attached to the draft when it was handed into the office of the bank here in London.[16]

What the Report describes can be summarized graphically, as shown in Figure 3.06.

The consequences of such a transaction will be explained in a minute. Again, the Report speaks for itself:

> 'But now [i.e. after 1876] [the merchant] draws on the consignee to whom he sends out a shipment?'—To a large extent. There are still some merchants who draw in Manchester on London. There are two ways in which it is done. He may draw on London and run his risk of the exchange, waiting till the proceeds came home. 'That is a method which has been given up?'—To a large extent. The other way is often done. He draws on London for the sake

nineteenth century. To this lack of telegraph was added the slowness and uncertainty of transport by sailing vessels. [...] Not only merchants, but also manufacturers, were probably forced to maintain a large inventory of raw materials if they wanted to insure the smooth working of their factories, because of the uncertainty of supply. Thus inventory investment appears to have played a much more important part than in the present day and the financing of these goods in store must have been a great burden on the money market.   (1971, pp. 77–8)

[16] *Report of the Royal Commission Appointed to Inquire into the Recent Changes in the Relative Values of the Precious Metals; with Minutes of Evidence and Appendices.* 1887–8. London: Eyre and Spottiswoode, pp. 160–1.

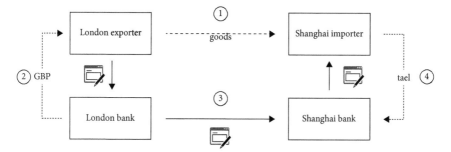

Figure 3.06. The flow of goods, bills, and money (remittances/advances) in the case of the export of merchandise from Great Britain to East Asia, after 1876; the use of silver-denominated drafts
Source: illustration created by the author

of getting cheap money, and at the same time telegraphs to his correspondent in Shanghai to buy forward as much exchange in sterling as the proceeds of the goods will amount to, thus ensuring himself a certain return for the goods when the proceeds come home. [However,] there is no forward business with Shanghai, or very little.[17]

There existed, however, serious problems with the settling of such transactions. As we see in Figure 3.06, the merchant sent out his products to East Asia (1), and bought a tael-denominated bill (*chūgoku-ate gin tegata* 中国宛銀手形) on Shanghai from his London banker (2). The latter sent it on to the Shanghai office (3), where the money was collected, at the bill's maturity (4), from the importer in China. In terms of accounting workflow, however, this posed new challenges, as can be seen in Figure 3.07.

Again, steps (2)–(4) are quite straightforward. The British exporter draws a bill on Shanghai in tael, and the London bank buys this bill. The London bank credits the merchant's account to the amount for which it has purchased the bill, and books the bill as 'debit' as a bill bought (2). Next, when sending on the silver-denominated bill, it debits its 'nostro' account with the Shanghai office (in tael), and books the bill to its credit as a 'bill bought' (3). The Shanghai office, on the other hand, credits the London office's 'vostro' account, and books the bill to its 'debit' as a 'bill receivable'. Once it debited the Shanghai importer's account with the bank for the amount due, it could book the bill as 'bill received'.

---

[17] *Report of the Royal Commission Appointed to Inquire into the Recent Changes in the Relative Values of the Precious Metals; with Minutes of Evidence and Appendices.* 1887–8. London: Eyre and Spottiswoode, pp. 160–1.

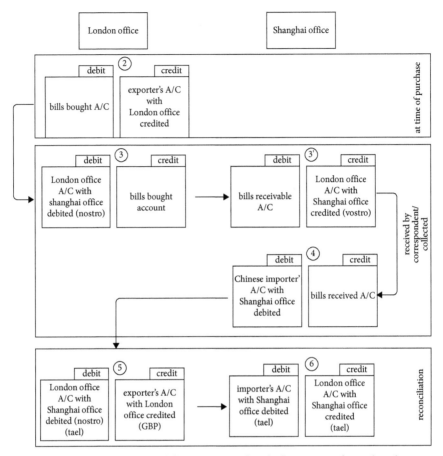

Figure 3.07. Accounting workflow associated with the export of merchandise from Great Britain to East Asia, after 1876; using a silver-denominated currency draft

Source: illustration created by the author

From the settlement in (5) and (6), however, it is clear that the London office faced a mismatch. It had engaged in a foreign exchange transaction, and found itself carrying the exchange risk for the period between the purchase of the bill and the latter's maturity, several months later. One understands the Gold and Silver Commission's surprise that the risk had effectively been transferred to the bank, whereas a reverse 'cover' transaction was not possible (Kitabayashi, 1987, p. 7).[18]

---

[18] Compare, furthermore, *The Economist*: 'The present system throws all the risk on the bank, which should not incur it [...]' 'Why Have the Anglo-Indian Banks Fared So Badly in 1881?' *The Economist* (London, England), Saturday, Apr. 22, (1882, p. 469, Issue 2017).

If anything, this 'Achilles heel' (Kitabayashi, 1987, p. 12) was at odds with the conservative exchange banking attitude of the pre-1870s, when the banker's bets were automatically hedged, thanks to the then stable gold-silver ratio. Mr Provand was very direct in his indictment: 'it is a speculation',[19] no more, no less, as there appeared to be no commensurate exchange cover. This, he assumed, explained the high rates for trade insurance with China and Japan (according to the report, frequently into 12 per cent *per annum* or more):[20]

—There is no forward business with Shanghai, or very little. As the produce business from India enables the banks to buy bills on London 'forward,' they in turn sell their own bills on London 'forward,' chiefly as remittances for proceeds of imports sold in India. They thus obtain 'cover' transactions, [...]. All the before-mentioned [sic.] conditions are wanting in the trade with China and Japan. There is nothing similar to India Council bills sold on these countries, and China and Japan have only two principal exports, tea and silk, most of which is shipped between June and September, and tea cannot be sold 'forward,' but only after it has arrived and been sampled. The banks are, therefore, unable for the greater part of the year to obtain 'cover' business in China and Japan as they do in the trade with India, and on this account they will not buy drafts on China and Japan against shipments, except at rates which cost the merchant about 12 per cent, for the use of the bank's money while the draft is running, and he must either pay this to the bank to be relieved of the risk of a fall in exchange, or wait the return of his proceeds, meanwhile taking the risk himself.[21]

To a certain extent, Mr Provand was right. Although hedging strategies definitely existed (cf. Chapter 4), they may not have been equally opportune or feasible to certain exchange banks. Also, banks may not have been willing to hedge their exchange transactions.[22] As we know from Suzuki Toshio's work on the Oriental Bank Corporation (OBC), expectations of a rebound of

---

[19] *Report of the Royal Commission Appointed to Inquire into the Recent Changes in the Relative Values of the Precious Metals; with Minutes of Evidence and Appendices.* 1887–8. London: Eyre and Spottiswoode, p. 161.

[20] *Report of the Royal Commission Appointed to Inquire into the Recent Changes in the Relative Values of the Precious Metals; with Minutes of Evidence and Appendices.* 1887–8. London: Eyre and Spottiswoode, pp. 161ff..

[21] *Report of the Royal Commission Appointed to Inquire into the Recent Changes in the Relative Values of the Precious Metals; with Minutes of Evidence and Appendices.* 1887–8. London: Eyre and Spottiswoode, p. 161).

[22] Possibly informed by misleading contemporary journalistic coverage, the idea that hedging strategies were unknown at the time persists until today. For a very recent example, see Bonin et al. (2015, esp. pp. 11ff.).

the silver price in the late 1870s fueled the willingness to take the silver risk and take long positions on silver,[23] to the detriment of pretty much all exchange banks in India at the time (2012). Especially the decision to lock up their working capital in long-term Indian government securities cost the banks very dearly. *The Economist* put it as follows: 'The bank which buys stock with the view of selling out at a possible profit, instead of with a view to hold for investment purposes, is simply gambling, and deserves a gambler's fate.'[24]

Against the backdrop of these flawed managerial decisions, there was however also a structural problem. Again, Nishimura must be credited with discovering how the 'structural problem' of 1870s bill finance related to earlier developments. Put simply, the ameliorations in both speed and distance had caused the usance of bills to become considerably shorter (typically, from six months to four months).[25] This is also clear from his computations (usance goes back up again afterwards, for reasons that we will explain in later paragraphs) (Figure 3.08).

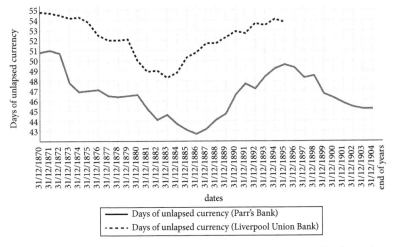

Figure 3.08. Bill usance, 1870-1904: nine year moving average of unlapsed currency of bills held by Parr's Bank and Liverpool Union Bank

Source: illustration created by the author, after Nishimura (1971, p. 98, p. 130)

[23] Mr Murray Robertson, the then Chairman of the Chartered Mercantile Bank of India, London and China relates his bank's decision to the monetary conferences discussed in Chapter 2: '[Our] bank took a wrong view of the result of the Paris Conference': 'Why Have the Anglo-Indian Banks Fared So Badly in 1881?' *The Economist* (London, England), Saturday, Apr. 22, 1882, p. 469, Issue 2017.

[24] 'Why Have the Anglo-Indian Banks Fared So Badly in 1881?' *The Economist* (London, England), Saturday, Apr. 22, 1882, p. 468, Issue 2017.

[25] References in *The Economist* with regard to this discussion abound. See 'Usance of Indian Bills.' An East India Merchant. *The Economist* (London, England), Saturday, June 30, 1866, p. 769, Issue 1192; 'The Shortened Usance of Indian Bills'. *The Economist* (London, England), Saturday, July 7, 1866, p. 792, Issue 1193; 'Usance of Indian Bills'. An East India Banker. *The Economist* (London, England),

Arduous demands—mostly from journalistic outlets such as *The Economist*—to reduce the bills' usance, plausible as they might have seemed at the time, drew sharp criticisms from merchants.[26] They argued that the transportation of goods from India to London took four months and that, until the sale of the goods had been effected, six to ten months after shipment were necessary.

From a banking perspective, however, bringing down the usance of bills was even more problematic, as it squeezed the market: now there were fewer bills in circulation against which opposite claims could be bought. Consequent 'excessive competition for exchange business' had not only brought down profits. It turned out, again according to *The Economist*, that it had also given rise to 'illegitimate' competition: 'in the competition for exchange business, latterly, "options" have been granted, allowing a merchant to call for his telegraphic transfer when it suited him best, and, of course, with money rising in India, when it suited the banks least'.[27]

It is nowadays commonplace to point to the reduction of bill usance as a main factor behind the fate of the once mighty OBC (Kitabayashi, 1982; Suzuki, 2012). Yet this issue was obviously not confined to OBC, so it is difficult to blame it on ill-inspired managerial decisions within the OBC cadre alone.[28] It turns out that *all* exchange banks, with the notable exception

---

Saturday, July 7, 1866, p. 798, Issue 1193. 'Usance of India Bills'. Australian Merchant. *The Economist* (London, England), Saturday, July 14, 1866, p. 823, Issue 1194; 'The Bill Circulation of the United Kingdom'. *The Economist* (London, England), Saturday, June 28, 1873, p. 775, Issue 1557; 'The Usance of Eastern Bills'. *The Economist* (London, England), Saturday, Dec. 28, 1878, p. 1520, Issue 1844; 'Eastern Usance of Bills'. W. Rathbone. *The Economist* (London, England), Saturday, Jan. 25, 1879, p. 94, Issue 1848; 'The Usance of Eastern Bills'. Exchange. *The Economist* (London, England), Saturday, Feb. 1, 1879, p. 124, Issue 1849; 'Usance of Bills from the East'. *The Economist* (London, England), Saturday, Mar. 1, 1879, p. 234, Issue 1853; *The Economist* (1882, p. 472, Issue 2017.

[26] Nishimura provides a summary of the debate (1971, pp. 36–9). Interestingly, and with a hint to the difference between 'real bills' and 'finance bills', *The Economist* argued against long usance from the viewpoint of 'sound' vs. 'unsound' finance:

> [W]ith the introduction of steam and fast sailing clipper ships, the need for such a long credit was removed, and by the subsequent opening of the Suez Canal the conditions of business have been so changed that long bills are now not only unnecessary, but positively mischievous. They afford dangerous facilities for reckless financing, for, as transactions with China can now be readily enough completed within three months, the employment of six months' bills enables a trader to have the use of money for several months after the goods, which constituted the security for the advance, have passed out of his possession. [...] *Goods have been shipped to or from this country, not with a view of realising a profit upon their sale, but simply as a means of raising money.*
> (*The Economist* (London, England), 9 Nov. 1878, p. 1315; italics mine)

I surmise this distinction most probably found its roots in the aftermath of the Overend-Gurney crisis (Flandreau, Ugolini, 2013). Suzuki Toshio has provided a very thorough history in Japanese (1998).

[27] 'Why Have the Anglo-Indian Banks Fared So Badly in 1881?'. *The Economist* (London, England), Saturday, Apr. 22, 1882, p. 468, Issue 2017.

[28] For examples of such an approach, see McGuire (2004); Sheehan (2019).

of the Hong Kong and Shanghai Banking Co (the latter did not adhere to the agreement of bringing usance down) (MacKenzie, 1954) saw sharp drops in their semestrial amounts of 'bills receivable'; their business results for the late 1870s were comparably abysmal (Kitabayashi, 1982).

Realizing that a shorter usance of Eastern bills was not in their interest, the associated banks unsurprisingly reversed the earlier decision in 1882 (MacKenzie, 1954, pp. 64ff.). *The Economist* dryly noted:

> The shorter usance, it was stated, was, in a manner forced upon certain of those institutions by the London banks, who refused to re-discount bills with more than 4 months to run; but as other of the Indian banks, who had not been similarly coerced, took 6 months papers, those who attempted to restrict themselves to 4 months' bills believe they have suffered in the competition.[29]

4. The Rise of 'Interest Bills' ('Advance Bills')

Financial innovation did not come to a standstill in 1876. Yet another year would turn out to have a profound impact on nineteenth-century bill financing. Not surprisingly, it was again a crisis that triggered a shift in banking practice. The year was 1886, and the events were a series of serious losses by the until then successful Hongkong and Shanghai Banking Corporation (HSBC) (King, 1987, 318ff.).[30]

This had several implications. For one, it was behind the debate about HSBC's often-misunderstood hedging strategy, the 'even keel', which is the subject of Chapter 4. Yet it also turned around exchange banks' expectations with respect to long-term evolutions in the gold-silver ratio. Startled by HSBC's misguided bets, and with the memory of the fall of the Oriental Bank still fresh, exchange bankers realized that even the slightest hint of taking on exchange risk would not fly with their shareholders anymore.[31] This translated, first, in a public relations campaign to assuage the public that the business of exchange banking was not 'gambling'. In the parlance of the day, the objective became to demonstrate that 'the principle of banking is to turn over money, and not bury it in the East'.[32]

---

[29] 'The Usance of Indian Bills'. *The Economist* (London, England), Saturday, Apr. 22, 1882, p. 472, Issue 2017.

[30] For a conjecture of why this happened, in spite of the 'even keel' policy, see Kitabayashi (1992, pp. 54ff.).

[31] Suzuki shows that the shares of all exchange banks, including HSBC, took a hit around 1879 (Suzuki, 2012, p. 99).

[32] *The North China Herald*, Sept. 10, 1886, p. 288.

In the field, it also led to the creation of the interest bill (*ritsuki tegata* 利付手形), designed with the explicit aim of avoiding all exchange rate risk.[33] Interest bills were a quite radical innovation indeed, and not only because of the interest clause they contained ('with interest added at…% per annum, from the date hereof to approximate due date of remittance in London'). More importantly, and in contrast to all of the above examples of bills, interest bills concerned a *deferred* exchange transaction (*ato-barai* 後払い), that is, the exchange was not effectuated at the time of buying the bill yet at the time of its collection. For that very reason, they had to contain an exchange clause (*kawase monku* 為替文句), typically formulated as follows: 'Payable at the current drawing rate…at sight on London'. Figure 3.09 shows how the flows of bills and payments were affected.

A typical example of an interest bill:

£1,000   London, July 10, 1904

At three months after sight, pay this First of Exchange (Second and Third unpaid) to the order of………………………………………………………, the sum of One thousand Sterling with interest added thereto at 7% per annum, from date hereof to approximate due date of remittance in London.
Payable at the current drawing rate for the International Banking Corporation's draft at sight in London.

Yokohama Specie Bank   Value received,
Yokohama, Japan   Signed by
                                                      (name)
                                                      (address)

Source: Ishikawa (1907, pp. 72-3).

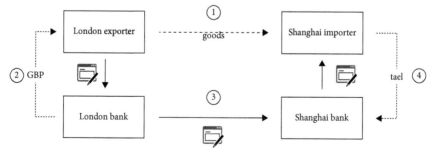

Figure 3.09. The flow of goods, bills, and money (remittances/advances) in the case of the export of merchandise from Great Britain to East Asia, after 1876; the use of sterling-denominated interest bills
Source: illustration created by the author

---

[33] For a very concise discussion of the latter, see Spalding (1917, pp. 60ff.).

Although it is not immediately clear from Figure 3.09, the British exporter's role in the transaction is finished at the moment he sells his bill to the London bank. His account is credited, and that is it (2). The bank sends the bill on to Shanghai (3), where it will be presented at maturity to the importing merchant, who pays the bank the amount due, not at the rate of the day but at the rate expressly stipulated in the bill; and he pays the interest accrued from the date of sending in London until the date of remittance to London (4). Note again that the exchange transaction is not concluded at the moment the British exporter sells his bill in London, but when the importer in Shanghai remits his money (hence the alternative term 'advance bills') (MacKenzie, 1954, p. 46).

What had led to the use of such instruments? According to the *Report for the Year 1892 on the Trade of Shanghai* within the British Foreign Office Diplomatic and Consular Reports on Trade and Finance, the shift to drawing sterling-denominated bills for imports into Shanghai (i.e., what, from the viewpoint of Great Britain, would be considered 'export finance') was related to what it called the 'Alteration of Mode of Import Business—Indent Trade':[34]

The long-continued fluctuations in the exchange values have been compelling merchants to alter their mode of doing business, especially in the import trade. Instead of holdings goods on stock or to arrive to meet the requirements of the market, merchants prefer to sell to the native dealers before ordering the goods in England. They settle the price in silver and the exchange at the same time, and then transfer their orders by telegraph to Manchester. The buying and selling and the fixing of the rate of exchange are thus practically simultaneous operations; the bank takes the risk of exchange and the foreign importer has no farther [sic.] interest in the transaction than earning his commission, which he deducts when he hands over the goods and gets paid by the Chinaman. The latter is the real merchant, for he takes all the risk and gets all the advantage for a favourable turn on the market, while the foreigner is relegated to the inglorious role of a mere commission agent. *The banks have the risk of exchange, but they again protect themselves by buying and selling bills to the same extent* [cf. infra], so that, however

---

[34] Foreign Office. 1892. Annual Series. No. 1266. Diplomatic and Consular Reports on Trade and Finance. China. *Report for the Year 1892 on the Trade of Shanghai.* Reference to previous report, Annual Series No. 1101. P. 4. A partly corrective review of the latter appeared in the *North China Herald.* 1893, Oct. 20, pp. 601–2, Volume LI, Issue 1368. For a rare explanation of the indent system in secondary literature, see Motono (1994).

exchange may vary, a loss on the operations one way is balanced by a corresponding gain on the other.[35]

Doubtlessly aided by the telegraph, (mostly British) import merchants in Shanghai had, by the late 1880s,[36] relieved themselves of the former necessity to maintain large inventories. Instead, they changed their roles from traders into commission agents by collecting orders (hence: 'indent trade' or 'indent system', or *kaitsuke itakusei* 買附委託制) from native Chinese traders. The latter possessed a superior knowledge of the demands of their clientele, but instead had to incur the exchange risk involved in the transaction. The Shanghai-based (British) merchant, on the other hand, could avoid exposure to exchange risk by entering into forward exchange contracts (*sakimono kawase keiyaku* 先物為替契約) with his banker (Kitabayashi, 1987, p. 12). For the exchange bank, trade contracts embodied in sterling-denominated interest bills were even more attractive. Not only were they to receive the lucrative (high) interest rates attached to such bills. As they received remittances for such bills in British pound, they could once more cleanly settle inter-branch accounts by using the proceeds of sterling-denominated interest bills in order to balance obligations accumulated by bills bought in Shanghai for imports into Great Britain (cf. supra, §2) and denominated in the same currency.

Let us then briefly review the accounting workflow. Figure 3.10 shows how, first of all, the bank in London credits the British export merchant's account, and debits its bank acceptances account (2). When the bill arrives in Shanghai and is collected at maturity by debiting the Shanghai merchant's bank account, the Shanghai branch credits its account with the London branch (4); next, *only after the remittance reaches the London branch*, the latter debits the Shanghai branch account with itself, and credits its own bank acceptance account, and, not to forget, the 'interest account' (4'). It is through this creation of a foreign exchange transaction at the Shanghai branch that (a) the London office wards of exchange risk, and (b) the Shanghai office replenishes its tael holdings at the rate of the day.

---

[35] Foreign Office. 1892. Annual Series. No. 1266. Diplomatic and Consular Reports on Trade and Finance. China. *Report for the Year 1892 on the Trade of Shanghai*. Reference to previous report, Annual Series No. 1101, P. 4. Square brackets and italics mine.
[36] Kitabayashi (1987, pp. 13ff.), relying heavily on the reporting of the *North China Herald*, perceives the early roots of the indent trade system as soon as 1887, that is, in the wake of another bout of severe silver depreciation and volatility.

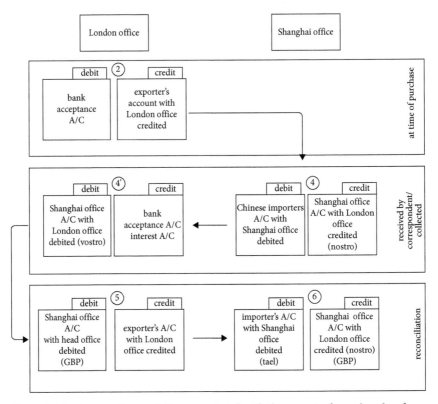

Figure 3.10. Accounting workflow associated with the export of merchandise from Great Britain to East Asia, after 1876; using a sterling-denominated interest bill

Source: Illustration by the author

5. Interest Bills and the Debate on 'Real Bills' vs. 'Finance Bills': A Nineteenth-century Carry Trade

If not for the nineteenth-century exchange banker, interest bills pose some serious interpretative hurdles for the financial historian. Looking forward to the discussion on the construction of the database underpinning most of this book's findings, these bills were, at least for the period 1898–1908, not included in the mid-term reports' flow data, but treated as a particular category under 'statement of loans and bills discounted' (*kashikin oyobi tegata waribiki no koto* 貸金及ビ手形割引ノ事).[37] Why is this? Second, and more puzzling, what explains, at least in the case of the YSB, their continued transfer

---

[37] This very fact has caused considerable misunderstandings among students of YSB foreign exchange operations. Notably Taira, who pioneered the network approach to YSB flow-of-funds, surmised that interest bills were listed in both 'statement of loans and bills discounted' and the 'statement on foreign exchange holdings and movements'. Hence, he omitted them from his analysis as it would

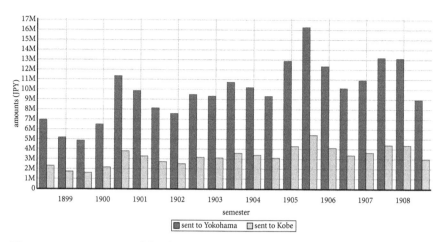

Figure 3.11. Estimates of the distribution of interest bills sent from YSB London branch to Yokohama headquarters and Kobe branch, June 1898 to June 1908 (unit: JPY)

Source: Calculations by the author

from the London (and New York) branch to the Yokohama headquarters *after* 1897 (Figure 3.11), in other words after Japan adopted the gold standard? Tokyo's decision to move onto the gold standard had at least eliminated exchange rate risk between Japan, on the one hand, and Great Britain and the US on the other. One would expect that instruments to hedge such risk had lost their rationale as well (Kobayashi 1910, p. 741). Ishii Kanji's conjecture that interest bills 'were very profitable' (1994, p. 12) so as to justify their use well into the early twentieth century is not particularly helpful, I feel.[38]

otherwise amount to double-counting the data (1984a, 1984b). Ishii, on the other hand, has convincingly argued that the interest bill data cannot have been included in the statement on foreign exchange holdings and movements, as Japan's trade deficit with Great Britain in this period should in any case have resulted in very large transfers of funds from Great Britain to Japan (as exports from Great Britain to Japan would have been financed by bills bought in London and sent to Yokohama and Kobe for collection) (1999). Consequently, Taira's analysis, which seems to show a reverse flow-of-funds from Japan to Great Britain, must be mistaken. Yet another interpretation can be found in Bak (Park) (1992). In his view, interest bills functioned as remittances (*sōkin* 送金) of foreign exchange which were sent by the branch/office in charge of collection (*toritate-ten* 取立店) to the branch/office that had purchased the bill (*kaitori-ten* 買取店). In other words, Bak believes that interest bills were a means of settling accounts *between branches* (in Japanese referred to as reimbursing (*kaikin* 回金) (as opposed to remitting)). In this view, including the interest bills in the flow-of-funds also amounts to double-counting, yet in a way different from Taira's interpretation. However, as is clear from, for example, interest bills handled by the New York office, *interest bills were also used for trade transactions*.

For primary evidence on the nature of interest bills handled by YSB's New York office, see the bank's internal journal: *Yokohama shōkin ginkō sōmubu kōhōkakari* 横濱正金銀行總務部行報係. 1911. 行報 *Kōhō* (*Bank Tidings*). 横濱正金銀行總務部行報係. Feb. 16. http://ci.nii.ac.jp/ncid/AA12169139

[38] Ishii sees the profitability of these instruments for banks, but it is not unthinkable that buying an interest bill (an exchange cover) may have been *cheaper* (rather than buying an uncovered bill) for the

Perhaps the key to the interest bills riddle is again to be found in Nishimura's seminal discussion of late nineteenth-century bill finance. As seen in §3, Nishimura traced the shortening of bill usance after the 1860s to the proliferation of the telegraph and drastic improvements in transportation technology. Much to his surprise, however, bill usance lengthened once again in the second half of the 1880s, that is, more or less with the introduction of interest bills (Nishimura, 1971, pp. 27-8). Clearly, this shift cannot be related to a renewed deterioration in technological circumstances. Other reasons can be ruled out as well. Increases in bank overdrafts for domestic trade certainly shrunk the share of shorter term inland bills in the total amount of bills held by banks, and would thus naturally have translated in a longer average usance (Nishimura, 1971, pp. 55-64); but such longer average could not possibly grow to such long terms as suggested by Nishimura's calculations (the nine-year moving average being more than forty-five days for Parr's Bank and fifty days for Liverpool Union Bank).[39] What, then, is behind this change?

In an almost buried passage, we do find, however, clear hints of the possibly shifted nature of the bills from his sample. This cannot be easily demonstrated in quantitative terms, nor do we find much direct evidence in journalistic outlets of the day, but, as we shall see, we possess considerable evidence to conclude that what follows is the only explanation possible. Concretely, Nishimura conjectures that the higher average usance of bills especially throughout the 1890s must be explained by the high number of *finance bills* in his sample.[40] He reaches this conclusion by a comparison of the discount rate of three months' and six months' bills with the general level of interest in the period (Figure 3.12). It turns out that, when the level of interest was low, the discount rate of six months' bills was higher than that of

---

buyers of those bills as well. Given the availability of information on interest rate differentials and forward discounts (/premia) published in the so-called *course of exchange*, they could have calculated their relative gains with approximate certainty (Kobayashi, 1910, p. 778–9). Einzig (1937, p. 41ff.), and later Bloomfield (1963, p. 39), came to similar conclusions in the context of exchange dealings in Russian ruble and Austrian crown, arguing that these operations were almost always covered, including *after* their stabilization in terms of gold.

[39] In the hypothesis that bills were renewed only once, these averages amount to a usance of respectively three months and 3.3 months.

[40] Nishimura has picked the term 'finance bills' after Spalding's seminal works on bill finance, I presume; Spalding himself distinguished these finance bills from earlier, and similar, uses of bills for smoothing the liquidity of firms and credit houses. At the time, however, there appears not to have been a unified terminology for such kind of trade contracts. One sometimes finds 'accommodation bills'; sometimes, they are referred to as 'acceptance credits'—both terms do, however, originate in earlier banking practice on the European continent (Rogers, 2004).

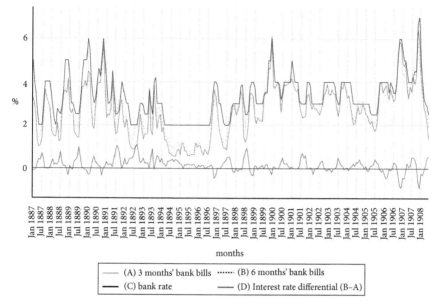

months

—— (A) 3 months' bank bills	······· (B) 6 months' bank bills
—— (C) bank rate	—— (D) Interest rate differential (B–A)

Figure 3.12. Note that, as we define the interest rate differential as the difference between the rates of 6 month's bills resp. 3 month's bills (B–A), we allow for a negative differential in case the rate for 3 month's bills is higher than the former. *Source*: illustration by the author, after Nishimura (1971, pp. 122–127)

three months' bills; yet, if the level of interest was high, the discount rate of three months' bills was higher.[41]

In case bills would only have been drawn for an underlying commercial transaction (i.e., if those bills were 'real bills', in the antiquated parlance of the day), the (positive (+) or negative (–)) value of the differential between the discount rates of six-month and three-month bills (R_{6m}-R_{3m}) would be largely proportional to the general interest rate level; in other words, the supply of six-month bills would be procyclical. After all, the drawing of commercial bills was a mere function of economic up- or downturns. In the case of an economic boom, increased demand for bills would not only cause the interest rate level to go up. It would also result in a sharp increase in six-month bills (and a consequent higher discount rate for the latter), as merchants would want to secure the use of money largely irrespective of its cost. In the case of an economic downturn or bust, a fall in demand for bills in general would also imply a decrease in six-month bills greater relative to three-month bills. In other words, their supply and discount rate were *positively related* to the general level of interest.

[41] Although never stated explicitly, I surmise Nishimura's discussion was inspired by several remarks formulated earlier by Spalding (1915, pp. 192ff.). An earlier mentioned contemporary hinted at a similar dynamic, but does not address the issue of finance bills (Kobayashi, 1910, pp. 778–82).

Finance bills, however, were radically different in that their supply was(/is) sensitive to the level of interest, and not the other way around (Spalding, 1915, pp. 192 ff.). For obvious reasons, and contrary to the aforementioned commercial bills, their supply, and the aforementioned differential (R_{6m}–R_{3m}) was *inversely related* to the interest rate level (this is also clear from Figure 3.12, in which the bank rate is plotted against the differential between longer and shorter term bills):

> When the general level of interest rates was low, banks and bill-brokers would have been ready to discount six month's bills. Foreigners who wanted to tap cheap money in London would have wished to draw six month' bills on London and discount them there, for a six months' bill would have ensured the use of cheap money for six months. Therefore, more six months' bills would have been drawn, which meant that the supply of these bills was greater, so that their discount rate would have been higher than that of three months' bills.   (Nishimura, 1971, p. 42)

One passage in *The Economist*, apparently unknown to Nishimura, links the sharp increase in London finance bills expressly to the Sino-Japanese war: 'It is true that, speaking generally, there is not much to be said against these finance bills themselves, and [...] with the recent transfer to this country of the proceeds of the Japanese Indemnity Loan, they have played a useful part.'[42,43] Fast growing use of finance bills is further corroborated by other leads we possess about bill finance for East Asia. For one, it might explain why interest bills continued to be sent from YSB's London and New York offices to the Yokohama headquarters after 1897, as pointed out above. If thought of as finance bills, this would imply that they were not used by merchants to insure against silver risk (which obviously did not exist anymore), but rather used by the Eastern exchange banks to take advantage of low British interest rates and make handsome profits from the differential with (high) rates within Japan (and Shanghai).[44]

---

[42] 'London Bankers and French Finance Bills'. *The Economist* (London, England), Saturday, Oct. 12, 1895, p. 1331.

[43] It turns out that another contemporary publication corroborates the role of the Sino-Japanese War in popularizing the use of interest bills (Sano, 1905).

[44] Note, furthermore, that, in times of high rates in London, the process was reversed. In other words, when the Bank of England signaled a desire for tightening the money supply, the Eastern banks were quick to get their money out of 'risky' operations in Asia, into 'safe' securities in London. This corroborates other evidence on the procyclical nature of capital flows to and from the periphery, which was reported by Bloomfield (1963).

We know that the possibility of such *carry trade* continuously existed, especially in view of evolutions in the London acceptance market towards the end of the nineteenth century.[45, 46] For bills related to East Asia, one bookkeeping manual from 1907 provides the following narrative evidence:

> The interest rate in London is, on average, between 3 and 4 per cent. [The international exchange banks] there purchase 'Eastern bills' [i.e., interest bills] on India, China and Japan. Given that the interest [on the latter] is normally around 6%, and given that they purchase Eastern bills by means of low-interest London funds, they are obviously running a very profitable business.
>
> (Ishikawa, 1907, p. 67)

This was certainly so after the Russo-Japanese War. According to the same source: 'The interest on interest bills to East Asia is normally 6%, but last year, due to problems in Russo-Japanese relations, the rate was increased to 7%' (Ishikawa, 1907, p. 76).[47] In other words, even when estimating the yearly cost of London acceptance credit to be around 5 per cent in the 1900s, arbitraging must have been a lucrative affair (Nishimura, 2012, pp. 65-6). And indeed, the share of interest bills in the total 'bills sent' portfolio of YSB London is very high (consistently more than 60 per cent after 1898).[48] Looking at the absolute numbers, shown in Figure 3.11, interest bills were, to no one's surprise, particularly attractive in the aftermath of Japan's war with Russia (1904-5), when another wave of military build-up resulted in a domestic credit squeeze.[49]

Yet another lead are the YSB mid-term reports. As said before, interest bills were for the period of 1898-1908 not categorized under flow data, yet under

---

[45] Nishimura (1971, pp. 55-64) notes in particular the rapid increase of deposits (and, because of the latter, bank offices) in the city of London around 1890 and later, and the consequent search for high-yielding investments this brought about.

[46] For the 1890s, *The Economist* mentions finance bills drawn from the European continent and finding their way to the London market: 'London Bankers and French Finance Bills'. *The Economist* (London, England), Saturday, Oct. 12, 1895, pp. 1331-2. This is taken up as well by Spalding (1915, pp. 75ff.). Later, that is, at the beginning of the twentieth century, American finance bills increasingly found their way to London. See in this respect: 'The Money Market.' *The Economist* (London, England), Saturday, Sept. 6, 1902, p. 1380; US borrowing by means of finance bills was especially massive in 1906. 'The United States.' *The Economist* (London, England), Saturday, Mar. 17, 1906, p. 451; 'The Monetary Position in the United States and Its Effect upon International Markets.' *The Economist* (London, England), Saturday, May 5, 1906, pp. 758-9.

[47] Nishimura (2012, pp. 64-6), in another publication, takes the rate to have been continuously between 6 per cent and 8 per cent.

[48] A table showing the percentage of interest bills within the total of London bills drawn on Japan (all branches) can be found in Ishii (1999, p. 248).

[49] The first wave of militarization was enacted as the 'postbellum fiscal administration' in the aftermath of the Sino-Japanese War (1894-5). For discussions of the latter, see Ōkurashō (1900); Nōchi (1981); Hyōdō (1996, 1998, 1999); Ono (2008); Schiltz (2012a).

'statement of loans and bills discounted'. A look at the explanatory notes to these tables reveals that bills were mostly drawn against collateral, typically

> for interest bills bills drawn by the Head Offices and sent to Hongkong and Shanghai, cotton; [...] for bills drawn by the London office and sent to Yokohama, Kobe, [...], spinning products, iron products, pharmaceuticals and sundry goods [*zakka* 雑貨], [...]; for bills drawn by the New York office and sent to Yokohama, Kobe, Shanghai, machinery and ironware [...].
> (Yokohama Shōkin Ginkō, 1898, p. 23).[50]

Especially because the mid-term reports chose to list these assets, it seems to suggest that the latter were not goods that were the object of a commercial transaction, but conveniently collateralizable assets, pledged to obtain credit; it tried, in other words, to reassure its shareholders that these lending operations were safe. If the above conjecture is true (and it seems hard to come up with a viable alternative explanation), then the story ends with a remarkably twenty-first-century twist: a great deal of transactions related to interest bills may thus well have been early examples of commodity finance...[51]

---

[50] Square brackets mine. Similar remarks can be found in later mid-term reports. Interestingly, the mid-term reports also report a breakdown of the amounts of funds per branch being lent against particular types of commodities. From such tables it becomes obvious that certain financial instruments, such as bonds, stocks, and deposits could also be pledged (Yokohama Shōkin Ginkō, 1898, p. 23). In this respect, I must add that, because of the intangible nature of such securities, branch managers were urged to exercise restraint in accepting them (Yokohama Shōkin Ginkō, 1908, pp. 361ff.).

[51] The implications of the use of commodities (typically, copper) as collateral for loans in the Chinese economy has become hotly debated in twenty-first-century financial journalism. Sadly, because of the opaque nature of the transactions and the general lack of documentation about this part of the Chinese 'shadow banking' system, the topic is struggling to find its way in the academic literature. For some very rare examples: Peck (2001); Tang and Zhu (2015).

4

'On an Even Keel'

Hedging Exchange Rate Risk on the Branch Network Level

A word next as to our Exchange policy. There seems to be a mistaken idea that our sterling deposits are remitted to the East for investment there, and I may tell you, gentlemen, plainly and at once, that this is not the case. We have today some 4¾ millions of sterling deposits, which are exclusively employed for the purchase of outward mercantile bills, silver bullion, Mexican dollars or council bills for shipment to the East, pending the arrival of homeward bills purchased simultaneously by the Eastern branches, both operations being legitimate Banking transactions. It will be easily understood that by following this policy, large sterling deposits can be used without the price of silver affecting the position in the least, the money deposited having in reality never left London. The management has taken and will take particular care that *the bank keeps on an even keel with regard to both gold and silver*; beyond the comparatively trifling differences from day-to-day business, neither a rise nor a fall in the dollar exchange can injure or benefit us to any appreciable extent.

> (Mr. Davies, Chairman of the Hongkong and Shanghai Banking Corporation (HSBC) in an address at the Ordinary Half-Yearly Meeting at the Hongkong City Hall, at noon, Aug. 20, 1892. *North China Herald*, Sept. 2, 1892, p. 344; italics mine)

1. Introduction

In Chapter 3, we reviewed the accounting specifics of the most representative type of bills exchange banks dealt with in the second half of the nineteenth century. We demonstrated that, in the case of an imaginary bank existing of two branches with a different metal as unit of account, the key to recouping

Accounting for the Fall of Silver: Hedging Currency Risk in Long-Distance Trade with Asia, 1870–1913.
Michael Schiltz, Oxford University Press (2020). © Michael Schiltz.
DOI: 10.1093/oso/9780198865025.001.0001

funds incurred by branch X when sending on a bill to Y (X_y) was to engage in a reverse transaction, with a bill flowing in the opposite direction (or Y_x, as it concerns a bill branch Y sent on to branch X). In a concrete example: a branch sold, for local currency, remittances to importers in order to recover the same amount in local currency it had spent on buying bills from exporters. The idea of an exchange bank's workflow can thus, in its most general and symbolic form, be expressed as: $X_y \leftrightharpoons Y_x$. We also saw that, ideally, operations were executed simultaneously or, in other words, at the same rate of the day, in order to avoid exchange rate risks and, by extension, in order to avoid situations in which the working capital of the branch was affected.[1]

Yet how do sets of such binary relationships translate on the branch network level? This question is a pertinent one. Most importantly, does the above relationship imply that *every* liability/asset incurred by X on Y should be matched by a liability/asset of the same amount incurred by Y on X? Although this situation might seem logically implied, it is patently improbable in a real-world scenario. As we know, the balance of trade between nations is typically in disequilibrium rather than in equilibrium. Is it therefore not to be expected that imbalances in interbranch assets and liabilities are offset by, say, triangular relationships (at the time known as three-cornered transactions)? Clearly, this must be the case. But then, if so, how can this be organized? Concretely, which currencies are more likely to be used as the vehicle for offsetting others? Related to the latter, can currencies be clustered into a basket and treated as isomorphic? How can branches protect against highly volatile exchange rates? Were bankers aware of hedging techniques? On the branch network level, can the network be organized into a core-periphery structure, with certain key branches put in charge of monitoring the business activity of lower tier ones? And put into an intra-bank comparative perspective, why were some banks apparently more successful in their hedging strategies than others?

2. From the Fall of the Oriental Bank to Hongkong and Shanghai Banking Corporation Losses

The above questions turned out to be topics of great contention in the 1880s, when the once mighty Oriental Bank Corporation had been forced into

---

[1] A similar description can be found in one of the contemporary accounting manuals, under the heading *kawase no deai* (為替の出合, 'exchange cover') (Tomita, 1894, pp. 76–83). The manual stresses that not covering his dealings, or running an exchange imbalance (in Japanese referred to as *kata-kawase* 片為替) would 'amount to speculation, which was not in the true character of the exchange banker' (*tōkiteki no michi ni hairu ha ginkōsha no honshoku ni arazu* 投機的の道に入るは銀行者の本色に非ず).

liquidation (Suzuki, 2012).[2] A few years later the debate gained even more traction, when the until then profitable HSBC suffered unexpected losses 'by advancing against sugar in Manila', as Mr Provand explained to the parliamentary commission of Chapter 3.[3] It was this event that triggered, among others, the parliamentary hearings that provided the greater deal of evidence for Chapter 3.

Yet the debate had many facets, not least, concerning the activities of the British exchange banks in Asia. More specifically, people came to focus on the question of how to turn exchange banking into a profitable business in the long run, or, in other words, unaffected by volatility in the gold price of silver. That the latter had become problematic after 1876 does not need any repetition here. In a remarkable opinion piece from 1882, *The Economist* hinted at the urgency of reconsidering the complexities of the silver problem on the micro-level in the following manner:

Why have the Anglo-Indian banks fared so badly in 1881? To find any really satisfying answer to the above question is a matter of difficulty. By all the laws of legitimate banking, the profits of the Indian banks should have increased last year, not diminished. [...] There was a much increased demand for money, thus enabling banks to employ their resources more completely, and at higher rates, than in 1880. Further than this, the export trade of India grew rapidly, and means of remittance to pay for Indian produce were in considerable request. At the same time, far from the banks holding diminished funds, their deposits were increased, and so were their notes in circulation; they discounted more bills, advanced more money, and under almost every head their business operations gave unmistakable signs of expansion. Neither can there be said to have been any losses due to the depreciation of silver. [...]. Yet, with it all, they have lost ground in profits, in dividends, and in market values.[4]

---

[2] The paper is all the more remarkable given that the bank's archives were destroyed at the time of its bankruptcy. For obvious reasons, however, contemporary journalistic evidence remains: 'The Failure of the Oriental Bank Corporation.' *The Economist* (London, England), Saturday, May 10, 1884, pp. 567, Issue 2124; 'The Liquidation of the Oriental Bank.' *The Economist* (London, England), Saturday, Dec. 6, 1884, p. 1480, Issue 2154.

[3] Again, according to Mr Provand in 1887. *Report of the Royal Commission Appointed to Inquire into the Recent Changes in the Relative Values of the Precious Metals; with Minutes of Evidence and Appendices. 1887–8.* London: Eyre and Spottiswoode, p. 166.

[4] 'Why Have the Anglo-Indian Banks Fared So Badly in 1881?' *The Economist* (London, England), Saturday, Apr. 22, 1882, pp. 468–9, Issue 2017.

As we argued in Chapter 3, *The Economist* blamed only part of these outcomes on flawed managerial decisions; it also identified reduced usance of bills as a culprit behind the numbers.

Yet more important for the following discussion is that the authors appeared unhampered by macroeconomic concerns, and felt free to delve into aspects of managerial decisions. They thereby transcended the ideological cleavages that were so typical of many discussions of the time. They did, for instance, explicitly and emphatically deny any condemnation of bimetallist premises that may have played a role in the judgment of the Anglo-Indian bank managers ('they are probably beyond the reach of argument', as the article states). What matters, so the authors argued, are the interests of the banks' shareholders and depositors; and the managers' decisions should be judged only in terms of the latter. Something that stood out, however, was the fact that the few profitable banks operated on terms that were quite different from all others:

> one point strikes us with regard to the [profitable banks]. The Bank of Bengal makes up its accounts in rupees; the Hongkong and Shanghai Corporation in Mexican dollars. What reason is there why the Anglo-Indian banks should not render their accounts in the currency of the country where their business lies? [...] As far as capital is concerned, we hold that a bank should always consult its customers' convenience first; but as regards the deposits, where at present so large an element of risk lies, there is everything to be said in favour of a change of form. Rupee securities are becoming more and more popular over here, and there is room for a converted Anglo-Indian bank, which instead of taking deposits in sterling would take them in rupees.[5]

The logic behind the argument is clear: have the London branches of the exchange banks opt to acquire their liabilities (deposits) in the silver currencies of the Eastern countries, so that, when the export bills—which were purchased with those deposits—fell due months later in Asia at the rate of the day, there would be no exchange risk to incur. Put differently: if liabilities acquired by the London branch had the same unit of account as the remittances the Eastern branches sold to the Eastern importers, the banks could neutralize the vices of the 'present system', which 'throws all risk on the bank, which should not incur it'.[6]

[5] 'Why Have The Anglo-Indian Banks Fared So Badly in 1881?' *The Economist* (London, England), Saturday, Apr. 22, 1882, p. 469, Issue 2017.
[6] 'Why Have the Anglo-Indian Banks Fared So Badly in 1881?' *The Economist* (London, England), Saturday, Apr. 22, 1882, p. 469, Issue 2017.

The idea is simple enough. Yet, as it turns out, the managing of exchange risk was at the time, just as it is today, not so easily understood. On second sight, the proposal was not only impractical, but even oxymoronic. Given that the depositors' base of the exchange banks' London branches was mostly composed of British importers (who wanted to remit silver currencies but had their accounts otherwise in British pounds) and British exporters (who wanted to receive remittances in British pounds), rupee or other silver-denominated deposits in London would imply a transfer of risk from the bank to the depositors, *who had turned to the bank for insuring against exchange risk in the first place.* Clearly, such cannot have been the objective.

More subtle but equally important, the above reasoning implies that the *only* way to eliminate exchange risk was by means of adopting a uniform unit of account because, *The Economist* concluded, 'we may be very sure we shall never find the gold and silver mixing amicably in [the exchange banks'] accounts'.[7] Moreover, the reason that *The Economist* proposed rupee securities in London (and not: gold-denominated securities in Asia) has to be seen against the overall liquidity condition of London vis-à-vis the money markets in Asia. As the former was the financial center of the world, it was *de facto* the place where the exchange banks held the lion's share of their capital. Consequently, the reasoning went, the only place where a change of unit of account could practically be implemented was in the gold centers; the periphery was too liquidity poor.

3. Hedging Exchange Risk: From Unit of Account to the 'Even Keel'

The reason we highlight the premises of the above proposal is not so much because they were correct (as we will see, they were in many ways mistaken) but because they were so widely held at the time, even among those intimately involved in the import and export trade with East Asia. We find, for instance, a similar argument in the testimony of Mr Provand before the parliamentary commission in 1887 (cf. supra):

'does not the fact that [the exchange banks] make small profits, although they charge large interest, show that there is a good deal of risk in their

---

[7] 'Why Have the Anglo-Indian Banks Fared So Badly in 1881?' *The Economist* (London, England), Saturday, Apr. 22, 1882, p. 470, Issue 2017.

transactions?'—Yes. 'And is not the very heavy charge for interest due to the existence of this risk?'—It is. 'Quite as much as to the question of exchange or fall in silver?'—*It is the exchange which is the risk, and if there had been no fall in silver there would have been no question of exchange.* [...] Every decline in silver since 1873 has caused the banks severe loss. Their capital is in sterling and also their chief deposits. These were sent to the East when exchange was high and stand in the banks' books at nearly 2s. per rupee. But since the decline in silver they have written down this value, which has cost them several several hundred thousand pounds, and much of their profits have gone in doing this. [...] The Hong Kong and Shanghai Bank's capital is in silver, because it is a local bank out there, and its profits have chiefly derived from local business. [...] I believe it would be infinitely better today if silver and gold were tied together again as they were before 1873.[8]

Note the fundamental similarities with the aforementioned reasoning: (1) exchange rate risk is a question of the unit of account, and (2) the only ways to eliminate the risk is (a) by fixing the values of gold and silver,[9] or, as in the case of HSBC, (b) by adopting the unit of account of the liquidity poor Eastern countries and focusing on local business in East Asia.

Yet was the unit of account the only key to managing exchange rate risk? In a rare series of heated exchanges in the *North China Herald* of 1886, we find this notion fundamentally challenged, notably by whom we can very safely assume to have been managers at the Hong Kong and Shanghai Bank. Their timing for throwing light on their exchange strategy is important. This was the first time that the bank had run considerable losses, as said before because of managerial mistakes in Manila, but also because of the unfortunate decision to have laid down funds for an exceptionally bad tea harvest in China. This, together with another episode in the silver drama,[10] and the fall of the Oriental Bank only two years earlier (Suzuki, 2012),[11] had shaken confidence in the business of the exchange banks. Now, managers of the HSBC too had come under fire. The critique voiced in the *North China Herald* by a certain C. S. Taylor[12] was particularly damaging, as it, echoing the above-described

---

[8] *Report of the Royal Commission Appointed to Inquire into the Recent Changes in the Relative Values of the Precious Metals; with Minutes of Evidence and Appendices.* 1887–8. London: Eyre and Spottiswoode, pp. 166–7; italics mine.

[9] Clearly, *The Economist* did not espouse this option in view of its strong antagonism to bimetallism.

[10] The silver price had fallen from 32:4d to 3s:0½d, or 8.8 per cent (!) in the first six months of 1886. For evidence of the full episode, see the *North China Herald* (several issues).

[11] For a more descriptive story, see McGuire (2004).

[12] According to several directories of foreigners in China at the time, C. S. Taylor seems to have been a clerk with the Chinese Marine Customs Administration. See, for example: *The Directory & Chronicle for China, Japan, Corea, Indo-China, Straits Settlements, Malay States, Siam, Netherlands*

common understanding of trade with East Asia, questioned the fate of the bank's sterling deposits in London:

My [...] question has reference to the $69,664,853 of Deposits. How is this amount made up? How much is there in sterling, and at what rate of exchange is this sterling converted into [Hong Kong] dollars? [I assume] that the London sterling deposits are converted into dollars each half year at the ruling rate of exchange. [...] Taking this as my basis, and looking at the accounts as presented at the half yearly meeting of shareholders, I find that [based on the manager's statement that about one third of the deposits is in sterling] the Bank must have written off, since the 30th June last year, for loss on sterling deposits no less a sum than $2,840,553 and since the 30th June 1880 $3,905,063 as the following figures show: —

		Sterling		Sterling
	Deposits	1/3rd.	Exchange	Deposits
June '80	$21,000,000	$7,000,000	3/9¾	£1,334,000
June '81	$30,000,000	$10,000,000	3/8⅝	£1,859,000
June '82	$35,000,000	$12,000,000	3/9⅜	£2,268,000
June '88 [sic.]	$46,000,000	$15,000,000	3/7½	£2,718,000
June '84	$46,000,000	$15,000,000	3/8½	£2,781,000
June '85	$53,000,000	$18,000,000	3/6¼	£3,168,000
June '86	$69,000,000	$23,000,000	3/6½	£3,496,000

[...] The question is simply whether the Bank has or has not written down its sterling deposits, to the present actual rate of exchange, for if it has not, the Reserve Fund [which the Bank reported to stand at $4,5 million at the time] exists only on paper [...].[13]

A reply from the HSBC managers was swift and condemning. Their reaction in the same issue, and signed with L.S.D (a pun on *'librae, solidi, denarii'*,

---

India, Borneo, the Philippines, &c: With Which Are Incorporated 'The China Directory' and 'The Hong Kong List for the Far East' ....1892. Hongkong Daily Press Office, p. 116. The Jardine Matheson Archives at Cambridge University contain a letter, dated Sept. 6, 1886, from presumably the same C. S. Taylor in their 'Letters from Shanghai': ref. MS JM/B22/3.

[13] *North China Herald*, Sept. 10, 1886, pp. 287–8 (square brackets mine). Mr Taylor calculated the losses (and gains) on changes in the exchange rate as follows:

During the year 1880–1 you write down £ 1,344,000 from 3/9¾ exchange to 3/8⅝ exchange; loss £33,000 or $182,478. During the year 1881–2 you write up £1,859,000 from 3/8⅝ exchange to 3/9⅜ exchange; gain £31,000 or $163,966. During the year 1882–3 you write down £2,268,000 from 3/9⅜ exchange to 3/7½ exchange; loss £106,000 or $584,827. During the year 1883–4 you write up £2,718,000 from 3/7½ exchange to 3/8½ exchange; gain £63,000 or $339,774. During the year 1884–5 you write down £2,781,000 from 3/8½ exchange to 3/6¼ exchange; loss £141,000 or $800,945. During the year 1885–6 you write down £3,168,000 from 3/6¼ exchange to 3/6½ exchange; loss £432,800 or $2,840,553.

the old expression for the pre-decimal British pound?), rejected the letter as an 'ungracious charge' which 'goes out of his way to question a very straight-forward statement'. L.S.D continued:

> Mr. Taylor ought to know that the principle of banking is to *turn over money*, and *not bury it in the East*, as he appears to think it is done. The London Deposits may come out to the East half-a-dozen times in the course of the year, and be returned at a profit or a loss as the case may be, which shows itself at the end of every half-year.[14]

What this 'straightforward statement' meant was addressed in yet another contribution. It upset all of the assumptions listed above, and sought out the unit-of-account argument in particular:

> Those who did not take the trouble to study the half-yearly reports of the Bank, and ascertain from them how the funds were distributed, who took it for granted that all its deposits must necessarily be employed in loans and discounts in the East, had a notion [...] that when the London deposits came to be paid off, there would a considerable loss, unless silver recovered its value of two or three years ago, in the meantime. [...][15]

This was simply not the case, its authors stressed. The unit of account did *not* play any role of significance in the bank's dealings; neither a fall nor a rise in the silver price would affect the bank's capital. As we will explore later in greater detail, what did matter, and in which respect HSBC differed from

---

[14] *North China Herald*, Sept. 10, 1886, p. 288.
[15] *North China Herald*, Sept. 10, 1886, p. 273–4. Note, hereby, that the authors of the piece charged the unit of account argument to be intellectually dishonest as well, that is, a way by means of which the proponents of bimetallism sought to influence British policy making towards some kind of bimetallic compromise:

> it always seemed that those who held the opinion that a liability for the depreciation existed, considering it a contingency which would disappear, when the relative values of gold and silver came to be adjusted. It was not looked upon as bad debts and business losses are looked upon, as required to be provided for at once. [...] Probably this was mainly owing to the unreality of the opinion, even in the minds of those who held it; to their considering the possibility of loss not sufficiently imminent, or as something that a turn of the wheel might remove, when the American Government or the Indian Government did something,—or bi-metallism was universally adopted,—which should send the price of silver up again.

(most of) its competitors,[16] was the *even keel*[17] (*kingin kinkōsaku* 金銀均衡策), that is, a *management strategy* whereby:

1. the uses of funds in one particular metal (silver/gold) were kept within the boundaries of the sources of funds in that metal (silver respective to gold); or, in other words, a 'moving' of funds between the gold and silver regions was ruled out; and

2. the exchange rate of every transaction was 'locked in':

   a. On the branch level, managers were supposed to avoid, as much as possible, an uncovered exchange position (*kata-kawase* 片為替). Ideally, the banker's positions were offsetting: the buy position was, in that case, equal to the sell position.

   b. On the *branch network level,* the amounts of bills bought and bills sold were *at all times kept identical,* in other words, the position was *squared.* The relative appreciation/depreciation of aggregated assets and liabilities at the silver branches would thus be offset by the depreciation/appreciation of assets and liabilities held by the gold branches, to the same degree. The bank thus significantly reduced exchange rate risk. At no point would the bank *as a whole* tilt towards one metal (hence the 'even keel').

   c. Although this may seem obvious now, the difference was made through an innovation in communication technology. Because of telegraphy, branches could at all times inform each other about how much was due by whom to whom, and use that information vis-à-vis their customers (for instance by lowering the discount rate at a time foreign exchange was plenty).

---

[16] It is unclear when exactly the bank chose to adopt this strategy. From the evidence presented by King (1987, p. 209–11), it is clear that no hedging strategy was in place when James Greig was the bank's Chief Manager; he appears to have been urged to step down exactly in view of his misjudgment of the course of the silver price. As far as I can see, the 'even keel' policy was distilled in conversations between then Manager of the London Office, David McLean, and Thomas Jackson, Greig's successor. We locate the birth of the strategy, possibly arbitrarily, around 1878–9.

[17] From the title of the first volume of Frank King's (1987) official history of HSBC, the reader might get the impression that the 'even keel' was the accepted terminology among contemporaries. This is, however, not the case. In one of his recent publications, Suzuki Toshio (2014, p. 350, fn. 325) stresses that the word is nowhere to be found in the bank's surviving archives. On the other hand, the relatively regular occurrence of 'even keel' in the online databases of *The Economist*, and the *North China Herald*, more specifically in the context of money and finance demonstrates that it functioned as a generic term for all matters related to maintaining a form of balance (typically: 'keeping one's finances on an even keel'). It follows therefore that one should be careful not to make too much of a term that, at least for the contemporary observer, may not have carried the meaning of a specific hedging strategy.

3. Concretely, short-hedging happened by means of different, yet related operations:

   a. Typically, the proceeds of the bills falling due (bills for collection (B/C)) at a branch (or a cluster of branches on the same metal) at a certain date formed the funds out of which bankers of that branch (/branches) paid out their obligations (bills for payment (B/P)) for the same date. In other words, branches engaged in 'swap' transactions: they swapped future cash flows for flows that were the result of contracts falling due at a certain date.

   b. *At the same time*, the banker of this branch (/branches) sold remittances (mostly telegraphic transfers) in order to remit to the branch (/branches) on the other metal.

   c. After consulting with the correspondent banker overseas, the proceeds of the sales of the remittances (+ any possible surplus of B/C in (a)) were used to buy export bills that would fall due several months later at a branch (/a cluster of branches) on the other metal.

   d. The latter branches were informed by telegraph of the realized amount of bills for collection, so they could in turn plan to balance amounts of bills sold and bought at the same future date.

4. In short, bankers at branches thus saw to it that identical amounts of different instruments (B/C and B/P) were set off against each other. They tried to set them off *simultaneously*, in other words, at the rate of the same day. Branches thus avoided a situation in which their working capital was affected, and, at the same time, averted exchange rate risk. (Kitabayashi, 1992)[18,19]

Although the discussion in the *North China Herald* mostly focus on point (2b) of the above (and then only on the branches in Asia), it suffices to understand the banker's point of view:

---

[18] Stuart Muirhead's mention of 'simultaneous transactions' within CMBILC seems to hint at a comparable mechanism (1996, p. 218).

[19] According to Frank King, it was the 'matching of sources with sterling uses of funds by sterling sources of funds—and similarly in silver—was to be known as "keeping on an even keel"' (1987, p. 277), but this is mistaken, as it only pays attention to what above is outlined as point (1) of the strategy. Furthermore, as is also indicated in contemporary journalistic sources, uses of funds in a certain metal were not 'matched' by sources of funds in the same metal; the latter had to exceed the former (if only slightly), in order to retain a safe margin. We will discuss this aspect of the strategy below.

The accounts of the Bank to the 30th of June show very clearly that none of its gold deposits can have been used in Loans and Discounts in the East. The Capital and the Reserves are about balanced by the Cash held, and a large part of this asset is necessarily in gold. The Deposits amount to 69 millions of dollars, and if the local advances, 37 millions, are deducted therefrom, there is a balance of 32 millions of dollars, which is employed in the exchange business of the bank, and for which it is altogether insufficient. *These 32 millions of dollars are represented in the Bills Receivable, which are the remittances made to London*, and it will be seen that in addition to the 23 millions of dollars, or one third of the deposits, which the General Manager of the Bank stated was about the amount of sterling deposits, there are some nine millions of silver deposits employed in exchange. And as one of our correspondents correctly showed, a great part of these funds are kept in London in order to provide for the telegraphic transfers which the Bank sells every day, and in which the bulk of merchants' remittances are now made. Against these sales of transfers the bank purchases mercantile paper at four and six months' sight, and this course of business necessitates the keeping of a very large amount of funds in London.[20]

Let us briefly review this. First of all, the deposits referred to can be broken down schematically as shown in Table 4.01.

Obviously, these numbers in the half-yearly reports are a mere snapshot of a banking business characterized by a constant turnover. What was missing from Mr Taylor's argument, is the fact that the liabilities (bills payable and the sales of telegraphic transfers) and assets (bills receivable and proceeds of telegraphic transfers sold) can constantly be kept in a very *liquid* state. Chains of exchange operations in which the proceeds from bills collected at a branch in a certain metal were shorted, that is, by immediately buying export bills that will fall due at branches in the other metal, make it possible to run a large business with limited capital.[21] This is the meaning of L.S.D.'s point that 'London Deposits may come out to the East half-a-dozen times in the course

---

[20] *North China Herald*, Sept. 10, 1886, p. 274.

[21] In the jargon of exchange banking, these operations are therefore also referred to as 'simultaneous transactions.' Stuart Muirhead (1996, p. 218) briefly touches upon these transactions in his discussion of the Chartered Mercantile Bank. In his view, 'head office were not particularly in favour of continually carrying out "simultaneous transactions" because the profit was so small.' Regardless of the fact whether this factually was a concern uttered by head office personnel at the time, this is nevertheless mistaken as it confuses the branch level with the branch network level. As is clear from our discussion of YSB, inter-branch differences in exchange positions could be very wide, yet were then flattened out on the network level.

Table 4.01. Breakdown of Hongkong and Shanghai Banking Corporation deposits for Jan. 1, 1886 to June 30, 1886

Deposits total: $69 million		
	Gold deposits: $23 million	Silver deposits: $46 million
Employed for advances in East Asia:	0	$37 million
Employed for exchange (bills bought and telegraphic transfers)	$23 million	$9 million

Source: Created by the author, after *North China Herald*, Sept. 10, 1886, p. 274.

of the year' (cf. supra). The one thing that made matters more complicated were (1) the differences in usance (for export bills: four months for bills on New York, six months for bills on Lyon; for import bills: two months) (Ishii, 1999, pp. 244-5) among types of bills; (2) seasonal fluctuations in demand for the latter; and (3) the type of underlying contract. However, these could be flattened out relatively easy depending on the skills and foresight of the bank's accountants. The use of 'forward contracts', which became more and more common after 1890, clearly facilitated the banker's business (Engel, 2015). They enabled a very accurate assessment of outstanding assets and liabilities at all times.

The reader will notice that in such operations the risk on exchange fluctuations was transferred from the exporters and importers to the banker, and the margin of profit which the latter made on the rates was be increased or diminished in proportion to the rise or fall in the exchange (Spalding, 1915, p. 144).[22] Also, the fact that these operations were valued at different rates did not need to affect the bank's working capital. Because 'the exchange is adjusted once a week by mail, or daily by wire',[23] all outstanding exchange transactions

are valued at the rate of exchange actually ruling, and at which they could be closed, at the end of the half-year. This enables a just estimate of the profit and loss account to be made, and the lapse of a few days or weeks makes the estimates certainties.[24]

---

[22] His discussion is based on a lesser known discussion by Charles Addis, once HSBC banker (Schiltz, 2019a).

[23] *North China Herald*, Sept. 10, 1886, p. 288.   [24] *North China Herald*, Sept. 10, 1886, p. 274.

4. Specie Points, Exchange Rates, the Even Keel, and Managerial Success

Importantly for our discussion, the adoption of the even keel effectively neutralized the falling price of silver vis-à-vis the profitability of the bank's operations. The rate at which the banker sold foreign exchange had become a relative matter. Paraphrasing HSBC banker Charles Addis, this rate was determined by the rate at which bankers were able to cover their drawing operations (Schiltz, 2019a, p. 3).[25] The banker could, as we know, buy bills directly on London; or he could buy in a third country and remit funds there to pay for them; or he could ship bullion directly. Ultimately, two factors played a role in this. First of all, there was the *market* price of silver and in London, both spot and forward; and second, there was the rate of the exchange to determine the relative cost of bullion in different markets. Based on the latter, the banker decided whether to ship gold or silver as commodities (bullion) or as currency (i.e., in the form of a bill). Taking the aforementioned example of remittances to London, the banker proceeded as follows. He calculated the market price of silver in London *expressed in Chinese tael* and compared it with the local silver price. The former formed the natural limit above which, after adding importing charges (comprising the costs of shipping, insurance, assaying, stamp duties, etc.) the rate could not rise. Vice versa, it formed the limit below, after deducting exporting charges (from London to Shanghai), it could not fall.[26] Beyond those limits, bill business would not take place; the banker would opt to settle by means of bullion shipments.

In order to appreciate the full extent of what his statement on (a) exchange rates and (b) relative bullion prices in different markets implies, it is instructive to take a step back in time and explore the situation that was prevalent *before* 1873. The latter has been elucidated in an arguably definitive account by Flandreau (1996b, 2000a),[27] whose discussion is in turn based on the manuals of contemporary bullion brokers and exchange specialists as William Tate (1842), Ottomar Haupt (1870, 1871, 1872, 1874), and Ernest Seyd (1868).

---

[25] There exists a very rare manual describing the calculations needed to arrive at the aforementioned bullion points, written by a Shanghai-based bullion broker at the time (White, Kinnear, 1903).

[26] Nowadays, late nineteenth- and early twentieth-century *vademecums* containing the 'tables of exchange' are the only remaining witnesses of the arcane rules behind the 'daily exchange quotations' Charles Addis referred to (White, Kinnear, 1903; Martinho-Marques, 1908; Bell, 1919).

[27] This proposition marks a difference with the more common analysis of specie points, according to which the mint parity functions as the benchmark of (bullion) arbitrage. Flandreau's approach has recently been applied in the context of Singaporean silver absorption before 1873 (Kobayashi, 2019).

From their discussions, Flandreau reconstructed the equations needed to determine the lower and upper limits between which the *exchange rate* had to remain in order to enable the sustenance of bill business and avoid the settlement of international trade transactions by shipping bullion. When applied to the trade between London and, say, Shanghai, these equations are as follows. Defining $X^£$ as the rate(s) at which the banker in Shanghai will sell/buy bills (the price of GBP expressed in tael), c as the cost (in *percentages* %) of shipping silver(/gold) to (SHS→S (SHG→S)) or from Shanghai (SHSS→ (SHGS→)) or any other Eastern market, and p as the price of silver(/gold) in Shanghai (SS (GS), expressed in tael) or London (SL (GL), expressed in British pounds), the following relations held (Flandreau 2000a, pp. 99–100):

$$[1] \quad (1\text{-cost}_{SHS \to S})^* p_{SS}/p_{SL} \leq X^£ \leq (1+c_{SHSS \to})^* p_{SS}/p_{SL}$$
and
$$[2] \quad (1\text{-cost}_{SHG \to S})^* p_{GS}/p_{GL} \leq X^£ \leq (1+c_{SHGS \to})^* p_{GS}/p_{GL}$$

Equations [1] and [2] mean the following. The exchange rate of the British pound (or the number of tael that had to be given up to acquire one British pound) in the Shanghai market should not fall below the level at which it became profitable to buy silver(/gold) in London, ship it to Shanghai and convert it into Shanghai tael (the silver/gold import point).[28] Vice versa, it should not rise beyond the level at which it would become profitable for the Shanghai banker to move out of the bill business with London, and, instead, pay for charges and enter into the bullion shipment business (the silver/gold export point). Put simply, the lower and upper bounds of the exchange rate constituted an interval or a 'band' of so-called *specie points* or the *arbitrated pars of exchange* between which bill business could go on. Beyond those points, merchants would prefer to settle their transactions by means of bullion shipments.

Remember, however, that Addis made it clear that not only exchange rates but also *relative bullion prices* determined the means of settlement of

---

[28] Transmission costs implied more than just transportation costs. As argued by Flandreau, and corroborated by bullion brokers' handbooks, it included a wide range of costs. We mention: brokerage, transportation (broken down into: wharfage dues, packing, freight, insurance, landing, portage, municipal dues, etc.), assaying, and interest loss (Flandreau, 1996b, pp. 423ff.). For the concrete case of operations to and from Shanghai, see White and Kinnear (1903). White's account clearly documents and differentiates the amount of charges applying to each market, and identifies so-called 'constants' which contain the charges pertaining to different markets. In absence of a calculator, the local banker simply had to multiply the constant by the quotation in market 1 in order to obtain the equivalent exchange value in market 2 due to or from the customer. Differences in assaying practices are detailed in a pamphlet found at the Toyo Bunko Library in Tokyo (Schiltz, 2019b).

international transactions. Reformulating the above equation, it is clear that there also existed constraints to the latter. The silver (gold) price in London, when converted into Shanghai tael should not fall under the level at which it became profitable to ship silver to London. Alternatively, it could not rise beyond a level at which a converse operation was preferable.

$$[3] \quad (1-cost_{SHS \to S})^* p_{SS} \leq X^{\pounds *} p_{SL} \leq (1+c_{SHSS \to})^* p_{SS}$$
and
$$[4] \quad (1-cost_{SHG \to S})^* p_{GS} \leq X^{\pounds *} p_{SL} \leq (1+c_{SHGS \to})^* p_{GS}$$

One of the centerpieces of Flandreau's argument is the demonstration that, in the pre-1873 monetary system, the so-called *bullion points* described in equations [3] and [4] *were endogenous*, because of France's role as *arbitrageur* of last resort (1996b, p. 422).[29] As France was a buyer of the depreciating metal, and a seller of the appreciating one, it checked the degree of divergence between the points. Reflecting the relative scarcity of the silver and gold in Paris and other major financial centers, the bullion points adjusted, expanding or shrinking the band while at all times exhibiting a corrective potential: shipment of one of two, or both metals, in both directions acted in the direction of stabilizing any initial disequilibrium between markets. The level of the exchange rates was informative too. By virtue of its relative distance to the specie points described earlier, it determined the direction of bullion flows (concretely: it settled the question whether imbalances would be cleared by means of silver imports from location 1 to location 2 or gold exports from location 2 to location 1, or the other way around).

After 1873, the aforementioned equations [1] and [2] did not change per se, as is clear from Addis' quote (cf. supra). As before, bankers in both London and Shanghai could still settle transactions using bills of exchange (mostly telegraphic transfers), gold bullion or silver bullion; their choice depended, as before, on the comparative returns of each operation. What had become different, however, was the breakdown of former mechanisms that had the effect of stabilizing international disequilibria. France's decision to 'unfix' the silver price—first temporarily (1873), then permanently (1876)—did not only sabotage the traditional arbitrage mechanism of the pre-1873 period. It killed the innately transnational and multilateral nature of international monetary arrangements, as well. After 1873, the specie points were thus no longer

---

[29] Note as well the subtle distinction between bullion points and specie points (Flandreau, 1996b, p. 422, fn. 12).

endogenous. In other words, when France took down the notion of a floor price for silver, it abandoned its role as the clearing house for pre-1873 world trade.

Personnel at the Eastern exchange banks were most certainly taken aback. Initially, they did not possess the means to grapple with the most pertinent results of the calculations producing the arbitrated pars. These results related to (a) the *width* of the band (under bimetallism, bullion points were included within the gold points, hence the band was, by definition, smaller than in a gold standard regime (Flandreau, 1996b, pp. 435-6));[30] and (b) *movements of the band* itself.[31] The latter, in particular, was behind the fall of the traditional Eastern exchange banks as the Oriental Bank Corporation. Unaware of strategies for hedging exchange rate risk (or, perhaps, unwilling to consider them), their business was incapable of accommodating short- to mid-term variations in the gold price of silver. As seen before, they initially experimented with bills of shorter usance, a strategy that had to be abandoned soon. Later, their bill and bullion businesses were drastically curtailed. Typically, the semi-annual reports of, for example, the Oriental Bank Corporation are witnesses to the shrinking nature of its bill business and the consequent drop in the latter's return on assets (ROA) and share price (Suzuki, 2012).

The even keel, however, was a game changer. Because of the newly discovered ability of setting off amounts of bills bought with equal amounts of bills sold, the Eastern exchange banks were able to accommodate not only a higher variability in the bandwidth of import and export points. They were also immune to the sometimes substantial movements *of the band itself*.[32] As Addis pointed out, the settling of transactions by means of bullion shipments was brought down to a level of virtual insignificance (Schiltz, 2019a, p. 4). Even in the absence of the pre-1873 bimetallic way of stabilizing imbalances in the vicinity of the legal ratio of gold and silver, the even keel thus gave the Eastern exchange banks the chance to become the *arbitrageur* of last resort in mercantile relations between the European core countries and the Asian

---

[30] This variability does not only relate to the relative time (sometimes several months) over which exchange rates could fluctuate but also to the higher charges for importing/exporting bullion. The longer distance and time of the East-West trade entailed substantially higher transportation and insurance costs; bankers naturally had to allow for a larger interest loss as well. An undated pamphlet (supposedly from around 1920, i.e. many decades after 1873) puts the period for interest loss at 'six weeks'; the total of charges was put at 1.8125 per cent (Schiltz, 2019b, p. 669).

[31] To this one may also add the concrete composition of the 'effective band.' By mentioning silver shipments to Shanghai (from London) and gold shipments away from Shanghai (to London and Osaka) only, contemporary *vademecums* make clear that the import point was constantly the silver import point, and the export point the gold export point (White and Kinnear, 1903).

[32] For this reason, it is safe to assume that all surviving Western banks in Asia adopted an 'even keel' strategy of some sort. Unfortunately, only narrative evidence remains (Meuleau, 1990, pp. 102ff).

periphery.[33] At the same time, it boosted each surviving bank's relative importance, because the capability of arbitraging post-1873 was only available to them and institutions with a comparable network of branches in both European centers and the Asian periphery (Hamashita, 1980, p. 344).[34]

Taking into account the aforementioned fact that the bank worked towards a situation in which the London-based sterling deposits were at all times replenished by sterling remittances from silver-using regions in Asia ('heavy remittances are constantly on the way to London, making the position there impregnable'),[35] it is clear that the HSBC was running a safe business indeed. What remained of the exchange risk were the 'comparatively trifling differences of the day-to-day business' referred to in the epigraph to this chapter.

HSBC's strategy worked. Whereas its competitors struggled, or went out of business altogether, the company thrived, as can be concluded from its share price during the period under discussion (Figure 4.01). In terms of trade volume too, its record was impressive. Several authors estimate that, in the early 1880s, HSBC was responsible for financing half of all trade to and from Hong Kong; the Chartered Bank accounted for some 25 per cent, whereas the other exchange banks competed for the remaining quarter (MacKenzie, 1954, p. 75; Ishii, 1999, p. 58).

5. The Even Keel: Stock vs. Flow data

Unfortunately not further developed in the otherwise excellent discussion by Kitabayashi (1992), HSBC's management principles (largely copied by Yokohama Specie Bank (YSB) in the 1890s and later) were of such a nature as to necessitate a distinction between *stock data*, on the one hand, and *flow data* on the other. In this context, Mr Buchanan (another shareholder of HSBC) reminds us once more that trade from and to England was financed by means of different types of contracts: 'since the extension of the telegraph to China the method of finance has changed. While shipments from China are generally drawn against 4 months' sight, the proceeds of imports are usually remitted by electronic transfer.'[36] This explains the *discrepancies* that emerge *in the*

---

[33] This role of *arbitrageur*, and the suspected ability of price fixing through cartelization, was often contested by the Asian host nations, which often reacted by establishing their own exchange banks. This explains, for instance, the creation of the YSB, but also the Imperial Bank of China (中国通商銀行 *chūgoku tsūshō ginkō*) (Hamashita, 1980).

[34] See, again Hamashita (1980).   [35] *North China Herald*, Sept. 2, 1892, p. 344.

[36] *North China Herald*, Sept. 10, 1886, p. 288.

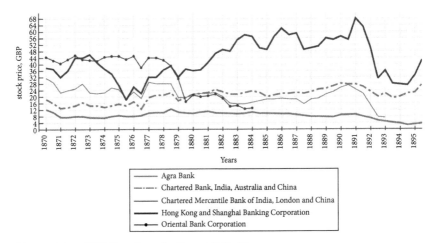

Figure 4.01. HSBC against the Rest, 1870–95

Source: figure created by the author, after The Economist, 'Bankers' Price Current' (until 1880) / 'Stock Markets Price Current' (from 1880), multiple issues. Data were taken half-yearly, i.e. for the months of January and July.

stock data when comparing the amounts of bills receivable and bills payable, as he illustrated by means of Table 4.02.

Note hereby once more the implications of the changes in the methods of financing of which Mr Buchanan spoke, and which we explored earlier. Whereas, in the early 1870s, bills receivable (i.e., gold-denominated remittances from China to London) and (silver-denominated long-term) bills payable are more or less in balance, the late 1870s show a tendency for a slightly higher amount of the former vis-à-vis the latter. This discrepancy can largely be explained by the fact that inland bills for international trade could be renewed, whereas currency drafts, which went out of the country, could not (cf. supra); a longer usance naturally caused the amounts of outstanding bills receivable to be higher. Yet later, that is, around 1880, coinciding with the growing popularity of telegraphic transfers for remittances to Great Britain, amounts of bills receivable became consistently and markedly higher than those of bills payable: the Chinese exporter could not afford to wait for a remittance and, therefore, drew in sterling and settled the rate of exchange (i.e., he sold his bill to an exchange bank).

And yet, as Mr Buchanan also pointed out, '[i]n the end, Bills Receivable and Bills Payable balance each other.'[37] This is a very important remark, and it is therefore regrettable that nobody has ever attempted to explore its meaning quantitatively. Yet, as we will see in a minute, it is arguably for this reason that

---

[37] *North China Herald*, Sept. 10, 1886, p. 288.

Table 4.02. Statement of bills receivable and payable (in millions and thousands of HK$s)

Date of account	Bills receivable	Bills payable	Date of account	Bills receivable	Bills payable
June 30, 1873	$24,7	$29,4	June 30, 1880	$17,8	$14,9
Dec. 31, 1873	26,9	26,1	Dec. 31, 1880	28,2	14,6
June 30, 1874	18,7	22,5	June 30, 1881	17,9	8,7
Dec. 31, 1874	21,7	17,8	Dec. 31, 1881	30,1	15,3
June 30, 1875	15,5	17,8	June 30, 1882	26,5	18,5
Dec. 31, 1875	18,1	15,7	Dec. 31, 1882	35,5	17,9
June 30, 1876	19,6	18,7	June 30, 1883	30,4	8,8
Dec. 31, 1876	28,9	24,4	Dec. 31, 1883	36,9	16,0
June 30, 1877	25,4	20,1	June 30, 1884	27,9	12,7
Dec. 31, 1877	34,0	24,0	Dec. 31, 1884	34,3	15,6
June 30, 1878	30,9	28,3	June 30, 1885	33,8	14,1
Dec. 31, 1878	28,2	22,3	Dec. 31, 1885	46,5	20.7
June 30, 1879	25,7	27,9	June 30, 1886	44,9	14,2
Dec. 31, 1879	27,2	20,8			

Source: Created by the author, after *North China Herald*, Sept. 10, 1886, p. 288.

YSB, which, as said, emulated HSBC's exchange management strategy in the early 1890s, chose to include an elaborate section of *flow data* in its mid-term reports. After all, they make it possible to measure something fundamentally different. Whereas stock data report *total* amounts of assets respective to the liabilities acquired and incurred at the point for which the balance is struck, flow data allow us to study *how assets and liabilities have been distributed among branches* (or branch clusters) *over an interval of time* (in the case of YSB, a semester). In other words, they offer insight into the *net* transfer of assets and liabilities, and, by extension, are a means of judging whether, on the branch network level, a net transfer of, say, funds from the gold branches to the silver branches has been offset by a commensurate flow in the other direction. Although we cannot illustrate this for HSBC, for want of the relevant flow data,[38] that YSB was indeed on an 'even keel'[39] after 1893 can be seen in Figure 4.02.

A few remarks are in order here. Importantly, the graph in Figure 4.02 should not be interpreted in a tautological manner, as if it were to mean that

[38] The absence of flow data notwithstanding, there have been some creditable efforts at reconstructing the flow-of-funds using the contemporary Inspector's reports, the general ledger balances, etc. (Nishimura, 1993, 1994, 2007; Yasutomi, 2003).

[39] As is well known, the notion gained currency through Frank King's (1987) tetralogy on the history of the HSBC: it even figured on the title page of Vol. 1. Yet, the tetralogy has important drawbacks; notwithstanding the importance of the 'even keel' strategy, its meaning was never quantitatively addressed.

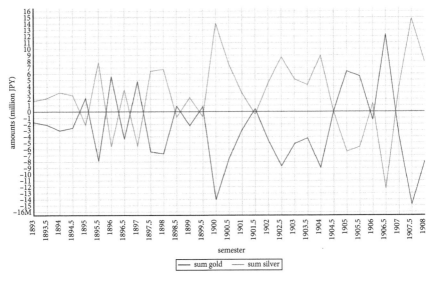

Figure 4.02. YSB on an 'even keel', 1893–1908
Source: calculations by the author

'what is sent by silver(/gold) branches is received by gold(/silver) branches.' What we see represented above are, in the strictest sense of the word, origin-destination data, or, in other words, amounts being transferred from one type of branch to another type of branch, irrespective of the fact that these amounts are positive or negative ones. Concretely, the graph describes that, at any time, *an aggregate positive transfer* (a surplus of 'bills bought' over 'bills sold') *from branches on one of two metals is countered by a nominally equal, aggregate negative transfer* (a surplus of 'bills sold' over 'bills bought') *from branches that have the other metal as unit of account.*

If considered as such—and this is indeed the intention behind consider-ations about the making of the database—then similarities to what we have seen above about HSBC's exchange risk hedging are too obvious to ignore: the aggregated flows of funds sent by the silver respective to gold branches are almost perfect mirror images of each other (factually, very minor differences do exist, but they are to be explained by issues of rounding and the exclusion of yet other, more exotic, types of bills).[40]

---

[40] Discrepancies are most pronounced for the semesters December 1896 and June 1897. A look at the respective mid-term reports reveals the existence of categories of bills that are not listed in other mid-term reports, and that, for reasons of formatting of the matrices in the database, could not be included. More specifically, the reports mention—admittedly very limited—amounts of 'gold coin bills sent' (*kinka sōkin tegata* 金貨送金手形) from the London office to the Yokohama head office. Determining the specific nature of these bills—is there perhaps a relationship with the repatriation of gold bullion in the context of the remittance of the Chinese indemnity after the Sino-Japanese War?—must be left for future research.

6. An 'Asymmetric' Even Keel? The Role of Silver Deposits

It is equally important to try and understand the fact that, for the larger part of the period under discussion, the net transfer of the silver to the gold branches is positive, and, vice versa, the transfer from the gold to the silver branches is negative. In Chapter 3, we explained in the rather sterile vocabulary of contemporary accounting practice that this must mean that the amount of bills bought by silver branches (for exports to gold standard countries) plus the amount bills sold on them (i.e., sold by gold branches to exporters in order to pay for imports from silver countries), on the one hand, outdid the amount of bills silver branches sold plus bills bought on them, on the other (cf. supra). If considered in the monetary geographical terms that inform this book, however, it will be clear that such discussion tends to underestimate the pivotal role of banking in East Asia's silver periphery.

Several people, among whom the aforementioned L.S.D., have, partially erroneously, been led to stress that the focus of managers' attention was, in the end, with preserving the value of the bank's gold assets and liabilities. The Hong Kong and Shanghai Bank was, so he said, 'operating on a gold basis',[41] as the amount of its gold-denominated assets (bills receivable) was much larger than its silver-denominated liabilities (bills payable). There is something to be said for that, but it is, at the same time, certainly not the whole story. Although strictly speaking not untrue, I tend to believe that this claim should be studied as a contemporary effort to reassure the doubtful London investor: for, if considered more carefully, it would have been more adequate to point out that *this very operating on a gold basis was, in itself, wholly dependent on the maintenance of large silver deposits in Asia.* Factually, L.S.D did so much as admit this when referring to the 'large amounts of Bills Receivable'.[42] After all, the latter could only be sold to Asian importers *with money (deposits) at the Asian branches.* Similarly, these deposits formed the funds out of which the bank could buy bills which were to fall due in London or any other gold branch. Yet, as these deposits were solicited in liquidity poor Asia, they naturally bore a higher interest rate than those in the European centers.

Understanding this and comprehending the nature of this liability was the catch to a successful hedging strategy, and it probably explains why HSBC managers were, in the strict sense, exchange operators aware of the problems that manifested themselves in daily trading routine.[43] Seen through their

---

[41] *North China Herald*, Sept. 10, 1886, p. 28.   [42] *North China Herald*, Sept. 10, 1886, p. 28.
[43] *North China Herald*, Sept. 10, 1886, p. 28.

eyes, liquidity in particular lifted banking operations in the periphery, especially the soliciting of deposits, to a higher, asymmetric, level of importance. David McLean, manager of HSBC's Shanghai office from 1865 to 1873, understood the centerpiece of HSBC's hedging practice perfectly, and therefore vehemently resisted every plan to expand the bank's capital base, which could only be done with capital raised in the city of London:

> Our great success *depends upon the Eastern people being interested in the Bank,* besides if more than one-half were on this register the London shareholders might some day, for some reason or other, attempt to get the HO [head office] transferred to London, which in my opinion would not be for the good of the concern.[44,45]

For the YSB, liquidity in the silver regions similarly became a concern, first after the opening of the branch in Shanghai (1894), then when extending its network of branches and agencies in other towns in China and, yet later, in Manchuria (after 1905). Judging from the elaborate transcripts that survive in the bank's archives, the Meetings of the Managers of Asian Branches of YSB (*tōyō shitenchō kaigi* 東洋支店長会議) were, as late as 1908, organized especially in view of the problem of finding cover for the exchange dealings of the silver branches; put simply, demand for silver resources needed to finance the bank's 'legitimate' business exceeded the available supply. Having experimented with several management systems (cf. infra), the managers would eventually agree to appoint the Shanghai branch as the office in charge (*tōkatsuten* 統轄店) for offsetting imbalances in the silver branches' overall exchange position (*kawase-jiri* 為替尻): apparently, it was the only money market in East Asia with the depth to accommodate the sometimes large daily imbalances (Yokohama shōkin ginkō, 1908).[46]

Even then, as is clear from Figure 4.03, the bank struggled considerably to raise sufficient silver deposits. Although the graph is a little bit distortive in that its amounts of gold deposits also include the (very) high amounts of

[44] David McLean in a letter to John Walter, March 12, 1886, 'Private Letters', Vol. 253; David McLean Papers (MS 380401), Library, School of Oriental and African Studies, University of London (King, 1987, p. 303). Italics and square brackets mine. The prospect of moving the head office to London had been an issue of contention almost since the bank's establishment. Compare: King (1987, pp. 98, 99ff., 275ff., 342ff., 420ff.).

[45] Nishimura Shizuya reaches an identical conclusion (2012, pp. 117–18).

[46] I used a copy in my personal collection. The transcripts for 1908 pay particular attention to the sometimes difficult relationship between the Shanghai and Kobe branches. Especially Chinese traders within the city of Kobe were supposed to be engaged in large speculative transactions.

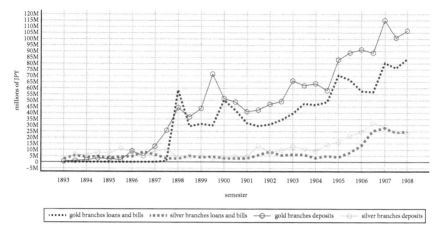

Figure 4.03. Gold respective to silver deposits vs. gold respective to silver loans and bills

Source: calculations by the author

'separate deposits' (*betsudan yokin* 別段預金) or 'escrow accounts'[47] at the Yokohama Headquarters and the London Branch (which in turn explains the much larger gap between the amount of deposits on the one hand and amounts of loans and bills at the gold branches), the difference between gold and silver branches is striking. What is more, deposits for the silver branches were at several times so low as to make breaches of HSBC's first rule (keeping the use of funds in one particular metal within the boundaries of the sources of funds in that metal) inevitable. In any case, as can easily be ascertained, the amount of loans and bills at the silver branches (especially around 1900) constantly flirts with the limits set by the amount of available deposits.[48] However, as we will see in a minute, the situation was more complex than that.

For HSBC, there was an interesting flip-side to this determination to check the bank's course of business by means of East Asian business conditions (or in other words, the determination to keep silver-denominated assets and liabilities separate from gold ones). Together with the relative ease of raising capital in London, it *ipso facto* had to lead to the rationing of deposits there. Again in McLean's words, and clearly hinting to the 'even keel' strategy,

---

[47] See, with regard to the origin of these accounts: 「大蔵省ノ部 正金銀行ヘ別段預入規則修正ノ件」. JACAR Ref. A07060571100.

[48] As the reader observes, there is one instance in which such 'breach' seems to be the case as well for the gold branches; it concerns the difficult transition period from the silver standard to the gold standard in the second half of 1897. It is therefore not immediately clear to me what causes this data mishap. Is it perhaps a mismatch caused by the change in denomination within the period? Or is something else at play?

'surplus on the water is no use to us'.[49] The half-yearly reports of HSBC, reprinted in the *North China Herald* and other Asian journalistic outlets of the day,[50] contain plenty of references. A report from 1888 had already hinted that the interest issue was related to the bank's prudent management,[51] but, in 1892, then Chairman Davies put it more poignantly:

> Towards the end of 1891, it was considered that, by our constantly increasing deposits, we were getting more money than we could profitably employ, and the consequent loss of interest was a heavy drag on our earnings. It was, therefore, decided to attempt to lessen the amount of London deposits by reducing our rate of interest there from 4½% to 4%, and the result was quite satisfactory, deposits falling off in just the proportion we had expected and wished to see.[52]

For YSB, I hasten to add, similar devices were never so easily available. Being a Japanese bank with headquarters in Yokohama, YSB had to take into account credit conditions within Japan proper. The latter were, especially in the years after YSB's establishment, rather averse to the prospect of competing with the other—mostly British—international banks. Saitō Hisahiko, relying on the reporting of the *Tokyo Nichi Nichi Shinbun*, points out that the annual interest YSB paid on fixed deposits (*teiki yokin* 定期預金, arguably the most important source for running an exchange business) in 1900 amounted to 6 per cent. This was not only a major liability. If compared with the 3.3 per cent interest YSB's foreign competitors in Yokohama paid, one understands that the bank had to rely on extensive government back-up, either in the form of direct subsidies and/or rediscounting facilities with the Bank of Japan, in order to play a role of significance in regaining Japanese control of import and export finance (Saitō, 1986, p. 71). It certainly explains the low ROA that characterized YSB's early history (Figure 4.04).

---

[49] David McLean in a letter to J. J. Winton (Singapore), August 22, 1879, Private Letters II 225; David McLean Papers (MS 380401), Library, School of Oriental and African Studies, University of London (King, 1987, p. 299). Admittedly, McLean used these words in the opposite context of superfluous remittances towards London, but the idea is clear.

[50] Several of these newspapers (e.g., *Straits Times and Singapore Journal of Commerce*) can be browsed/searched at NewspaperSG, an online resource for historical Singaporean and Malayan newspapers, maintained by the Singapore government. See: http://eresources.nlb.gov.sg/newspapers/

[51] '[W]e are convinced that at 4 per cent., we shall get as much money in London as we can profitably employ. Even if our sterling deposits do diminish to some extent, it will not be an unmixed evil' (*North China Herald*, Sept. 7, 1888, p. 273).

[52] *North China Herald*, Sept. 2, 1892, p. 344; for yet other references to the London deposit issue, see *North China Herald*, Mar. 10, 1893, p. 345; *North China Herald*, Mar. 2, 1894, p. 325; *North China Herald*, Aug. 31, 1894, p. 357. *North China Herald*, Aug. 28, 1896, p. 364.

One is also not surprised that, because of the high interest paid on them, these deposits could not be used for purchasing low-yielding bills of exchange. Instead, they were only employed as funds for YSB's lending operations ('advances', *kashidashi* 貸出), which obviously yielded a higher profit (Ishii, 1999, p. 244). Basing himself on a testimony in the *Transcripts of the Meetings of the Managers of Asian Branches* (Yokohama Shōkin Ginkō, 1908),[53] Ishii insists that YSB's comparatively low dependence on deposits (see Table 4.03) was also caused by the desire not to compete with other Japanese banks in this field (Ishii, 1999, p. 239), but I tend to believe that the former explanation carries more weight.

Related to the above, YSB also lacked the prestige so typical of HSBC for most of its career. Kasuya Makoto reports that, as late as 1930, when YSB had arguably outgrown the problem of credibility that plagues nascent financial institutions, the bank had a middle-class rating.[54] This situation must have certainly been worse at the beginning of the century. Interestingly, this very issue was brought up at the second meeting of the Managers of Asian Branches (May 1909), in the particular context of competition among the exchange banks. At the time, the manager of the Bombay Branch, Kodama Kenji 兒玉謙次, put it as follows:

> when I travelled through Shanghai and Hong Kong the other day, I hap-
> pened to look at the rates of interest on deposits of [other] exchange banks,
> as these are listed in the English newspapers. I noticed that, in Hong Kong,
> the interest rate on time deposits of HSBC and the Chartered Bank is 4%,
> while [ours] is 5%; in Shanghai, the interest rate on time deposits of HSBC
> and the Chartered Bank is 4%, while [ours] is 5½%. Knowing that this
> [information] was out there in the open, I could not but feel pity [for the
> bank]; and I wondered whether this policy did not result in attracting
> unnecessary amounts of deposits.
>
> (Yokohama Shōkin Ginkō, 1909, pp. 158-9)

Other branch managers were quick to correct him. The higher rates of interest were not the cause of the bank's credit rating, they said, but rather a symptom

---

[53] 横濱正金銀行. 1908. 第壹東洋支店長会議録. [横浜正金銀行], pp. 37ff. http://ci.nii.ac.jp/ncid/BN04887997

[54] 'YSB obtained "Prime-¼ up", while out of 159 banks, 101 banks obtained "Prime", 9 banks had "prime-⅛ up", 12 banks had "prime-¼ up", and 37 banks had a worse rating' (Kasuya, 2012, pp. 215-16).

of the latter. A concrete proposal from Suzuki Shimakichi[55] 鈴木島吉 (Manager of the Shanghai branch) to cut rates in Shanghai to 5 per cent, again in view of the bank's 'standing',[56] therefore fell on deaf ears. Chinese deposits were direly needed, so it was reasoned, and consequently, 'a lowering of rates is unnecessary' (*shina kakuten yokin risoku hikisage hitsuyō naki ya* 支那各店 預金利息引下ノ必要ナキヤ), as one of the captions went (Yokohama Shōkin Ginkō, 1909, pp. 274ff.).

7. An Intermittent Conclusion: The Microstructure of the 'Even Keel'

Concluding this chapter, one last remark is in order. In recent scholarship concerned with the question why countries opt for a certain monetary standard, in this case the gold standard, much has been made of the fact that the adoption of the gold standard is, for whatever reason, correlated with a growing trade volume with gold standard countries. For instance, in what seems to have become the obligatory reference, Ernesto López-Córdova and Christopher Meissner have reported

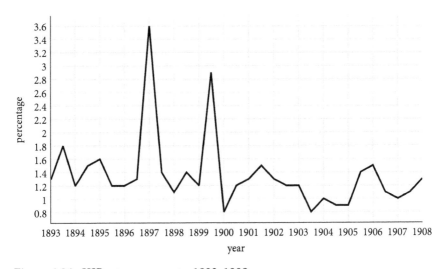

Figure 4.04. YSB return on assets, 1893–1908

Source: figure created by the author, after Kasuya (2012, p. 177).

[55] Suzuki Shimakichi would eventually go on to become President of the Industrial Bank of Japan (*nippon kōgyō ginkō* 日本興業銀行) (tenure: 1927–30).
[56] The transcripts use the literal transcription *sutanjingu* (スタンヂング), after the English original ('standing').

Table 4.03. The ratio of deposits vis-à-vis the aggregate amount of capital (*shihonkin* 資本金) and reserve fund(s) (*tsumitatekin* 積立金) (deposits/ (capital+reserve fund)).

Bank	Year			
	1890	1900	1911	1925
• YSB	0.57	1.99	2.89	2.95
• HSBC	6.52	6.85	6.38	6.51
• Chartered Bank	6.55	6.92	5.80	7.30
• International Banking Corporation			3.16	
• Russo-Chinese Bank (from 1910 onwards Russo-Asiatic Bank)			6.29	
• Deutsch-Asiatische Bank			5.13	
• Banque de l'Indochine			1.76	
• Nederlandsche Handel-maatschappij			2.07	
• Oriental Bank	5.47			

Source: Created by the author, after Ishii (1999, p. 239).

strong evidence that coordination on a similar commodity money regime is correlated with higher trade and some evidence that monetary unions are associated with large increases in trade [...] we find that gold standard countries trade up to 30 percent more with each other than with nations not on gold.   (2003, p. 344)

Around the same time, Estevadeordal et al. claimed that a large part of the change in trade volumes between 1870 and 1914 'can be explained by a "common currency" effect, related to the rise and fall of the gold standard' (2003, p. 362). Absence of a common currency, as in the period after 1914 and later, after 1960, is in their view directly related to the fallback of worldwide trade volumes at the time. The payments frictions arising from the currency regime, they argue, must therefore be considered equally important to 'conventional' commercial policy frictions such as tariffs.

This has led others to turn the argument inside out, and inquire whether such increase in the trade volume with countries on an identical standard may have been the motivation behind gold standard adoption in the first place. In the concrete case of Japan, Mitchener et al. have therefore turned to the vast legislative debates of the 1890s; in their view, 'evidence of [these] debates suggests that policymakers believed gold standard adoption could impact borrowing costs, debt issuance, domestic investment, and trade' (2010,

p. 28). What is more, they say, history proved the gold proponents right. Using estimates from a gravity model of Japanese exports at the time, they find that gold standard adoption boosted the country's trade volume even more than the adoption of the silver standard (which is obviously also a hard peg, and one it shared up to 1897 with the bulk of East Asian countries).

For reasons that cannot possibly be covered exhaustively here, the 'common standard → increased (bilateral) trade' hypothesis does, however, suffer from grave oversimplifications, against which arguments existed before their formulation. Some have pointed out the multicollinearity of trade and protectionism, thereby indicating that the direction of causality is not an obvious given (Flandreau, 2000b; Flandreau and Maurel, 2005). Put simply, the desire to move one's country onto the gold standard (a *selection* effect) may itself be borne out by an already increasing trade volume with gold standard countries, or the anticipation of the latter (a *contagion* effect). In short, it constitutes a case-study of the Lucas Critique (1976).

If put in the microeconomic context of exchange banking, as in this chapter, it is easy to see that the model needs a great deal of further specification. After all, given its cognitive bias towards the inevitable emergence of a *common* monetary (gold) standard (and because of the difficulties of counterfactually quantifying the effects of the survival of bimetallism), it cannot but treat the boost of Japanese banking and business activity in silver China and Manchuria after 1897 as anomalous.[57] Yet, in our empirical analysis the anomaly does not only disappear; it must even be treated as a *prerequisite* to expanded trade with gold standard countries, and this especially in view of the share an exchange bank as the YSB had in the financing of Japan's foreign trade (Table 4.04).

The empirics of exchange banking practice (and the typical attention for the 'flow-of-funds') thus naturally invites an extended focus on the latter's reflection, namely the corollary 'flow-of-goods' (*ryūtsū* 流通). This is the subject of the following chapter. Again, a host of primary and secondary sources in Japanese will be our guide.

Whether the inclusion of banking and corollary accounting practice factually invalidates the 'gold-standard-and-trade-hypothesis' is something that cannot be concluded here. It does, however, demonstrate the distinct

---

[57] Factually, Mitchener et al. (2010) find that gold standard adoption also resulted in an increased trade volume with countries on a different monetary standard ('remarkably, even bilateral trading volumes between countries that had previously shared the silver standard increased significantly'), but explain it away ('while silver was good for trade, joining gold was much better'), in a typical example of confirmation bias. The technicalities of trade *finance* are not given any attention.

Table 4.04. The evolution of the share of YSB in Japan's total export and import finance, 1892–1912

Year	1. Amount of total Japanese exports	2. Amount of total Japanese imports	3. Amount of YSB in Japanese export finance	4. Share of (3) in (1) %	5. Amount of YSB in Japanese import finance	6. Share of (5) in (2) %
1892	91,103	71,326	21,644	23.8	9,828	13.8
1893	89,713	88,257	20,712	23.1	17,991	20.4
1894	113,246	117,482	30,397	26.8	18,460	15.7
1895	136,112	129,261	28,500	20.9	23,942	18.5
1896	117,843	171,674	64,808	55.0	46,916	27.3
1897	163,135	219,301	75,101	46.0	67,690	30.9
1898	165,754	277,502	59,045	35.6	110,979	40.0
1899	214,930	220,402	88,193	41.0	80,766	36.6
1900	204,430	287,262	97,155	47.5	95,025	33.1
1901	252,350	255,817	112,622	44.6	84,267	32.9
1902	258,303	271,731	109,842	42.5	96,216	35.4
1903	289,502	317,136	89,153	30.8	118,049	37.2
1904	319,260	371,361	122,075	38.2	107,251	28.9
1905	321,534	488,538	173,543	54.0	138,469	28.3
1906	423,755	418,784	176,099	41.6	141,172	33.7
1907	432,413	494,467	181,653	42.0	205,964	41.7
1908	378,246	436,257	145,221	38.4	143,332	32.9
1909	413,113	394,199	177,558	43.0	140,033	35.5
1910	458,429	464,234	173,328	37.8	189,146	40.7
1911	447,438	513,806	202,302	45.2	230,290	44.8
1912	526,981	618,934	245,155	46.5	284,118	45.8

Note: Amounts are given in: ¥1,000.

Source: Created by the author, after Nishimura (2014, p. 1282).

advantages of integrating an understanding of the contracts and operations associated with trade finance in the historically circumscribed context of late nineteenth-century Asia. Indeed, we argue that existing macroeconomic analyses may need to be updated with micro-historical findings. In particular, we challenge economic historians to take the micro-structure of, among others, exchange banking, much further. It may also make it possible to address some of the paradoxes that appear in the existing macroeconomic literature.

In the end, the empirical demonstration is that, at least for the Japanese case, the analysis must necessarily take into account the realities of a world that is multipolar (or, at least, bipolar). The preference for a certain monetary standard thus does not imply a preference pro or contra trade partners on a certain monetary standard. Instead, the decision is, ultimately, a *financial* one, that is, one of *insurance against mismatch*, as I have argued elsewhere (Schiltz, 2012a). The fact that Matsukata chose gold rather than silver was the outcome of a cost-benefit analysis; by siding with the core currencies of the world (which, after the 1870s, all happened to be on gold), he avoided the liquidity premium that a 'silver insurance' would have entailed...

5

Yokohama Specie Bank
Flow-of-Funds Analysis

1893–1908

1. Introduction

Our analysis of the flow-of-funds within particular time frames must commence in 1893, for a reason not only hinted to in other chapters, but also explored in earlier research. Simply put, YSB was not a full-fledged exchange bank before 1889 (Saitō, 1985, 2002), and until 1893 it did not actively choose to hedge its foreign exchange operations. Hence, it is only after that date that YSB accountants chose to separate, in a clear manner, the flow-of-funds within the branches network from the bank's dealings with correspondent banks and their offices. Not accidentally, they presented the types of bills in a more systematic manner. Underlying this shift in accounting style and itemization, however, was a pre-history that illuminates core characteristics of the bank after the 1890s.

This story takes us back to the late 1870s, when several countries started to challenge the role of the Mexican dollar as the currency for settling intra-Asian transactions. As we have seen before, German, French, British, and American authorities all understood the benefits that would accrue if the coins of one of their institutions managed to obtain a position of prominence. Tokyo, however, defined the stakes as invariably higher. Aware that it would be costly and difficult to redraw the monetary map once a new equilibrium had been reached, it decided to embark upon a nation-wide scheme of mobilization against foreign influence. Whereas the latter has often been described as anti-foreign—and it is undeniable that these elements were also present—it is actually more appropriate to describe it as a kind of reactive imperialism, an attempt to 'occupy' and regain those political, judicial, and economic domains which it considered key to its sovereignty. In monetary affairs, therefore, the intention behind the creation of the *bōeki gin* (貿易銀; a Japanese

Accounting for the Fall of Silver: Hedging Currency Risk in Long-Distance Trade with Asia, 1870–1913.
Michael Schiltz, Oxford University Press (2020). © Michael Schiltz.
DOI: 10.1093/oso/9780198865025.001.0001

trade dollar) was not just to 'drive off the Mexican dollar' (Matsukata, 1899, p. 11). We know that its rationale was to

> give our trade dollar sufficient sway to turn around the Mexican dollar's monopoly position, become the main means of exchange for the regions in the East, and be the measure for assessing the value of the region's myriad currencies.[1]

As is clear from the above quote, the concerns of Japanese policymakers were squarely focused on liquidity and prestige. This was no more and no less than Tokyo's audacious attempt at creating a 'vehicle currency' *à la* Devereux and Shi (2013).

As a semi-national institution, the Yokohama Specie Bank (YSB) was in the vanguard of policy developments from the very beginning. Under the auspices of finance minister Matsukata Masayoshi, its relationship with the Bank of Japan (BOJ), in particular, became very close. As is well known, Matsukata regarded them as key to his plan to take back Japan's mercantile sovereignty (商権 *shōken*). According to the same plan, their differences concerned the domestic respective to external dimensions of the nation's finances. Simply put, the BOJ's mission related to price stability and liquidity provision in times of crisis. The YSB, on the other hand, was to be in charge of all matters related to the stability of the yen's exchange value.[2] Importantly, this also implied efforts to give the yen sufficient critical mass as an international currency.

Because competition was fierce (Ishii, 2002), the latter necessitated considerable government back-up, especially in the days of the bank's inception. Ishii Kanji (1994) must be credited for explaining how the early adoption of a government-sponsored system of authorized documentary bills or *goyō gaikoku nigawase-tegata* (御用外国荷為替手形) bypassed even the most competitive British banks at the time (Tamaki, 1990).[3] The policy was mostly

---

[1] In the original:

「我貿易銀ニ一層ノ勢力ヲ与エ従来洋銀ノ専有セル地位ヲ変転シテ我貿易銀ノ
有トナシ東洋地方到処該銀貨ヲ以テ各地ノ為替ヲ取組ミ百貨ノ価格ヲ擬定
セシムルニ至る」

(waga bōeki-gin ni issō no seiryoku wo atae jūrai yōgin no sen'yū seru chii wo henten shite waga bōeki-gin no yū to nashi tōyō chihō tōsho gaiginka wo motte kakuchi no kawase wo torikumi hyakka no kakaku wo gitei seshimuru ni itaru).

(Naikoku Kirokukyoku, 1891, p. 205)

Compare furthermore Ono (2001, pp. 92ff.); Schiltz (2012a, p. 1152).

[2] This division of roles originally caused resentment among the BOJ cadre. A comprehensive and definitive history of the latter can be found in (Yoshino, 1974).

[3] YSB's role as a facilitator for mostly Japanese exports was stipulated in the bank's regulations: 『横浜正金銀行条例ヲ定ム』, JACAR A15111453100.

aimed at the nascent Japanese community of silk and tea producers, who felt particularly disadvantaged by the fact that the export market was controlled by foreign buyers. Given the seasonal nature of the produce, warehouses tended to be flooded (輻輳ス *fukusō su*) with these products at certain times only, a situation which foreign merchants were quick to exploit; they then bought the merchandise at giveaway prices (Shiratori, 2012, p. 229).

YSB set out to correct this situation, and to protect Japanese producers against the losses that naturally came with such a buyer's market. At the same time, it used the situation to accumulate specie. The mechanism worked as follows.[4] When the producers sold their bills to YSB branches, they were given paper currency, provided to YSB by the BOJ; YSB sent the bills on to its agent in, say, London or Lyon. The latter collected the payment, which he then converted into bullion and remitted the latter by telegram to the Yokohama head office. The arrival of specie at Yokohama closed the transaction. Specie was transferred from the bank to the government, which used a considerable part of it as reserve for BOJ silver convertible paper notes. Provided the BOJ managed to uphold the credibility of its notes, that is, by being able to guarantee their convertibility, Japanese merchants had an incentive to turn to YSB for having their bills discounted.

Given its success, this system was soon expanded to include Japan-based foreign customers. The trading house of Jardine Matheson, for instance, dramatically increased its share of export bills with YSB after 1883. Again, it was Ishii who discovered that strong Japanese government support wrought the exchange business out of the hands of foreign banks. His research (1984, esp. pp. 353ff.) makes it clear that it was not exceptional for YSB to buy Jardine Matheson export bills *at a higher rate* than the Hongkong and Shanghai Banking Corporation (HSBC), the Chartered Mercantile Bank of India, Australasia and China, or the Comptoir d'Escompte (Ishii, 1984, esp. pp. 353ff., 1979a, 1979b). Furthermore, the brittle state of the foreign banks and the bankruptcy of the Oriental Bank (1884) inadvertently furthered YSB's interests.[5] In any case, the bullionist nature of the *goyō gaikoku nigawase* system was behind the steady inflow of specie into government coffers. What was more, YSB did not have to take the risk of the exchange. For that reason, and because of deficiencies in the inspection of the quality of Japanese

---

[4] For a narrative drawing on primary sources, see Shiratori (2012, pp. 232ff.).

[5] The bank acquired the responsibility of handling the outward transfers of Japanese government funds (官金の回送 *kankin no kaisō*), a business that was formerly held by the Oriental Bank Corporation (OBC).

exports,[6] the government abruptly ended the system in 1889, and changed it into a system of cheap rediscounting facilities (up to ¥10 million at a rate of two per cent) with the BOJ.[7] From then on, YSB was responsible for exchange risks arising out of its transactions.

Yet old habits die hard. Although the bank did some efforts to streamline its operations, for instance by establishing an exchange fund (為替基金 *kawase kikin*) in London, this was mostly achieved by *transferring yen funds* (to the amount of £500,000) from the head office rather than by raising deposits locally. Especially in the mirror of the fall of the OBC, this appears as an odd strategy. As also explained in Chapter 4, the fact that Japanese (silver) funds were transferred to a branch on a different metallic standard implied that the rate at which these funds were converted (YSB used the average rate for demand drafts of the preceding two years (Yokohama Shōkin Ginkō, 1920, p. 118)) was not locked in; those funds were, in other words, sensitive to fluctuations in the future gold price of silver.[8] And indeed, as explained in the bank's official history (Yokohama Shōkin Ginkō, 1920, p. 118):

> This rate was to be corrected 2 years later on the basis of the average rate for demand drafts during the next two years. In case a surplus was arrived at, then this surplus was to be left 'as is' [其儘ニ据置き *sono mama ni sueoki*]; in the case [the bank would face] a deficit, then that was to be provided from the profits of that period [其季ノ利益金カラ補充スル *sono ki no riekikin kara hojū suru*].

Were YSB managers still betting on the continuing depression of the silver price? Or were they oblivious to the possibility of hedging its operations? We may never know for sure. In any case, the Sherman Silver Purchase Act (1890), which obliged the US government to purchase millions of ounces of

---

[6] It turns out that YSB ran into a considerable problem with badly performing loans (Yoshihara, 1979, 1995; Shiratori, 2012, pp. 232–3).

[7] The prelude to this policy change was a dispute, notably between Finance Minister Matsukata and then BOJ Governor Tomita Tetsunosuke 富田鉄之助, about which institution was to be in charge of foreign exchange operations. The dispute ended with Tomita's resignation; the BOJ would not handle foreign exchange operations until after the Russo-Japanese War (Yoshino, 1974).

[8] This is an important point, which, even among contemporaries, was not well understood. In an early report, to which we will later return, one YSB exchange manager claimed 'that swings in the gold silver parity had, in fact, been the main source of profit to the foreign banks present in Shanghai [金銀比価ノ変動ハ現今上海ニ於ケル外国銀行ノ主要ナル利原ヲナセリ *kingin hika no hendō ha genkin shanhai ni okeru gaikoku ginkō no shuyō naru rigen wo naseri*]' (Sano, 1905, p. 72), but Ishii has correctly pointed out that the very uncertainty concerning the fluctuations of peripheral currencies had, in reality, been behind the fall of many an exchange bank, and that one should therefore be careful to draw rash conclusions (1999, p. 119, fn. 79).

silver and monetize the latter, briefly sent the silver price soaring, and knocked the bottom out of a strategy that had factually been discredited many years earlier. A ¥1,5 million loss arising from YSB's long position on bills payable in gold, together with another loss of ¥500,000, due to the failure of one of its customers, caused the bank 'for the second time since its establishment, to face extreme difficulty (大難 *dainan*)' (Yokohama Shōkin Ginkō, 1920, p. 123). The consecutive effort at recuperating these losses caused a heavy drain on the bank's reserve fund. A comprehensive reform of its management strategy proved inevitable. Then YSB Governor Hara Rokurō 原六郎 commissioned his subordinate Sonoda Kōkichi 園田孝吉 to 'save this bank from peril' (危地カラ救ウ *kichi kara sukuu*) (Hagino, 1926, p. 164).

2. Sonoda Kōkichi 園田孝吉 and the Birth of a YSB Hedging Strategy

Sonoda Kōkichi, who took over the helm after that, made it clear that such reform would go well beyond the lowering of the dividend of its shareholders. To be fair, he insisted on that as well. In the first paragraphs of an early memo, he dryly stated that the dividend, which had been at an all-time high of 20 per cent only a few years ago, would have to be brought down to 14 per cent (Hagino, 1926, pp. 166-7). Of immediate importance to our discussion here, he also proposed a plan for restructuring the bank, roughly based on three pillars: (1) the adjustment and/or liquidation of unhealthy businesses (不健全ナ財務整理 *fukenzen na zaimu seiri*); (2) (prolonged) cooperation between YSB and the BOJ (正金ト日銀トノ協調 *shōkin to nichigin to no kyōchō*); and especially (3) the establishment of a 'combinatory management style' (連合的営業法ノ創設 *rengōteki eigyōhō no sōsetsu*). The first two pillars more or less speak for themselves (Yoshihara, 1979, pp. 49-50). But what was implied in the so-called management style?

Sonoda put it as follows (Yokohama Shōkin Ginkō, 1920, vol. 1, app, p. 475). The bank should, he stated,

> change the old ways and habits [慣法 *kanpō*] that have persisted since the days the bank was handling *goyō gaikoku nigawase*, […], and strive towards a situation of exchange cover a) by continually balancing what comes in and what goes out [常ニ内外相応ジテ為替ノ出合ヲ求め *tsune ni naigai sō-ōjite kawase no deai wo motome*], […] and b) by neither overbuying gold

nor overbuying silver [金貨モ銀貨モ共ニ買越売越ヲ為サ ゝ ル *kinka mo ginka mo tomo ni kaikoshi urikoshi wo nasasaru*].[9]

Similarities with the 'even keel' strategy, discussed earlier, are obvious. As the reader will realize, the passage clearly refers to balancing the total amount of bills bought with an equal amount of bills sold, so that identical amounts of gold and silver claims were circulating at all times. The very ability to hedge its operations would be the key to becoming a 'perfect exchange bank' (完全ナル「エクスチェンジバンク」 *kanzen naru 'ekusuchenji banku'*) (Yokohama Shōkin Ginkō, 1920, vol. 1, app., p. 459).

The central problem in the period before 1891, Sonoda continued, was the fact that the bank's branches and agencies had been buying and selling exchange in an uncoordinated manner. The way to remedy this was to use the potential of the telegraph to the fullest and set up an information network to address this coordination problem. The attention naturally shifted to the composition of Japan's foreign trade:

> When reviewing the foreign trade of our country, it is obvious that Japan mostly exports goods to the United States and France, and that it imports products from Great-Britain. The agencies in the United States and France should be engaged exclusively in collecting payments for export bills and transferring (回送ス *kaisō su*) them to the London branch. The London bank should use these transfers as the funds with which it draws import bills on Japan, thus covering the exchange risk. Thus [it will be possible] to coordinate the different branches [and agencies] and achieve a perfectly closed exchange circle [為替ノ完結 *kawase no kanketsu*, i.e. by both 1) leaving the bank's working capital unaffected and 2) avoiding exchange rate risk at the same time].
>
> (Yokohama Shōkin Ginkō, 1920, vol. 1, app., pp. 475-6)

In conclusion, it was decided that the bank's branch network would be divided along two axes. One axis was to be led by the Yokohama head office, and comprised the Eastern branches, or, in other words, all branches with silver as the currency of denomination.[10] The other axis, headed by the London office, was composed of all offices in the gold standard areas (New York, San Francisco,

---

[9] The quote is a transcript of the resolutions voted on the daily meeting held on June 29th, 1991. Yoshihara provides a slightly mistaken quote (1979, p. 51).

[10] Note that, in 1891, the Kobe branch was the only other member of this group. Soon, however, it would be joined by several important Eastern exchange centers: Shanghai (1893), Bombay (1894), and Hong Kong (1896).

and Lyons; one year later, the Hawaii office joined this axis as well). Yokohama head office and London were to coordinate foreign exchange dealings between each other.

Concretely, the new management system entailed a set of rules and agreements with respect to reporting, not only of sales and purchases of foreign exchange, but also of exchange rate fluctuations, crisis situations, business difficulties, etc. (Yokohama Shōkin Ginkō, 1920, vol. 1, app., pp. 478ff.).[11] Lower-tier branches and agencies had to report these on a regular basis to the coordinating offices in Yokohama and London (統轄店 tōkatsu-ten). Drawers of bills had to inform the drawee of amounts it expected to fall due in the future; vice versa, drawees had to inform the former of what was realized, and so on. Equally tangible, and reminiscent of discussions in earlier chapters, were changes in accounting practice (Yokohama Shōkin Ginkō, 1920, vol. 1, app., pp. 481-8). Again, Yokohama head office and London were to be informed, by telegram, of the accounts of branches and agencies under their respective authority, just as the account of the other coordinating branch, including with itself (the so-called 'vostro' account); they also had to keep copies of all of these. Branches were required to submit, every Tuesday of every week, their exchange positions, to Yokohama or London. And every Wednesday, Yokohama and London would inform each other of the bank's overall position, and seek adjustments in case there had been instances of overbuying of gold and silver, respectively.

3. Flow-of-funds Analysis: Introduction

Several authors have attempted to map the resulting flow-of-funds within the branch network, with varying degrees of success (Yoshihara, 1979; Taira, 1984a, 1984b; Kikuchi, 1997; Ishii, 1999). In the following paragraphs, we will mostly compare our findings with those of Ishii, which are—correctly—considered to have rectified some of the earlier misunderstandings (see Appendix 1 of this book). We thereby stick to the script that YSB managers themselves produced when designing their policies.[12] Concretely, this means

---

[11] These rules were called 『為替営業方針改正ニ付支店支配人及出張所主任ノ心得』 *kawase eigyō hōshin kaisei tsuki shiten shihainin oyobi shucchōsho shunin no kokoroe* (plight of the branch officers and agency officials with regard to the reform of the management system of the exchanges).

[12] Ishii's analysis draws the demarcation lines slightly differently, but this should not bother us.

For the methodological and epistemological ramifications of our constructivist approach, see Luhmann (1995).

that the period between 1893 and 1908 must be studied as characterized by three sub-periods:

1. **1893-7**: the YSB branch network before gold standard adoption; flow-of-funds set up along the lines of a gold and a silver axis; adoption of the 'combinatory management style' (連合的営業法 *rengōteki eigyōhō*).
2. **1897-1905**: adoption of the gold standard and expansion in China; change from the 'combinatory management style' to the 'distributive management style' (分立的営業法 *bunritsuteki eigyōhō*); responsibilities of individual branches clearly outlined.
3. **Beyond 1905**: accelerated expansion in China, mostly in the region of Manchuria; YSB tapping into smaller silver-denominated commercial centers; Dairen upgraded to the status of coordinating branch for Manchuria; Shanghai cemented as the pivot in YSB's exchange circle.

One crucial difference with Ishii's analysis is that we will allow the analysis to be as granular as our ethno-historiographic method allows. This means, among others, that our analysis does not present data on an annual basis, but allows YSB biannual reporting to speak for itself. Second, we will not aggregate the data for branches and study the network on the national level; instead, our focus is with the role of individual branches.

There is a methodological reason for the latter. Nowadays, visualization techniques in social network analysis make it possible to explore the deep structure of networks to a degree that could not be achieved in earlier analysis. Typically, earlier research had to settle with an indication of the *amounts* of flows among branch clusters; network *structure* was mostly erased. The latter is misleading, as it is tempting to perceive a node's importance as directly proportional to the amounts it sends and/or receives. Separating the relative *centrality* of a branch from the *weight* of the aggregate funds passing through it is an important improvement upon the earlier literature. What is more, the advantages of such an approach were corroborated by our findings. As we will see, it makes it possible to derive hitherto unknown, and sometimes surprising, insights about the role and importance of certain branches. Importantly, they are also given further credibility when verified against contemporary descriptive evidence of the structure of YSB's branch network.[13]

---

[13] The practice of testing the plausibility of one's findings by contextualizing them through descriptive evidence provided by, in this case, primary sources is referred to as an 'ethnographic sandwich' and is considered a best practice in network research (Ofem et al., 2012).

4. Flow-of-funds, 1893–7

For the period before gold standard adoption (1897), we will use the second semester of 1896 (ending in December 1896) as the base period, as it represents YSB's branch network at a relatively mature point. After calculating the *net* amounts sent between branches (Schiltz, 2017a, 2017b) according to the accounting rules detailed in Appendix 1 (cf. infra), we obtain the matrix presented in Table 5.01.

Using the 'spring embedder' algorithms employed in social network analysis software, the above can be visualized as shown in Figure 5.01.

Clearly, our analysis confirms Ishii's findings. Figure 5.01 depicts a very basic network structure with a straightforward flow-of-funds, in which the London branch played the primary role. In Ishii's own words, and with attention to the most substantial (1994, p. 9):

> To the London branch the proceeds of the exported raw silk were sent from the Lyons branch […]. Using these funds the London branch financed the import of the machines and iron to Japan and sent funds to the Bombay branch in order to finance the import of raw cotton [into Japan].

Although not visible in our graph, we must also reiterate Ishii's findings with respect to the extraordinary role of government support and funding. Factually, government back-up was a recurrent and continuous characteristic of YSB development until its demise in 1946. For the early period, we remind the reader of the *goyō gaikoku nigawase* system and, later, the availability of cheap rediscounting facilities with the BOJ (Ishii, 2001, pp. 53–8). In the aftermath of the Sino-Japanese war, however, official support for YSB was due for a shake-up. Not only was the bank told to make an effort to diminish its reliance on official support, it was also urged to concentrate and expand its activities with respect to trade with China. The result of Tokyo's policy shift was immediate. Not only was YSB actively curtailing exports from London, it also developed rules for rationing bill business at its Asian branches, again with the explicit aim of smoothing trade with China.

As we see in Table 5.02, government back-up, whether directly or through the BOJ, remained substantial, but caused a shift in priorities. In the aftermath of receiving the Sino-Japanese war indemnity, the (once fraught) BOJ-YSB relationship grew very close, factually turning YSB into an instrument of Tokyo's policy. Most visibly, it led to a much stronger presence of YSB in Asia, and a corollary expansion of its activities in the region, in particular in China. Later, this presence would be further accentuated.

Table 5.01. Net flow-of-funds in the YSB branch network, 1896–12 (unit: JPY)

	Y	K	L	NY	LY	SF	HW	S	B	HK
Y	0	3,213,137	12,971,567	1,463,816	2,784,368	337,832	82,566	0	0	18,045
K	0	0	0	0	0	0	63,875	0	0	0
L	0	5,873,678	0	26,818	0	205,175	983	1,797,277	8,057,481	1,047,366
NY	0	1,353,278	0	0	0	0	927	13,568	906	0
LY	0	53,175	4,207,907	14,931	0	0	0	0	0	0
SF	0	347,445	0	59,872	0	0	0	0	0	0
HW	0	0	0	0	0	825,712	0	0	0	0
S	518,131	1,270,761	0	0	2,735,948	83,136	91	0	0	1,150,048
B	1,459,797	3,830,780	0	0	0	0	0	2,782,948	0	1,187,377
HK	0	76,249	0	33,352	356,844	2,019,306	1,862	0	0	0

Source: Created by the author, after YSB Midterm Reports (multiple issues).

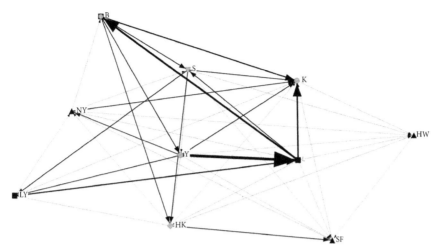

Figure 5.01. Y: Yokohama Head Office; K: Kobe; L: London; NY: New York LY: Lyon; SF: San Francisco; HW: Hawai; S: Shanghai; H: Hankow; B: Mumbai (Bombay); HK: Hong Kong; currencies are expressed by means of different node symbols (circle: JPY; square: £; up triangle: $; box: FF (here indistinguishable from the British pound because of the visualization in B/W); down triangle: CH¥; circle in box: Rs); branches are furthermore differentiated according to their metal of denomination: nodes in black are branches in gold-standard countries; nodes in grey use silver as the unit of account.
Source: calculations by the author

At the same time, Table 5.02 also highlights the particular importance of certain key branches. Take, for instance, the Kobe branch. Whereas Yokohama functioned as the port for Japanese silk and tea exports to Western destinations (London, New York, Lyon), Kobe clearly emerged as the crucial hub for linking Western Japan to Asia, that is, it was the port where the imports of primary materials (mostly cotton) from Asia arrived. This particular economic-geographical divide between Western and Eastern Japan was actually well known among contemporaries—in the early twentieth century, Japanese imperialist planners referred to China and Manchuria as the '"extension" (延長地 *enchōchi*) of Osaka and Kobe' (Schiltz, 2012b, p. 170)—but the financial networks behind the latter have only started to be discovered (Nishimura, 2012, 2014). Notably Nishimura Takeshi has described how China was the main source of (ginned) raw cotton for the industrialists in Osaka[14]

---

[14] The lack of a YSB office in Osaka at the time is striking. However, as explained by Ishii, traders in Western Japan tended to distrust YSB in the beginning, and were relying on private banks and money lenders in the region. Ultimately, when an Osaka branch was established in 1905, it quickly overtook the Kobe branch's business (Ishii, 2009).

Table 5.02. YSB uses and sources of funds, 1896-7 (unit: JPY 1,000)

Item	1896 (real)	1897 (projected/ planned)
Fund for imports from Western countries 欧米よりの輸入為替資金	13,921	14,170
London fund for telegraphic transfers (龍動)ロンドン電信為替資金	3,750	4,050
Fund for lending at Western branches 欧米支店貸出資金	870	900
Fund for exports to Western countries (held at Yokohama/Kobe branches) 欧米への輸出為替資金	15,145	16,000
Fund for domestic lending and Sino-Japanese exchange (held at Yokohama/Kobe branches) 国内貸出・日清為替資金	10,119	8,500 (Yokohama: 6,000) (Kobe: 2,000)
Fund for lending/exchange activities in Asia (shared among YSB Asian branches アジア貸出・為替資金	2,717	3,500 (Shanghai: 1,500) (Hong Kong: 1,000) Mumbai: 1,000)
Public debt certificates 公債証書	4,500	0
Total needed	51,022	47,120
Stocks/reserve fund 株金・積立金	13,510	15,300
Lent from BOJ 日本銀行より借用金	22,000	22,000
BOJ deposit in London (龍動)ロンドン預かり金	20,000	10,000
Total available	55,510	47,300

Note: For this period, YSB did *not* include deposits as a source of funds; this would have been very different at, for instance, the HSBC at the time. Also, note that the BOJ deposit appears to decrease from ¥20 million to ¥10 million; this is, however, the direct consequence of an earlier agreement to return ¥10 million to BOJ.

Source: Created by the author, after Yokohama Shōkin Ginkō (1920, vol. 2, app., pp. 592-6; Tōkyō Ginkō, 19—, vol. 1, pp. 25-9).

and Kobe before 1893. After that date, and coinciding with the establishment of the YSB Bombay office, the imports of Indian cotton grew exponentially.

This highly asymmetric relationship between the Kobe and Bombay branches (imports from Bombay to Kobe were much larger than the amounts of commodities flowing the other way) had pertinent implications. As the Bombay agency bought the bills that were to be collected in Kobe, most likely from Kobe-based Indian and Chinese merchants, the Bombay branch faced a chronic problem with respect to recouping its funds. Attempting to overcome heavy losses produced by such imbalances, YSB set up an exchange fund of ₨ 500,000 at this agency (it would be upgraded into an office in 1900) (Yokohama Shōkin Ginkō, 1920, pp. 151ff.). According to one observer, this became the incentive for Japanese trading companies to shift away from relying on, say, the Bombay agencies of HSBC and the Chartered Bank, and concentrating their business with YSB instead (Takamura, 1968, p. 29). However, this exchange fund soon proved insufficient for the voracious demands for Indian cotton.[15] This, in turn, shifts our attention to the large remittances from YSB's London branch to Bombay (amounting to more than ¥8 million in the second semester of 1896).[16] In the same period, YSB also started to encourage its non-domestic branches to collect deposits in their respective regions. At the Bombay branch, fixed deposits (the main source for bill finance) drew between 4 and 4.5 per cent interest per year. The share of rich Indian money changers (*shroffs*) in the latter was particularly large (Nishimura, 2012, p. 183).

Shanghai is yet another branch deserving our attention. Set up as an agency in 1893,[17] it would quickly grow into a major hub for YSB's operations in Asia. As early as December 1895, only two years after its establishment, YSB's cadre decided that the Shanghai agency was to be developed into an independent branch. Foreshadowing Furuta's analysis of this city as the pivot of Asia (2000), they noted that Shanghai was not only the largest harbor in the region, but that, because of the latter, it also was the one Asian market with the greatest financial depth (Yokohama Shōkin Ginkō, 1920, vol. 2., app., pp. 527ff.). It would be in the interest of the agency, they reasoned, to give it considerable independence when buying and selling foreign exchange, rather than making it dependent on decisions in the Yokohama head office. The branch was therefore given its own exchange fund (10,000,000 tael); in return, in order to shield other branches from losses arising out of this facility, the branch was to bear all the risks of its operations (貸記シ損益ノ計算ヲ自己ニ負担シ其見

---

[15] We should note the particular role of the Mitsui Trading Company in the latter. As noted by Sugihara, demand for trade finance was so large that it necessitated a continuing effort to curry favor with all exchange banks at the time (1996). This dominant position would carry over in Mitsui Bussan's expansion within China (Sakamoto, 2003).

[16] There exists an interesting YSB internal publication on the difficulties remitting from London to Bombay entailed (Nishimaki and Yokohama Shōkin Ginkō, 1910). Nishimaki and Yokohama Shōkin Ginkō describe how rampant speculation by bill brokers in the Bombay market caused YSB to develop precautionary measures when transferring funds.

[17] The establishment of the Shanghai agency was preceded by a bank-internal survey of business conditions in China, in particular the commercial centers of Shanghai and Hankow (漢口; nowadays transcribed as Hankou) (Schiltz, 2016d).

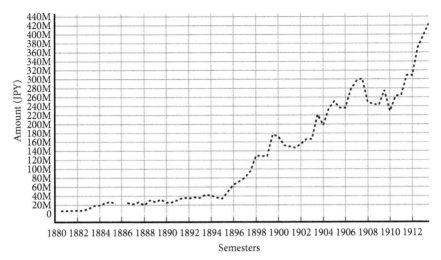

Figure 5.02. The evolution of YSB's balance sheet, 1880–1913
Source: calculations by the author

込ヲ以テ営業セシムル事 *kashiki shi son'eki no keisan wo jiko ni futan shi sono mikomi wo motte eigyō seshimuru koto*). It was the first step in a series of managerial shifts that would eventually lead to the branch's promotion to the linchpin in YSB's exchange circle.

Summing up, in 1896 YSB's branch network was composed of three types of branches: (1) coordinating branches 統轄店 *tōkatsuten*), (2) subsidiary combinatory branches (連合店 *rengōten*), and (3) independent branches (独立店 *dokuritsuten*).[18] Equally important, this set-up worked. After adopting the 'even keel' strategy, YSB's balance sheet would develop quickly, turning it into a formidable competitor of its European peers (Figure 5.02).

5. Flow-of-funds, 1897–1905

In 1897, a monetary decision in Tokyo profoundly upset the rationale and workings of the combinatory management style. Matsukata's decision to use the indemnity resulting from the Sino-Japanese war to bring Japan onto the gold standard changed the composition of Japan's foreign trade with the stroke of a pen. On November 15, 1897, when YSB managers held one of their meetings, they recognized that they would have to change their management

---

[18] These 'independent branches' were, as said, Shanghai, but also San Francisco (Yokohama Shōkin Ginkō, 1920, p. 157).

policy.[19] As two-thirds of Japan's foreign trade was with Western gold standard countries, and as the bank itself would also adopt gold as the unit of account, they argued that the bank 'would not be exposed to changes in the gold:silver parity as before' (金貨国ニ対スル為替ハ従前ノ如ク金銀比価変動ノ影響ヲ受ケザル *kinkakoku ni tai suru kawase ha jūzen no gotoku kingin hika hendō no eikyō wo ukezaru*). Hence,

> the need to cover all exchange dealings is less pressing. Consequently, we have reached the conclusion that the combinatory management style is obsolete. We will therefore abolish [this system] and will replace it with a distributive management style (*bunritsuteki eigyōhō* 分立的営業法).
>
> (Yokohama Shōkin Ginkō, 1920, vol. 2, app., pp. 586-7)

The authors explained that, apart from the sea change in the composition of Japan's foreign trade, the lack of accountability arising from the combinatory management style had played a role in their decision. In their view, there had been a tendency among second-tier branches to underestimate or even ignore the risks their foreign exchange operations entailed for other branches, and to prioritize their own profits over that of the bank as a whole. If anything, the newly adopted distributive management style thus did *not* mark a return to the early days when business was rather uncoordinated and when YSB did not take hedging exchange risk seriously. Quite on the contrary, it was a pretext for enhancing control within the network, and clearly distinguishing the responsibilities and penalties that would result from 'irresponsible' behavior. Concretely, every branch (甲店 *kōten*) would, from now on, (a) inform every other branch (乙店 *otsuten*) of any transaction that related to the latter. Also, (b) both branches were to inform each other of the amounts realized, and (c) this in accordance with the most recent rate, transmitted by telegraph (最近電報ノ相場 *saikin denpō no sōba*) (Yokohama Shōkin Ginkō, 1920, vol. 2, app., p. 588). In case there were fluctuations of the exchange rate between the latest quoted rate and the rate at which the transaction was realized, the differential between those rates (最終的ナ換算相場ト実際相場ノ差金 *saishūteki na kawase sōba to jissai sōba no sakin*), whether profit or loss, was for the account of the receiving branch.

As said, the plan also outlined penalties. These mostly related to 'uncovered positions', especially in cases a branch was (excessively) *overdrawing* its

---

[19] 「改正営業方針要領」 *Kaisei eigyō hōshin yōryō* (*Outline of the Policy for Management Reform*) (Yokohama Shōkin Ginkō, 1920, vol. 2, app., pp. 584ff.).

account with other branches (to put it more concretely, when a branch did not match the degree to which it engaged in import finance (bills sold) with a commensurate effort to engage in export finance (bills bought, to be collected at the other end)).[20] From now on, branches were to pay 2 per cent annual interest on the overdrawn amounts to the lending branch, and another 2 per cent to Yokohama headquarters, which the latter would add to the general ledger of loans. In other words, branches were made aware that they were responsible vis-à-vis the whole branch network, and not just one of their peers (Yokohama Shōkin Ginkō, 1920, vol. 2, app., p. 588).[21,22]

I surmise that this drive to cement checks and balances within the branch network must at least partially be explained by the prominent role YSB was from then on to play in upholding the country's gold standard. In itself, this had to do with several difficulties that posed themselves in the immediate wake of this monetary policy change. As I have explained elsewhere, the gold standard did not buy Japan instant credibility (Schiltz, 2012a). Instead, it functioned as some kind of insurance against mismatch when repaying loans raised in (gold-based) international capital markets (primarily London). As such, it was a second best choice, which came with quite a few strings attached. The necessity to keep a specie reserve abroad in a non-interest bearing account with the Bank of England was one of those. Not in the least, it also entailed a complicated trade-off between short-term instability, on the one hand, and long-term access to foreign capital, on the other. In the short-term, the consequences were severe. Domestically, it resulted in a credit crunch, for which Matsukata was held responsible (Figure 5.03).

Internationally, the yields on Japan's foreign loans even *went up* (Mitchener et al. 2010), very much contrary to the thesis according to which gold standard adoption would depress them.[23] After all, it was one thing to adopt the gold standard; it was yet another to *maintain* it. Gold standard adoption had, in other words, removed exchange risk for the time being but it had also

---

[20] For accounting technicalities related to export and import finance, see Appendix 1.

[21] A discussion hereof can be found in Shiratori (2008).

[22] Yet another effort at enhancing transparency and responsibility took aim at accounting practice at the bank. In particular Takahashi Korekiyo had complained about the lack of standardization among branches. A discussion hereof can be found in the transcripts of the first meeting of the directors of the Eastern branches (Yokohama Shōkin Ginkō, 1910, pp. 239ff.). In 1908, every branch was therefore sent a 'model book', outlining best practices for booking vouchers, types of bills, etc. (Schiltz, 2016c).

[23] This is the idea behind the 'gold-standard as a housekeeping seal of approval'-argument, which is now largely discredited (Bordo and Rockoff, 1996; Sussman and Yafeh, 2000).

Figure 5.03. 'the wound to the shinbone and the swelling of the forehead'. This scene depicts Finance Minister Matsukata, visiting a doctor. On his shinbone is written 'failure of the gold standard' (金制失敗 *kinsei shippai*). The characters on his forehead read as an 'admonition to step down' (辞職勧告 *jishoku kankoku*). Matsukata: "This wound to my shinbone already hurt, but the swelling on my forehead is a real problem. It keeps on growing bigger…!". [Doctor]: "This ointment may relieve a bit of the pain, but it looks like it will eventually become a serious condition."

Source: *Maru maru chinbun*, August 26 1897 (out of copyright).

heightened country risk![24] Discussions in, for instance, *The Economist* highlighted this problem from very early on.[25]

BOJ insiders must certainly have been aware of this, and for that reason approached YSB with a special request (Yokohama Shōkin Ginkō, 1920, vol. 2,

---

[24] In economic historical literature, this has only received limited attention. For an exception to the latter, see Mitchener and Weidenmier (2015).

[25] Compare, with particular attention to the price of Japan's foreign loans: 'The Political and Financial Situation in Japan.' *The Economist* (London, England) Jan. 8, 1898, pp. 39ff.; and 'Japanese Trade and Finance.' *Economist* (London, England) July 23, 1898, pp. 1076ff. Later, *The Economist* would also blame the 'intransparent' system of specie held abroad for Japan's monetary trouble. Compare: 'Japan's Gold Reserves in London.' *The Economist* (London, England) Mar. 9, 1912, p. 513. At the same time, yet unrelatedly (?), BOJ and the Ministry of Finance were alerted to the difficulties of maintaining Japan's international credibility. The viability of the specie-held-abroad system was particularly contested (Ishii, 2001, pp. 37–8).

app., pp. 568-9). Their arguments can be read as an endorsement of 'how global currencies work' (Eichengreen et al., 2017). Credibility of the newly adopted gold standard system was crucially dependent on the yen's liquidity, they said, which could only result from a wider use of the yen as a means for settling international transactions. In other words, market share was key, and YSB was in a unique position for providing the latter, for instance by giving preference to yen-denominated bills of exchange. In exchange for such services, BOJ declared itself ready to continue and even strengthen official support for YSB's operations. Realizing both the challenges and opportunities this would entail, YSB agreed:

> We are convinced that our bank has a strong responsibility in this respect, and are determined to do our utmost best within the boundaries of our possibilities
>
> 「当銀行モ最モ務ムヘキ責任ニシテ不肖ナカラ拙者共ニ於テモ深ク茲ニ服膺仕リ精々努力可仕覚悟ニ御座候」
>
> (tōginkō mo mottomo tsutomu beki sekinin ni shite fushō nakara sessha tomo ni oitemo fukaku koko ni fukuyō tsukamatsuri seizei doryoku tsukamatsuri kakugo ni gozasōrō). (Yokohama Shōkin Ginkō, 1920, vol. 2, app., pp. 570-1).

Through a system of interlocking directorships and oversight, YSB would remain in place as a semi-governmental institution until the end of World War II. Others have explored, sometimes at great length, how this set-up cut across YSB's functioning as a commercial bank, so we limit ourselves to pointing out relevant literature (Taira, 1984a, 1984b; Saitō, 2015).

Still, the decision came with a great deal of *opportunities* as well, and these have unfortunately been left out of the existing narrative. YSB bankers, educated in the mechanism of the even keel, realized that a safe business with silver regions was still perfectly possible, provided that raising funds (deposits) in those regions would not amount to a major liability (i.e., because of the interest to be paid on the latter). And if credit conditions were to turn out to be particularly tight, they must certainly have reasoned, YSB could experiment with issuing paper money, after the example of HSBC. In that case, *seigniorage* more or less amounted to the creation of deposits out of thin air; the only condition for *seigniorage* to work would be the stability of these notes.

We know that this is exactly what happened. In the immediate aftermath of gold standard adoption, YSB established the agencies (which later turned into branches) of Tientsin (天津 Tianjin, 1899), Yingkou (営口, 1900), and Peking

Table 5.03. Net flow-of-funds in the YSB branch network, 1904–6 (unit: JPY)

	Y	K	L	NY	LY	SF	HW	S	H	B	HK	T	N	TJ	NZ	P	D	LI	M
Y	0	14,869,775	0	9,881,163	12,275,535	0	68,686	906,655	0	1,013,968	1,091,982	0	0	0	212,431	0	0	50	0
K	0	0	0	0	0	0	278,674	229,315	0	0	191,016	14,609,666	472,622	199,682	2,928,527	0	0	40,125	0
L	16,262,461	3,308,757	0	3,792,438	0	2,784,205	0	0	0	2,488,490	0	10,308,281	65,818	17,325	0	0	0	0	0
NY	0	4,080,345	0	0	0	0	4,719	0	0	0	0	0	19,998	20,392	0	0	0	0	0
LY	0	11,171	14,397,029	276,811	0	0	0	0	0	0	0	265,005	0	0	0	0	0	0	0
SF	751,250	1,743,218	0	266,552	0	0	0	16,270	0	0	53,541	0	0	0	0	0	0	0	0
HW	0	0	1,303	0	0	2,408,585	0	1,274,841	0	0	0	0	0	41,807	111,935	33,882	0	0	0
S	0	0	5,886,051	295,984	1,171,034	0	0	0	0	0	136,066	0	0	0	0	0	0	0	0
H	0	0	0	0	0	0	0	0	0	0	0	0	0	0	0	0	0	0	0
B	0	2,453,110	0	0	0	0	0	0	0	8,173	0	98,240	0	13,658	0	0	0	0	0
HK	0	0	2,359,240	16,605	156,665	0	15,078	847,341	0	0	0	0	0	15,607	0	0	0	0	0
T	6,482,530	0	0	760,249	0	79,821	75,152	2,551,776	0	0	101,135	0	0	0	259,596	0	0	0	0
N	213,894	0	0	0	3,837	1,015	401	312,652	0	3,672	7,115	202,827	0	6,302	140,202	1,939	3,185	9,990	24,976
TJ	107,576	0	0	0	17,486	0	0	417,354	0	0	0	1,252,403	0	0	0	0	2,150	15	0
NZ	0	0	34,768	1,235	0	0	0	0	0	0	0	0	0	18,616	0	0	0	0	0
P	314	43,702	5,597	39,563	0	0	0	0	0	0	7,185	0	0	296,922	0	6,223	70,314	4,525	0
D	250	0	0	0	0	0	0	0	0	0	31	182,331	0	0	0	0	0	1,916	0
LI	0	0	0	0	0	0	0	0	0	0	0	0	0	0	0	0	0	0	0
M	0	0	0	0	0	0	0	0	0	0	0	0	0	0	0	0	0	0	0

Source: Created by the author, after YSB Midterm Reports (multiple issues).

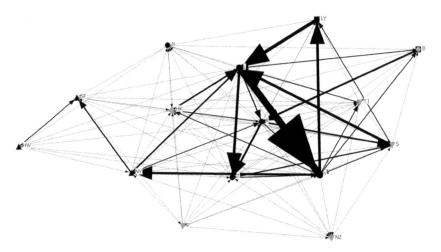

Figure 5.04. Y: Yokohama Head Office; K: Kobe; L: London; NY: New York LY: Lyon; SF: San Francisco; HW: Hawai; S: Shanghai; H: Hankow; B: Mumbai (Bombay); HK: Hong Kong; T: Tokyo; N: Nagasaki; TJ: Tianjin; NZ: Niuzhang; P: Beijing (Peking); currencies are expressed by means of different node symbols (circle: JPY; square: £; up triangle: $; box: FF (here indistinguishable from the British pound because of the visualization in B/W); down triangle: CH¥; circle in box: Rs); branches are furthermore differentiated according to their metal of denomination: nodes in black are branches in gold-standard countries; nodes in grey use silver as the unit of account.

Source: calculations by the author.

(北京 Beijing, 1902). Earlier (see Chapter 4), we have seen that YSB managers, when assessing the state of China's money market, judged the interest rate on deposits that YSB applied opportune in view of its own position in the country. From 1904 onwards, it was given further leeway to endorse the latter. From then on, YSB issued a silver-denominated paper money called *shōhyō* (鈔票) (Horesh, 2013), which would later play a formidable role in the management of its Manchuria business (Yasutomi, 1997; Schiltz, 2012b).

Yet what did all this mean in terms of the bank's flow-of-funds? Again, we use the last semester of this period (June 1904) as the basis for our calculations (Table 5.03 and Figure 5.04).

We note that, in terms of mere amounts of flow, the network has slightly changed from the way pictured in 1896–12. London, being the unchallenged financial center, still was the hub through which large amounts of funds were funneled and redirected. It received, by remittance, the massive proceeds of raw silk arriving in Lyon, and collected payments for the exported

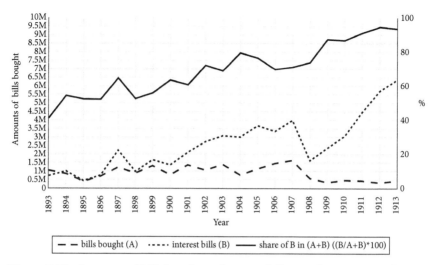

Figure 5.05. Amounts of bills bought and interest bills sent from YSB London branch to Japanese branches (in millions of JPY); share of interest bills in total amounts (as percentages; plotted on the secondary Y-axis)

Source: calculations by the author, after Ishii (1999, p. 248). For some years, only semestrial data could be obtained: 1895–06, 1896–12, and 1900–12.

cotton goods from China (mostly from the Shanghai branch). Funds were, as before, sent to the Bombay branch, in order to finance raw cotton imports into Kobe. A major difference, however, were the very large transfers from London to YSB branches in Japan (Figure 5.05). The overwhelming majority of the latter were interest bills (approx. 80 per cent of totals in 1904–6; cf. infra), as discussed in Chapter 3. They (mostly) did not represent exports but were used as finance bills. In early 1904, these amounts were probably further amplified as policymakers in Tokyo, preparing for war with Russia, attempted to build up a war chest by means of short-term private borrowing in London (Suzuki, 1994, p. 95).

In itself, this is a very important footnote to the commonly held assumption that Japan financed the war by means of sovereign borrowing in New York, through German-Jewish bankers (Best, 1972; Sherman, 1983; Smethurst, 2006; Gower, 2016). Although the government in London found it inopportune to support Japanese military operations in an overt manner, financiers in the City were clearly less constrained by political motives. After all, as indicated earlier, interest bills promised an easy and substantial return.

Yet, from an exchange banker's perspective, the whole operation cannot have been a straightforward matter. After all, this was a period in which the London branch was a large net exporter of capital, which would have preoccupied branch managers: how could funds be recouped? Second, because these capital flows were so massive, they were bound to become a macroeconomic conundrum. How could Japan counter the invariably downward pressure upon the yen's exchange rate? Would this not lead to the outflow of much-wanted bullion?

It is in this context that Japan's central bankers worked their financial magic. Kojima Hitoshi must be credited for discovering a 'gold device' that neutralised the 'rule' of the gold standard according to which specie outflow would lead to yen depreciation; and, eventually, a restoration of the balance of payments (Kojima, 1977). The specie held abroad was key. As soon as the yen's exchange rate approached the export point of gold and Japan-based foreign exchange banks demanded the conversion of paper yen into gold, the BOJ sold them pound-denominated exchange bills on London at a slightly better rate.[26] In London, these bills could then be paid from the part of specie held abroad that was *not* used as a reserve fund for currency issuance within Japan proper.[27] Although this account could in principle be run down in the long run, it was supplemented by specie held abroad held by the Japanese government.[28] Only by adding the proceeds of the sales of its loan issues to the latter, it managed to run the large deficits needed to pay for the military spending binges after both the Sino-Japanese and Russo-Japanese wars (Ohkawa, 1965) (Figures 5.06 and 5.07).

In the long run, however, this fueled the prospect of a massive Japanese default on its outstanding debt (Figure 5.08)—the latter could only be averted thanks to the unprecedented (and unforeseeable) demand for Japanese products in World War I.

[26] Interestingly, Japan also attempted to work towards a situation in which specie imports would be considered more favorable. According to a report by a bullion broker in Shanghai published in 1903, charges for minting bullion were 'in abeyance', presumably 'to encourage the import of metal into the country' (White and Kinnear, 1903, p. 72).

[27] Understanding the typology of specie held abroad is quite challenging for the novel researcher. Both the government and the BOJ had foreign accounts with specie, yet the BOJ accounts distinguished between 'foreign specie as currency reserve' (i.e., for currency to be issued within Japan proper) and foreign specie excluded from the latter. This second type (準備外在外正貨 *junbigai zaigai seika*) could be sold/transferred to a YSB account. Note however, that both Japanese government accounts and BOJ accounts abroad were managed by YSB, which is the source of confusion (Suzuki, 1994, pp. 170–3; Saitō, 2015, pp. 390–6).

[28] BOJ Director Fukai Eigo 深井英五 therefore argued in 1922 that, in the Japanese case, *foreign borrowing had been the means to maintain the gold standard*, a remarkable inversion of the assumption that countries adopted the gold standard in order to facilitate foreign borrowing (Suzuki, 1994, p. 174; Schiltz, 2012a).

Figure 5.06. 'the outflow of gold in the *maelstrom* [川瀬 *kawase*] of imports. Two boatsmen (Ministry of Finance officials?) exclaim: "In the exchange (為替 *kawase*) flood of imports to our country, gold coins are flowing abroad!" Note that maelstrom and foreign exchange are homonyms in Japanese.

Source: *Maru maru chinbun* January 30 1904 (out of copyright).

6. Flow-of-funds, 1905–8

In many ways, the Russo-Japanese War (1904–5) represented a turning point in international affairs. As it was the first war in which modern communications technology—the telegraph and photography—played a crucial role (Fraser, 1905; Gerbig-Fabel, 2008), it also was the first conflict in which 'public opinion', as the nascent corollary of modern technologies of communication (Kittler, 1999; Luhmann, 2000; Luhmann, 2005), was alerted to the horrors of modern, that is, total, warfare. For that reason, and for the fact that it paved the way for a worldwide conflict only a decade later, it has aptly been described as World War Zero (Steinberg, Wolff, 2006; Steinberg, 2008). In Russia, the massive unpopularity of the campaign certainly fueled the revolution of 1905. For Japan, it heralded its entry into a select club of empires that had hitherto been the exclusive domain of Western, and white, countries. In financial terms as well, it entailed a radical shake-up.

Figure 5.07. 'year's end for the military man'. This scene depicts two heavily decorated military officers having a lavish dinner. One of them says: "At the end of this incredible year (空前絶後 *kūzen zetsugo*) I stick out my breast and stick out my nose". 'To stick out one's breast (胸に懸ける *mune ni kakeru*) should be interpreted as being boastful; 'to stick out one's nose' (鼻に懸ける *hana ni kakeru*) means being arrogant.

Source: Tokyo Asahi Shinbun December 31 1906 (out of copyright).

It is instructive to put this development against the background of the existing Western literature. Several scholars have, after Fukuzawa Yukichi's famous editorial (1885) urging Japan to 'leave Asia' (脱亜 *datsu-a*), stressed that Japan's modernization and its acceptance within Western ranks was, at its core, the product of a society-wide embrace of Western institutions. In this view, the adoption of the gold standard—arguably a 'Western' standard[29]—is

---

[29] At the time, most observers added that gold was the 'Western' metal, in contrast to silver, the 'quintessentially Asian' one. As the reader may realize, we find this characterization misleading: the element in defining a currency's position within the international pecking order was, fundamentally, a function of *relative liquidity*, and thus not in itself a choice for or against a certain metal.

Figure 5.08. Debt hangover – The beloved tree of our ancestors.

Source: Hōchi chinbun, October 4 1911 (out of copyright)

yet another corroboration of the narrative. Although partially correct, this view nevertheless glosses over subtleties related to (a) the composition of Japan's foreign trade and, especially, (b) the practice of hedging that was necessitated by gold standard adoption in the first place. Without going so far as to argue that geography is destiny, there are a few elements that lead us to believe that the early twentieth century witnessed a tightly intertwined political and financial reorientation of Japan towards Asia. Together, they do not so much rewrite history as hint at an understanding of Japan's modernization that is more complex and contingent than the conventional portrayal.

This is most clearly visible in the network structure of YSB, the quintessential institution for projecting Japan's financial prowess abroad. Admittedly, the intensification of YSB activity in mostly Northeast China was noted before, in the Japanese literature. In a seminal contribution to YSB research, Kaneko has outlined the frenzy with the financial occupation of Manchuria after 1905.

However, YSB insistence on expansion on a silver rather than a gold basis remained a mystery, even to him (Kaneko, 1977, 1979). As discussed earlier, the micro-foundations of the even keel debunk the paradox. Hedging exchange risk with silver regions remained possible, and was only constrained by the costs of raising capital in markets that were traditionally characterized by low liquidity; the alternative, that is, a Japan-led monetary reform effort, would have been much more costly, including in political terms, and its outcome would have been insecure.

The ramifications for the structure of YSB's branch network can be deduced from Figure 5.09, depicting the flow-of-funds in the first semester of 1908. First of all, one is struck by the central role of the Shanghai branch. Turned into an independent branch in 1895 (cf. supra), it was promoted to the single most important central coordinating branch (中央為替統轄店 chūō kawase tōkatsu-ten) for YSB's network as soon as 1909. As a matter of fact, this development was behind the establishment of a separate assembly of the directors of the Eastern branches (東洋支店長会議 tōyō shitenchō kaigi), the records of which still survive (Yokohama Shōkin Ginkō, 1908). Citing a bank-internal publication, Shiratori indicates this move was inspired by a familiar vice: managers of both Western and Asian branches continued to put the profits of their own branches over the health of the branch network, so YSB needed a center in which exchange rate differences could be flattened out or manipulated to the benefit of the bank as a whole (Shiratori, 2008, p. 15).[30]

Concretely, Shanghai became the information hub of the network. Second-tier branches had to report uncovered amounts (bought and sold) to Shanghai, by telegram, on a daily basis, and apply for cover according to the rate of that day; the rate at which cover was realized was based upon the one telegraphed by the Shanghai branch on the day of realization (「為替相場ノ建方ハ日々上海支店ヨリ電報スル相庭ヲ標準トシテ之レヲ定ムル」 kawase sōba no tatekata ha hibi shanhai shiten yori denpō suru aiba wo hyōjun toshite kore wo sadamuru); importantly, the Shanghai branch had to comply with every application for exchange cover, including in cases this went against

---

[30] In the original:

「各店ニ於テ自店ノ利益ヲ主眼トシ全体ノ利害得喪ヲ第二ニ置クカ為メ為替ノ出合上往々不便ヲ感スルノミナラス金銀為替相場ノ危険ヲ冒スノ度合モ較々多大ナル憾アルカ如ク依テ此等ノ不便ト危険トヲ可成軽減スヘキ方法ヲ講究スルニ銀貨国及金貨国(欧、米、印ハ当分之ヲ除キ従前ノ通タルヘシ)ニ在ル各統務店及独立店ハ自今上海支店ヲ中央統務店ニ移シ整理スルヲ得策ナリト思考ス」.

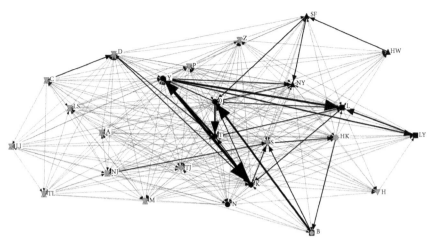

Figure 5.09. Y: Yokohama Head Office; K: Kobe; L: London; NY: New York LY: Lyon; SF: San Francisco; HW: Hawai; S: Shanghai; H: Hankow; B: Mumbai (Bombay); HK: Hong Kong; T: Tokyo; N: Nagasaki; TJ: Tianjin; NZ: Niuzhang; P: Beijing (Peking); D: Dairen; LI: Liaoyang; M: Mukden; LS: Lushun; A: Andong; Z: Yantai (Chefoo); O: Osaka; TL: Tieling; C: Changchun; currencies are expressed by means of different node symbols (circle: JPY; square: £; up triangle: $; box: FF (here indistinguishable from the British pound because of the visualization in B/W); down triangle: CH¥; circle in box: Rs; overlapping up/down triangle: Manchurian yuan); branches are furthermore differentiated according to their metal of denomination: nodes in black are branches in gold-standard countries; nodes in grey use silver as the unit of account.
Source: calculations by the author

the branch's profit. Taken together, these rules were meant to combat speculative behavior by branch managers.

The reason for putting this central coordinating branch in Shanghai, rather than, say, at the Yokohama headquarters, was directly related to the bank's role in the city. As said earlier, Shanghai was the most mature and largest financial center in East Asia. By further boosting activities of the YSB branch in the latter, it was an attempt to give YSB the role of a market maker. In this respect, several had declared victory as soon as 1896:

> In the beginning, the Eastern exchanges were largely the turf of the Hongkong and Shanghai Banking Corporation and the Chartered Bank; the Yokohama Specie Bank could merely follow the latter two's quotations. Nowadays, however, the situation has been reversed radically. The exchange that has to be sent

abroad, for instance to London, is sold exclusively by our bank; and the exchange needed to be sent from London to our mainland [Japan], Singapore, Bombay, Hongkong and Shanghai is exclusively bought by our bank. In other words, the Specie Bank now wields real power over the Eastern exchanges, and the Hongkong and Shanghai Banking Corporation and the Chartered Bank, which formerly controlled them, can do nothing but wait on YSB's beck (正金銀行ノ鼻息ヲ窺フテソノ取組ヲ為スニ至リシトナリ *Shōkin ginkō no hanaiki wo ukakafute sono torikumi wo nasu ni itarishi to nari*).[31]

Although this assessment was probably premature, in view of the bank's recurring problems with raising capital (Tōkyō Ginkō, 19—), one nevertheless gets a strong feeling of the intentions of YSB management.

Other descriptive evidence corroborates yet different findings of our network analysis. As the reader will have realized, *all* YSB expansion during or in the immediate aftermath of the Russo-Japanese war, with the exception of the domestic branch of Osaka, was *in silver territory*, and *on a silver basis* (i.e., the Manchurian silver yuan or M¥). Of particular importance is YSB influence in Manchuria. In rapid succession, branches were established in Dairen (1904), Mukden (1905), Changchun (1907), Tieling (later Kaiyuan 開原) and so forth. Here, the bank was involved in much more than trade finance. As explored by others, YSB engaged in note issuance, in order to redeem the large amounts of military scrip that had flooded the region during the Russo-Japanese War (Shiratori, 2008, pp. 18-21). After the example of YSB in China, it also consolidated the bank's venturing into long-term industrial finance in Manchuria. The bank's management was aware of the risks hereof (cf. infra),[32] but massive lending to, for instance, the Hanyeping Coal and Iron Concern (Jpn. *Kan'yahyō kōshi* 漢冶萍公司), was clearly a political move inspired by Tokyo. The Japanese government guaranteed the loans in several cases. In other instances, it even provided direct funding. In total, more than ten of these loans materialized; they were substantial enough to draw scrutiny from international observers (Remer, 1933; Schiltz, 2012b).[33]

---

[31] 「正金銀行東洋為替ノ実権ヲ握ル」 *Shōkin ginkō ha tōyō kawase no jikken wo nigiru* ('The YSB Grabs Real Power over the Eastern Exchanges'), in *Ginkō Tsūshinroku*, No. 123 (Feb. 10, 1896) (Yoshihara, 1979, p. 52).

[32] Notably Takahashi Korekiyo, YSB Governor from 1906 until 1911, was adamant about curtailing the bank's involvement in business activity other than trade finance. The transcripts of the assembly of the directors of the Eastern branches contain numerous references to the problem of capital immobilization as a consequence of long-term industrial finance.

[33] In turn, this fueled Japanese interest in Remer's findings (Minami Manshū Tetsudō Kabushiki Gaisha, 1934). For a very thorough treatment of these loans in Japanese, see Andō (1966a, 1966b); Kaneko (1977); Kubota (2011).

We are inclined to believe that YSB efforts at soliciting deposits in China and Manchuria were directly related to this industrial lending business. Several authors have argued that the paucity of Japanese government sources was behind the shift in YSB policy (Taira, 1986). And indeed, the BOJ had decided in 1903 to limit its supply of cheap capital to the YSB. Consequently, YSB used a 'China exchange fund' ((中国為替資金 *chūgoku kawase shikin* or 対支事業資金 *tai-shi jigyō shikin*), which constituted a portion of BOJ's cheaply supplied money) to fulfill its obligations to Western banks (Yokohama shōkin ginkō, 1920, vol. 2, app., pp. 598-604). Still, the decision to raise deposits in liquidity-poor regions (as repeatedly indicated before, they were a considerable liability because of the high level of interest paid on the latter, i.e. at least 4 per cent *per annum*) cannot have been connected to its bill business. Instead, it only makes sense as a means to partly offset problems of capital immobilization that long-term lending ensued. In any case, the pressure long-term lending put on YSB's profitability must have been substantial (Shiratori, 2008, pp. 21-2).

The fact that these deposits were raised within those regions in which Japan sought to gain a position of economic predominance furthermore suggests that the strategy fitted within a broader view of empire building: these regions were factually paying for their own subordination. This was possible because they were, as argued in Chapter 1, outside the Braudelian bell jar. Banks such as HSBC, the Chartered Bank, and YSB could fulfil a role that indigenous institutions simply could not. Put yet differently, foreign financial institutions were, because of their superior infrastructure and technologies, innately parasitic or even *parasitoid*[34] vs. indigenous ones: the latter were bound to disappear or, alternatively, to fulfil a second-tier role in the complex post-imperial economic set-up of the host country.[35] In the meanwhile, non-Chinese institutions thrived. YSB's Tianjin and Beijing branches, it turns out, were most active in the collection of deposits (Yokohama Shōkin Ginkō, 19—, vol. 1, pp. 67ff.). Apart from the money they used for their day-to-day lending, these banks channeled deposits to the Shanghai branch. There, these funds were used partly for so-called *chop-loans* extended to the local micro-banks (銭荘 *qianzhuang*), in an effort to enhance the bank's grip on the Shanghai capital market (Nishimura, 1998).

---

[34] We use parasitoid rather than parasitic, because we talk about institutions that established a symbiotic relationship that had traits of both predator-prey and parasitic relationships.

[35] Compare, in this respect, Nishimura's seminal analysis of so-called chop-loans in China's financial centers (Nishimura, 2005).

By 1908, YSB had attained a considerable presence in China's financial centers. Within Manchuria, Figure 5.09 clearly shows the position of Dairen and, to a lesser degree, Mukden. Subordinate to the Niuzhang branch at their inception, they soon climbed YSB's ladder. By 1908, their bill finance business had clearly already surpassed that of the Niuzhang branch. Two years later, in 1910, this shift was reinforced: from now on, Dairen was promoted to the coordinating office for Manchuria (Yokohama Shōkin Ginkō, 19—, vol. 1, pp. 226ff.). This decision, too, was bound up with Tokyo's strategy for the region. Coordinating with both YSB and the newly finished South-Manchurian Railway Company (SMRC), Tokyo attempted a shift in Manchuria's economic geography.

Traditionally, the original economic backbone for the region had been the River Liao, its harbor of Yingkou (where YSB's Niuzhang branch was located),[36] and the Chinese-owned Peking-Mukden Railway (PMR). This dominance was, for obvious reasons, resented by SMRC officials. They wanted to develop the region's economy along the corridor of Dairen (大連; Ch. *Dalian*)-Mukden (奉天; Ch. *Fengtian*)-Changchun (長春), the main line of the SMRC. Imperialist elements in the government were a natural ally of the latter, for they dreaded the fact that Manchuria's soybean trade would remain anchored within traditional Chinese merchant channels and local business communities.

Ultimately, geography proved a helping hand. After all, the Chinese route had one important disadvantage: the harbor of Yingkou was icebound during winter. Shippers choosing Yingkou therefore faced the costs and risks of stockpiling goods during several months of the year. Using this inconvenience as a political pretext as well as a commercial opportunity, the Japanese were quick to propose the Dairen strategy or 'Dairen-centrism' (大連中心主義 *Dairen chūshin shugi*). The harbor of the newly built city of Dairen was not only ice-free but also deep enough to accommodate oceangoing freighters. Although Yingkou might have sufficed for the time being (Yokohama Shōkin Ginkō, 1920, vol. 2, app., pp. 748-50), Dairen was clearly more suitable for future expansion (Yokohama Shōkin Ginkō, 1920, vol. 2, app., pp. 967-8).[37]

---

[36] There is a historical precedent for the misnaming Yingkou as Niuzhang. The place of Niuzhang indicated in the Tianjin treaty refers to the old town of Niuzhang. The British recognized, however, that the port of Yingkou, fifty miles farther down the river, was a more fitting place as a trading port. In Yingkou they set up a consulate which they called the 'Newchwang Consulate'—hence the misunderstanding (Chosŏn Ŭnhaeng, 1920, p. 16).

[37] Compare, in this respect, the explanation for promoting Dairen:

「満州ニ於ケル為替統務店ヲ大連ニ移スニ至リタル因由ハ主トシテ時勢ノ推移ニ伴ヒ處務ノ便宜ヲ謀リタルニ外ナラス候牛荘ノ地タル日露戦役前後ニ在リテハ南満州唯一ノ要港トシテ重要物産ノ集散地トシテ優越ノ地位ヲ占メ経済上ノ枢機専ラ牛荘市場ノ掌握スル所ナリシカ降テ大連ノ開港南満州鉄道ノ完成ヲ告

Figure 5.10. Yokohama Specie Bank officials posing for a photo with Sun Yat-Sen (孫逸仙 Sun Yixian) (seated in the middle of the picture). March 1913. At the time, Sun Yat-sen attempted to solicit Japanese support for organizing the second revolution against Yuan Shikai (袁世凱).

Source: Author's personal collection.

YSB, through its extensive facilities for lending (made possible by the system of special loan facilities or 特別貸付 *tokubetsu kashitsuke*, for which BOJ had been commissioned to extend a low interest loan to YSB), discounting, and so forth were essential in accelerating the port's expansion (Figure 5.10). A brief look at YSB's activities in bill finance reveals the obvious concentration of its capital and activities in Dairen. It was particularly involved in exports to Kobe and Osaka, by then the industrial hub of the nascent Japanese empire. Although not so much in name, Japanese finance had begun its return to Asia...

クルニ従ヒ満州内地トノ取引関係ハ更ニ大連ニ集中シ満州商業ノ中心漸次一変
ノ気運ヲ呈スルニ至レリ加之遼河ノ交通ハ冬季数月間杜絶ノ不便アルニ反シ大
連ハ終年凍結ノ患ナキニノミナラス海外電信ノ直通ハ各地トノ通信倍々機敏ト
ナリ其他開港トシテノ設備年ヲ逐フテ利便ヲ加ヘ曩ニ南満州鉄道ト上海航路ノ
連絡成リ頃者又欧州向直輸出ノ実行ヲ見ルニ至リ大連ノ将来ハ倍々発展ノ余力
ヲ認ムルニ足ルモノアリ如此大連ノ発展ハ同時ニ牛荘市場ニ影響ヲ及ホシ復昔
日ノ繁盛ヲ見ルニ能ス」.

Conclusion

Although a conclusion is mostly thought of as a recapitulation of findings in the preceding chapters and as an indication of the legitimation with regards to the way in which these findings build on one another, this is not my intention here. Instead, I am inclined to expatiate on what has been an encompassing interest that preoccupied many of the above findings, yet which I was not able to include because of the difficulty of proof. It concerns the question whether the 'even keel'—a hedging strategy pertaining to the bank branch network level of analysis—can be believed to have been conducive to strengthening trade ties between the gold standard Western countries and the East, either through

(a) decelerating, halting, and ultimately reverting the course of the gold price of silver in the mid-term to long-term; and/or

(b) resolving the effects arising from the disturbing volatility that had become so typical since the late 1880s.

Contrary to what an uninformed first analysis might lead us to believe, one should be very careful to draw any rash conclusions. With regard to the first question, this is more or less obvious. As is well known, the silver price did continue its free-fall roughly until 1903, after which the tide seemed to reverse in the white metal's favor, at least temporarily (until 1907) (Kemmerer, 1912). Yet the reason behind this course of events does not necessarily suggest a direct correlation with exchange banking practice. What mattered was the worldwide surge in demand for silver for subsidiary coinage (Kemmerer, 1912, pp. 227ff.), including for a country like Germany, which had once been famously looking for outlets for its surplus silver holdings.[1] Admittedly, the largest single factor in the increased demand for silver during the years 1904-7 was the monetary demand of gold exchange standard India, which was at least partly a function of the country's increased trade volume (and, hence, indirectly related to the exchange banks' proficiency in hedging

---

[1] Soetbeer, 1877, pp. 235–8. Compare as well Chapter 2 in this book.

Accounting for the Fall of Silver: Hedging Currency Risk in Long-Distance Trade with Asia, 1870–1913.
Michael Schiltz, Oxford University Press (2020). © Michael Schiltz.
DOI: 10.1093/oso/9780198865025.001.0001

exchange risk). As Kemmerer points out, however, India's commercial success was largely an effect of the rise of prices in gold standard countries, which was in itself caused by the large and increasing gold production over the period: '[t]he unit of value in India is the rupee adjusted to a 16d. gold par, and when that gold par depreciated in value the world over, Indian prices naturally rose' (Kemmerer, 1912, p. 231).[2]

I approach the second question with much more trepidation, if only because the timing of the coincidence between the rise of new types of financial instruments (especially the *interest bill*) and the expansion of worldwide trade from the late nineteenth century onwards seems so flawless. This has not escaped the attention of several Japanese scholars. Kojima (1978), in a thought-provoking paper, regards the (gold currency denominated) interest bill as the obvious driver behind the end of the Long Depression (1872-96). As the exchange banks did not have to worry about losses incurred through a flailing silver price, the argument goes, they were more willing to expand their holdings of silver denominated assets and liabilities, thus 'ending 4 centuries of dormant East-West trade' (Kojima, 1978, p. 137). At the same time as also China saw itself surrounded by an increasing number of trading partners on the gold or on the gold exchange standard, gold started to find its way into China in a steady pace (Suizu, 1911). Newly arising arbitrage opportunities in the Shanghai market (*Shanhai ni okeru kin no torihiki*, 19—) were bound to compress the limits between which exchange rate fluctuations were to occur. In other words, financial innovation had successfully subsumed (*hōsetsu* 包摂) the silver using Asian countries into the gold standard world center. Kitabayashi (1987, p. 16ff.) reckons that this process was bolstered by the introduction (roughly from about 1893) of forward exchange contracts to Chinese importers,[3] as the latter fed back into expectations with regard to the future spot rate of the GBP in the Shanghai market. Nowadays, even the most acknowledged Japanese observers credit interest bills with having smoothed exchange banking operations around the turn of the century (Ishii, 1999).[4] In this book, we demonstrated that matters of a *managerial nature* were equally, if not more, important when accounting for the steadily expanding balance sheets of the Eastern exchange banks.

---

[2] For a firsthand contemporary account in Japanese, see Horie (1907). Compare, furthermore, the early work by Atkinson (1898, 1903, 1909).

[3] The reader may remember that forward exchange business with China did not exist in the 1880s. See the testimony of Mr Provand in Chapter 3.

[4] For an earlier analysis, see Ishii (1979a, 1979b).

And yet, although financial innovation and hedging strategies played an undeniable role as tools through which exchange risks were alleviated, it would be a mistake to isolate them from a shift in the *structure* of the London silver market that had been fermenting since the early 1890s, and that culminated in the fixing of the silver price from 1897 onwards (the practice would notoriously continue until August 14, 2014). One observer has suggested that the origin of the latter sprang from 'the interest of the London market as a whole [to eradicate] competition and [to end] the erosion in commission rates by the four brokers' (Blagg, 2014, p. 19), but, as we shall discuss in a minute, I suspect that it is more plausible to suggest that it arose out of a demand from silver market participants, however contradictory this looks at first sight.

Why London was and remained the world's silver market at the time has been convincingly argued by Spalding, and thus needs no extensive repetition here (1922, pp. 179–80).[5] It suffices to note that London occupied the lion's share of the West's trade with East Asia, a reality that was further reinforced by the fact that all exchange banks, notwithstanding the location of their headquarters or their nationality, had a presence in London in order to tap into the depths of the world's financial center. And, second, although the world's largest silver producers were located in Mexico, the US, and to a lesser degree, Australia, their share of silver dealings with the Eastern countries remained relatively trifle when compared to the amounts shipped from London.[6]

By the end of the 1890s, the London silver market faced a curious mismatch between the expectations of the main market participants (both on the supply and the demand side), on the one hand, and the incentivization of speculation borne out by silver price evolution, on the other. As pointed out by Spalding long ago, none of the market participants had a remote interest in fluctuations in the price of the metal (Spalding, 1917, pp. 254ff.). The principal first sellers being the smelters,[7]

---

[5] A Yokohama Specie Bank internal report discussing the London money market is drawn along the lines of Spalding's seminal publication (Yokohama Shōkin Ginkō tōdoriseki chōsaka, 1934).

[6] It is possible to construct a reliable time series of bar silver movement from and to the United Kingdom by means of the annual circulars or bullion letters distributed by the London bullion brokers (Montagu (Samuel) and Company, n.d.; see, for instance: Montagu (Samuel) and Company, Ltd [from old catalog], ed. n.d. *Annual Bullion Review*. London.

[7] Since the 1850s, only a handful of bullion refiners were approved by the Bank of England. These were: Johnson & Matthey, Browne & Wingrove, Rothschild's Royal Mint Refinery, and H. L. Raphael's Refinery.

whose custom it is to sell their silver at the London market price and to buy at once a similar amount of ore at a corresponding price. The smelters obtain from the silver miners, or, rather, the mine-owners, a certain fixed sum in gold for each ton of ore to meet the charges incidental to smelting and selling. It is obvious, therefore, that the price of silver in reality determines the price of the ore, and, consequently, the profits of the first sellers are not materially decreased when the price of silver falls nor increased much if it rises.   (Spalding, 1917, p. 254)[8]

Perhaps surprisingly, an increase or decrease in the price of silver was also largely irrelevant to the demand side. The reason therefore was that the overwhelmingly large proportion of silver consumption was for subsidiary coinage, that is, it corresponded to a demand from governments.[9] And whereas it was admittedly in the interest of countries to obtain silver as cheaply as possible, their real source of profit was derived from *seigniorage*. Still, the 'spasmodic and irregular' (United States, 1903, p. 182) nature of the demand for subsidiary silver made the market unpredictable and liable to speculation.

Given the very existence of a spot and forward market for silver (contrary to the gold market, for which there existed only a spot market),[10] speculation must certainly have been rife. Spalding mentions *Budla* or *Budlee* operations in Bombay—after the Punjabi word for 'exchange'[11]—or, as it turns out, an option business in which speculators would carry over selling contracts from one date to the next, through buying 'ready' (spot) to meet deliveries for the first settlement and simultaneously selling 'forward' for delivery at the next

---

[8]   To this one must add: (1) improvements in metallurgic technology, which made processing silver much cheaper; and (2) a shift in the nature of mine owners producing silver. As argued by the Commission for International Exchange in 1903,

> [t]he largest single producer of silver in the United States is a distinctively copper mine. The cheapening of metallurgical processes has permitted of the working of ores, particularly those containing lead and gold in small quantities, to such an extent that from this source also a large proportion of the silver production of the world is obtained. The Broken Hills Proprietary Mine of Australia, a distinctively lead mine, is not only the largest producer of lead in the world, but also probably the largest producer of silver. At least 90 per cent, and probably 95 per cent, of all the silver produced in the United States is the product of lead and copper smelting, and the great increase in the production of silver in Mexico is entirely due to lead and copper smelting.   (United States, 1903, p. 181)

[9]   Spalding (1917, p. 252):

> [T]he amount taken for industrial uses is always a factor with which the market must reckon, since it is the industrial consumption which ultimately absorbs all surplus silver. Curiously enough, however, this consumption has little effect on prices, probably because buyers of silver for the arts and manufactures know that they are generally able to obtain the balance remaining after other demands have been satisfied.

[10]   For an explanation of the London gold market, see Spalding (1922, pp. 170ff.).

[11]   Starkey (1849). These operations are explained in (Bratter, 1933, p. 14).

settlement.[12] The aim was to 'corner'[13] or squeeze the market (including, I surmise, through something as a nineteenth-century equivalent of 'spoofing') at times government buyers were in open competition for the limited stocks of the sellers.[14]

Even in the absence of remaining archival evidence, it seems to me that silver fixing was called into existence as a way of countering artificial silver shortages by means of excluding information access to everybody except for a handful of London-based licensed bullion brokers.[15] As *The Times* put it much later, it 'is [in times of speculation] that the brokers who generally have orders of a discretionary nature use their powers to keep the movements within reasonable limits.'[16] In the vocabulary of Akerlof's famous thought experiment (1970), their *reputation* or *reputability*—and there is no shortage of references to the latter, in particular when describing their disengagement from / disdain for speculative practices—was the price the market paid for a price level 'keeping with the statistical position of the metal. By statistical position, we mean the actual, visible, and potential stocks of silver within reach of the market' (Spalding, 1917, p. 257).

If the above conjecture is true, it not only demonstrates that, when attempting to explain Asia's escape from the Long Depression, one may have to consider how hedging technologies, largely independent of governments' predilections for a certain monetary standard, conspired with, among others, the spread of the gold exchange standard *and* a shift in the London silver market to produce new, viable conditions for trade with the West. As in the epigraph to this monograph, it thus adds yet another 'little world' to account for this most fascinating episode in modern financial history.

[12] We know from bullion speculation in Shanghai thanks to a few contemporary reports (Suizu, 1911) (Imura and Shanhai, 1925).

[13] For a description of cornering in the context of the London copper market, see: "London Metals." *Financial Times* [London, England] 25 Nov. 1899, p. 3. Others described how the market reacted to a cornering operation breaking down: Correspondent. "Silver and Its Prospects." *Financial Times* [London, England] 17 Nov. 1908: n.p.; "A Swadeshi Corner in Silver." *Economist* [London, England] 16 July 1910, p. 115.

[14] '[I]t is known as "calling" and "putting", the charge for which is about 2 per cent on the value of the silver for which the option is taken, and, in addition, the buyer is charged the usual ⅛ per cent brokerage on the option' (Spalding, 1922, p. 182). One finds a reference to budlee operations in the *North China Daily News*, Volume 133, Issue 1935-12-03.

[15] Between 1720 and 1840, bullion brokering was a monopoly held by Mocatta, but in the mid-nineteenth century, this monopoly was broken to include Sharps & Wilkins, Pixley & Haggard (later Abell) and Samuel Montague & Co. For a description of the fixing process, see: Special Correspondent. 'London Bullion Market.' *Times* [London, England], June 20, 1933: 39. *The Times Digital Archive*. Web. Dec. 8, 2016.

[16] Special Correspondent. "London Bullion Market." *Times* [London, England] 20 June 1933: 39. *The Times Digital Archive*. Web. 8 Dec. 2016.

Construction of the Database and Methodological Issues

「私ノ意見テハ帳簿ハ銀行ノ生命テアル」

(In my opinion, account books represent the lifeblood of banks)

(Yokohama Shōkin Ginkō, 1908, pp. 240–2)

1. Introduction: Yokohama Specie Bank Primary Materials

The Yokohama Specie Bank (YSB) has had it fair share of historians, albeit it more or less exclusively in Japan. Or perhaps one should say 'historiographies' rather than historians, as literature on YSB could, at least until now, roughly be divided into two large strands—each of them related to discoveries of or access to large swaths of primary materials.

On the one hand, there has been a group of researchers focusing on the role of YSB in the (early) development of Japanese capitalism. Their origins must be traced back to a research group on the history of the port city of Yokohama that published its findings as early as 1960 in a massive series with the generic title *History of Yokohama* (Yokohama-shi, 1958-). The disclosure of related archives proved a boon for students of financial history. If anything, it drew the attention of many to the difficulties of fundraising in the 1880s and 1890s, a mere three decades after the country's traumatic 'opening up' (*kaikoku* 開国) and the chaotic process that led to the Meiji Restoration. Saitō Hisahiko (1973, 1976, 1978a, 1978b, 1986) was one of the first to study YSB's relationship with the Bank of Japan, which functioned as the former's facilitator (through channeling funds or providing redis- counting facilities); yet it must also be remembered for having set clear limits to YSB's development into an exchange bank with a 100 per cent commercial agenda. Taira Tomoyuki (1984a, 1984b), and later Ishii Kanji (1994, 1999), established the interest in a network understanding of exchange banking that persists to today, and that also informs this book.

Later, other publications started to draw attention to the role played by YSB in Asian development before World War II. Again, having (priority) access to previously unavailable primary materials, this time batches of YSB primary holdings for the interwar period proved instrumental. The publication of an edited volume on YSB's interwar activities must be credited for laying the groundwork of pretty much all later studies (Yamaguchi, Katō, 1988). Around the same time, Kaneko Fumio (1977, 1979, 1981a, 1981b, 1990) and Shibata Yoshimasa (1977) published about the role of YSB and other banks in upholding Japan's empire in East Asia, most prominently in Manchuria. Taira's research, in the mean- while, had started to concentrate on the role of several of YSB's key branches (1990, 1993, 1994, 1995a, 1995b).

Nowadays, the above dichotomy can be subverted thanks to the disclosure of the rich YSB Archives, held at the University of Tokyo (UTokyo). As described by

Takeda Haruhito 武田晴人,[1] until recently the archive's host, editor, and compiler, the history of the archives' wanderings and their ultimate destination in a Japanese university library has been closely bound up with the travails of Japan's financial institutions after the bursting of the country's proverbial bubble in the early 1990s. In 1996, in the middle of a seemingly non-ending wave of banking mergers, the Bank of Tokyo (BOT)—Mitsubishi Ltd emerged as the world's largest bank in terms of total assets (in 2006, it was absorbed into the mega-institution called the BOT Mitsubishi UFJ, composed out of five former financial institutions). The merger of a large bank with an even larger bank spelled the total dissolution of the former, and its archives.

Reminiscent of the archives of YSB's British peer, the Hongkong and Shanghai Banking Corporation (HSBC), they had been crammed into boxes and kept in a nondescript warehouse in Moegino もえぎ野 (near Yokohama) until 1999.[2] The latter turned out to be unfit for the conservation of already brittle pre-war bank archives; Takeda estimates that approximately fifty boxes were permanently lost due to humidity, unfavorable temperatures, and so on. If anything, the fact that the collection could be preserved for posterity is not an example of 'survivor bias'. In Autumn 2000, when word about their imminent destruction reached Hamashita Takeshi 濱下武志 of UTokyo's Institute for Advanced Studies on Asia (東京大学東洋文化研究所; IASA),[3] the university decided to act. Although the inquiry for hosting the archives originally went to IASA, Takeda explains that the archives were too bulky to be hosted there, and that, for that reason, negotiations were taken up with the Library of the Faculty of Economics of the university. Up to this day, they are housed in that library's Rare Materials Reading Room or *shiryōshitsu* 資料室.[4]

Importantly for our discussion, Takeda has also supervised a still-ongoing project aimed at the extensive disclosure of the YSB archives, including primary sources that were once deemed too sensitive to be included in the bank's earlier official histories (Yamaguchi and Katō, 1988). Microfilming started after 2003, after several years had passed for organizing the materials. Their current organization does not reflect the original order as thought out by the bank's archivists, but was determined by a combination of both logistical and commercial needs, that is, on the basis of the plan to microfilm those parts which were considered of higher priority than others. And indeed, the release of large microfilm corpora (somewhat confusingly referred to as 'periods' or *ki* 期; hereafter, we will refer to them as 'series')[5] can be said to be largely a function of their relevance to historians and, related to the latter, the collection's commercial appeal to university libraries.

For the discussion of this book, the following series have been of particular importance:

---

[1] See, for further information: http://www.takeda.e.u-tokyo.ac.jp/shihonshijoh/shokin_kaidai01. htm (visited Jan. 19th, 2015).

[2] The enormous work of finding a new home for the HSBC archives, and organizing them into material for the bank's official history is described in (King, 1987).

[3] Relationships between the Institute and the BOT, the YSB's successor in the post-war era, have been close. Since the late 1950s, the Institute has housed the majority of research reports, statistics, etc., compiled by the YSB's 'Research Department' or *chōsabu* 横濱正金銀行調査部.

[4] See, for a history of the Rare Materials Reading Room, with particular mention of collections of business archives: http://www.lib.e.u-tokyo.ac.jp/?page_id=11

[5] At the moment, fourteen of such 'series' have been published, amounting to (at the estimate of Kojima Hiroyuki 小島浩之, Head of the Rare Materials Reading Room) plus/minus half of all YSB material.

- Series I: in total 227 reels; containing among others YSB's business reports, YSB-related legislation, transcripts of board of directors meetings, shareholder meetings, and meetings of the directors of Asian branches; and
- Series II & III: respectively 156 reels and 163 reels; mostly focusing on the activities of and agreements among YSB branches, agreements with the Bank of Japan; and description of the economic situation within the respective regions of respective domains.

Being able to mine the granularity of daily exchange banking activity provided what could be called an ethno-historiographical insight that was necessarily absent from earlier literature, and what turned out to be an extremely valuable feedback tool for movements in the data that did not otherwise offer a straightforward explanation.

2. YSB Semestrial Reports

The foundations upon which the findings in this book were built are the YSB semestrial or 'mid-term' reports, called *hanki-hōkoku* 半季報告, or, originally, *kōkajō* 考課状 (literally 'assessment report'), notably for the period January 1893 until July 1908 (Takeda, 2003, reels E001–E018).[6] Although these reports occupy only a small part of the complete archival collection, their importance for our understanding of the activities and management of a late nineteenth-century exchange bank can hardly be overestimated. Highly reliable for especially the period around 1900, they provide the necessary shortcut for inter-branch connections that would otherwise be painstaking to reconstruct, for instance on the basis of the ledgers of each individual branch.

At first sight, they have much in common with the business reports of other exchange banks of the time. Their very semestrial publication to start with was common among other exchange banks as, for instance, the HSBC, or the French Comptoir d'Escompte. Yet they do not have a unified format, which is due to the absence of internationally accepted accounting standards in the pre-war period, shifts in management practices, and even the occurrence of certain political events. Just as is the case with HSBC reports and others, this makes their interpretation not always a straightforward matter (cf. infra).

In their most basic form, the mid-term reports almost all contain the following items:

1. a balance sheet listing the bank's main assets and liabilities (mostly included as fold-out in the back-cover) (*kashikari-taishōhyō* 貸借対照表)
2. a statement on the bank's shareholders fund; its reserve fund(s) (Jpn. *kabukin shotsumitatekin oyobi junbikin no koto* 株金諸積立金及ビ準備金ノ事)
3. a statement on deposits (Jpn. *yokin no koto* 預金ノ事)
4. a statement on loans and bills discounted (Jpn. *kashikin oyobi tegata waribiki no koto* 貸金及ビ手形割引ノ事)

---

[6] Originals are kept in the Rare Materials Reading Room of the Faculty of Economics Library, UTokyo, boxes 32–42.

5. a statement on its foreign exchange holdings and movements (Jpn. *kaigai kawase no koto* 海外為替ノ事)

6. a statement on inland bills (*naikoku kawase no koto* 内国為替ノ事)

7. a statement on rediscounting activity (*sai-waribiki tegata no koto* 再割引手形ノ事)

8. a statement on loans payable (*kari-irekin no koto* 借入金ノ事)

9. a statement on holdings of silver and gold money; cash on deposit (*kingin zaidaka oyobi yotakukin no koto* 金銀在高及ビ預託金ノ事)

10. a statement on holdings of public loans and other securities (*kōsai shōsho no koto* 公債證書ノ事)

11. a statement on property (*shoyūbutsu no koto* 所有物ノ事)

12. a statement on holdings of gold and silver bullion and foreign currencies (*jigane gin oyobi gaikoku kahei no koto* 地金銀及ビ外国貨幣ノ事)

13. a statement of income derived from the selling and buying of stocks (*kabushiki baibai jōju no koto* 株式売買譲受ノ事)

14. a profit and loss statement (*son'eki kin no koto* 損益金ノ事); and

15. a statement with respect to the allocation of profits (*riekikin bunpaihō no koto* 利益金分配方ノ事)

For obvious reasons, the balance sheet (1) represents the gist of the bank's assets and liabilities for each semester. It aggregates the balance data that one can find broken down under categories (2)(3)(4)(7)(8)(9)(10)(11)(12)(13)(14)(15). Note, however, that (5) and (6) are *not* included here. The latter are *flow data*, meaning that they consist of origin-destination data documenting the flows or migration of assets acquired and liabilities incurred, within the bank's branch network. Because these data comprise both assets and liabilities, they cannot conveniently be allocated to one of these categories. Rather, they help identify risks in inter-branch dealings, in our case typically related to difficulties with regard to finding 'matching funds', the relative 'exchange position' of a branch within the network, and so on. As we will see later, flow data are particularly revealing when assessing the characteristics of specific bank management systems.

In the case of the YSB (and, for that matter, in the case of any other exchange bank), flow data document the transfer of both foreign (5) and inland (6) bills of exchange. Concretely, they document, on the basis of the distinction between 'bills bought' and 'bills sold', how branches exchange liabilities and assets among each other, and thus they make it in principle possible to identify trade patterns between countries and/or regions (Figure App 01). In later paragraphs we will discuss how the latter relate to the former.

3. Interpretative Hurdles

This being said, the above accounting categories are not consistently uniform over time, or they are represented in a way that make longitudinal comparisons sometimes hard if not impossible. To a certain extent, this is to be expected. First of all, mid-term report editing reflects the limitations imposed by the growing business activity and corollary increase in the bank's branches worldwide. Especially after victory in the Russo-Japanese war, branches in Manchuria mushroom, in turn leading to further business activity in China proper, and

第百貳拾八回貸借對照表

昭和拾八年九月參拾日現在

資　産　(借方)	金　額		負　債　(貸方)	金　額	
債　權　勘　定	5,204,929,004	43	株　主　勘　定	251,465,504	80
政　府　貸　上　金	274,717	30	資　　本　　金	100,000,000	00
貸　　付　　金	1,076,049,841	82	積　　立　　金	147,150,000	00
滯　　貨　　金	1,813,194	80	特　別　積　立　金	2,500,000	00
當　座　貸　越	1,536,542,318	39	滯　貨　準　備　金	1,815,504	80
輸　出　爲　替　前　貸	428,312,428	30			
割　引　手　形	951,993,157	20	債　務　勘　定	7,334,016,685	50
買　爲　替　手　形	307,401,105	75	定　期　預　金	664,203,445	65
利　付　爲　替　手　形	194,888,282	73	當　座　預　金	1,752,863,903	34
當　座　預　託　金	305,251,925	85	通　知　預　金	353,933,458	70
別　段　預　託　金	348,979,863	83	別　段　預　金	3,758,759,800	99
公債元利支拂基預託金	96,120	16	普　通　貯　金	8,307,085	10
支　拂　承　諾　見　返	53,326,018	30	據　置　貯　金	2,881,246	59
			軍　票　引　換　基　預　金	60,131	48
假　　勘　　定			公債元利支拂基預金	12,341,657	52
假　　拂　　金	787,414,778	10	手　形　內　入　金	21,285,999	47
			賣　爲　替　手　形	77,492,650	31
他　店　勘　定			借　　用　　金	135,556,046	05
他　　店　　貸	76,837,924	33	別　途／借　用　金	59,947,983	27
			當　座　借　越	350,224,066	11
公債並債券勘定	2,028,282,302	71	再　割　引　手　形	81,762,774	01
公　債　證　書	1,955,918,950	93	引　受　軍　票	274,717	30
債　　　券	72,363,351	78	銀　　行　　券	195,671	31
			支　拂　承　諾	53,326,048	30
所　有　物　勘　定	20,497,758	49			
土　　　地	7,576,720	80	假　　勘　　定	1,052,664,738	59
建　　　物	11,456,642	80	未　拂　利　息	36,996,079	16
什　　　器	753,017	01	未　經　過　益　割　戻	33,604,809	02
債權執行取得物件	711,377	88	假　　受　　金	981,835,165	41
			未　拂　配　當	228,685	00
地金並外國貨幣勘定	9,928,793	95			
地　　　金	3,488,663	42	他　店　勘　定		
外　國　貨　幣	6,440,130	53	他　　店　　借	4,855,534	63
金　銀　勘　定			損　益　勘　定		
現　　　金	538,713,736	61	當　半　季　利　益　金	22,244,718	33
			(內前半季繰越金　¥ 18,263,890.21)		
			爲替戻換算差金勘定		
			爲　替　戻　換　算　差　金	1,357,116	77
合　　　計	8,666,604,298	62	合　　　計	8,666,604,298	62

Figure App 01. YSB balance sheet illustration

Note: a typical balance sheet in a Midterm report (this one from 1943, in the year Japan changed from the classical fiscal year (January-December) to the then newly used fiscal year (April-March)).

Source: Courtesy of the National Diet Library (out-of-copyright).

so on. A comprehensive discussion of business activity within all branches would be a boon for business historians, but would at the time have made reports unnecessarily bulky. For later years, business results have therefore been aggregated by region, rendering a branch-level analysis much more difficult. The latter is also, to no small degree, an implication of a change in managerial style, which we discuss in chapter 5.

Second, the mid-term reports are to a certain extent a function of the political positioning of Japan and its institutions. As we will discuss further below, this has had—ironically—its fortunate implications for the discussion here. At a time when the country was in fact too weak to unilaterally claim its place in the world order, YSB resorted to a sort of 'news propaganda' (Akami, 2012) that was carefully geared to the information-hungry investors in London, Paris, or any other global financial market.[7] As a result, early mid-term reports for 1893-1908 are very extensive, sensitively reflecting the market conditions that its branches faced, documenting the political and economic events that were to explain any volatility in its business record, and so on.[8] Put differently, early reports cleverly play into the discourse of the European (mostly British) liberal economic ideas by which observers since the 1930s have wanted to remember the first gold standard period. It is beyond doubt that such reports would be followed by leading financial outlets of the day: subtly, but con-vincingly, YSB demonstrated to an international readership that its knowledge of the expanding Asian market, bolstered by its presence in all but the smallest trading centers in the region, was second to none, apart perhaps the HSBC.

Alas, the darkening geopolitical climate of the 1920s and 1930s, and the economic and political bloc-ism that is so typical of the later period was also reflected in the contemporary exchange banker's incentive to document business conditions, profits and/or losses, economic forecasts etc. The latter becomes painfully clear for the mid-term reports after 1931, the year in which rogue Japanese soldiers engineered the famous Mukden Incident (consequently drawing the country into a large-scale military operation in Manchuria) and set the country on a collision course with the international community (Ferrell, 1955; Nish, 2000). YSB official reports then instinctively followed a radical course *against* trans-parency, for instance by aggregating results for all branches, and/or deceiving outsiders with respect to the accurate numbers of YSB foreign exchange holdings, and so on (Miller, 2007). From flow-of-funds data, in particular, it is impossible to extract any mean-ingful information; the reports mention one total (and unverifiable) amount of funds being transferred among branches, without any specifics.

4. The Flow-of-funds among Branches: Construction of the Dataset

As stated above, the latter is fortunately *not* the case for the mid-term reports that have formed the core of the following argument. Reports for the period under discussion are especially helpful as they provide non-aggregated data per *branch*, with clear indications of

---

[7] Although, to my knowledge, not being dubbed 'news propaganda' as such, a similar interest is at the core of a recent research strand in economic history (Bignon and Flandreau, 2011; Flandreau and Flores, 2009).

[8] As a matter of fact, the precision of the coverage in the reports between 1893 and 1908 was a topic at the first Meeting of the Managers of Asian Branches of YSB (*tōyō shitenchō kaigi* 東洋支店長会議; April 1908 at the Yokohama head office). Concretely, several managers worried that its foreign competitors might undertake a translation of the mid-term reports, causing valuable 'business secrets' of the bank to be 'leaked' (*naibu no himitsu wo morasu osore ari* 内部ノ秘密ヲ洩ラス恐レアリ) (Yokohama Shōkin Ginkō, 1908, p. 310). For HSBC too, secrecy was an ongoing issue (King, 1987, pp. 411–12)

Table App 01. Data organization in YSB mid-term reports

---

1. Bills sent from branch X to other branches

		Branch Y 支店	Branch Z 支店	Total 合計
Bills sold 買為替	Bills of exchange 為替手形			
	TT 電信為替			
Bills bought 売為替	Bills of exchange 為替手形			
	TT 電信為替			
[Totals]		[amount a]		

2. Bills sent from other branches to branch X

		Branch Y 支店	Branch Z 支店	Total 合計
Bills sold 買為替	Bills of exchange 為替手形			
	TT 電信為替			
Bills bought 売為替	Bills of exchange 為替手形			
	TT 電信為替			
[Totals]		[amount b]		

Notes: Note that the 'totals' in column 1, row 6 are not included in the original, but calculated by us; the mid-term reports do not mention total aggregates for the amounts of bills sold and bills bought, for reasons to which we will return. We do however include it in anticipation of the simple formula needed to express, in a generic manner, the amounts of funds being transferred between branches.

TT stands for 'telegraphic transfers'; we use it as such as it was a much employed abbreviation at the time.

Source: Created by the author.

subcategories (as, e.g., types of deposits and their respective amounts, etc.). For an analysis of the bank's flow-of-funds network (*shikin junkan* 資金循環), arguably the most defining feature of exchange banks, we turned to the exceptionally rich flow data of foreign bills of exchange (*gaikoku kawase* 外国為替) and inland bills of exchange (*naikoku kawase* 内国為替), included towards the end of the mid-term reports. For every branch, here for matters of convenience called X, they are listed in the format of Table App 01.[9,10]

---

[9] Note that the 'totals' in column 1, row 6 are not included in the original, but calculated by us; the mid-term reports do not mention total aggregates for the amounts of bills sold and bills bought, for reasons to which we will return. We do however include it in anticipation of the simple formula needed to express, in a generic manner, the amounts of funds being transferred between branches.

[10] TT stands for 'telegraphic transfers'; we use it as such as it was a much employed abbreviation at the time.

For our analysis, however, a branch per branch organization of data is inadequate. Mid-term report data have had to be organized into so-called 'adjacency matrices', or, in other words, into square matrices with as many rows and columns as there are actors (branches) in our data set. Also, the above distinction between foreign bills of exchange and inland bills of exchange cannot be maintained. Although strictly speaking different kinds of bills, a network analysis must treat them as necessarily isomorphic. After all, it concerns transfers of funds among branches, although obviously branches within Japan and thus transfers that do not imply a foreign exchange transaction.

Cells with a numerical value express (1) the existence of any relationship at all, and (2) the quantitative importance of that relationship, that is, an amount being transferred between two branches. In the simple case of the aforementioned data for branches X, Y, Z of the above example, a typical spreadsheet looks as shown in Table App 02.[11]

Table App 03 shows what this would amount to, in simplified form, that is, after the calculation of the total amount of funds transferred (as we shall see later, this is *not* the same as the aggregate of bills bought and bills sold (cf. infra)).

The direction is important: it must be remembered that in network analysis, by convention, the direction goes from the *rows* to the *columns*; in Table App 03, we have therefore added the upwardly curving arrow. Hence, the flow from X to Y, which we generically defined as [amount a] in Table App 02 can now be found as [amount a] in the second row, third column, under Y; vice versa, the flow from Y to X, defined as [amount b] can be found on row 3, column 2, under X. Note furthermore that we do, for obvious reasons, not allow flows from branches to themselves (so-called self-loops). As it concerns flows-of-funds within a banking network, we only want to consider transfers between different branches. Hence the diagonal can be left blank, filled with zeros, or represented as a concatenation of black cells. As we assume that matrix values can be zero or negative (as for instance in the case of a certain branch 'drawing' on another) (cf. infra), we prefer to leave the diagonal blank after all, a zero amount might as well imply that amounts sent and amounts received cancel each other out.

As a last remark, we add that the size of the matrices differs over time. This has to do with the growth of the YSB branches network: whereas, in the early 1890s, YSB had a limited number of branches in several of the world's financial centers, the number grows to include a lot of branches in relatively minor trading centers in the early 1900s, mostly in China and Manchuria.

5. A Methodological Issue: Amounts of Bills Sent or Amounts of Funds being Transferred?

But how did nineteenth-century exchange business work? How do we deal with the character of types of bills listed in Tables App 01 and App 02, but—for reasons of analytical convenience—left out of Table App 03? As we have seen, bank branches sent both 'bills sold' (to importers in their country of location) and 'bills bought' (from exporters in their country of location) to each other. Can we conveniently aggregate these amounts in order to calculate the relative exchange position of certain branches within our network? Although this is certainly tempting, and may even be legitimate depending on the research question, for instance in the case of measuring *activity* at branches, it is problematic in view of the accounting technicalities that were valid at the time.

---

[11] The complete spreadsheets related to YSB's flow-of-funds have been formatted in this manner and were uploaded to figshare (Schiltz, 2017a, 2017b, 2018).

Table App 02. Preparation of a spreadsheet for entries related to the flow-of-funds in a generic branch network with branches X, Y, Z

	A	B	C	D	E	F	G	H	I	J	K	L	M
1		**X**				**Y**				**Z**			
2	**X**	BS	b/e			BS	b/e	a		BS	b/e	a'	
3			TT				TT	b			TT	b'	
4		BB	b/e			BB	b/e	c		BB	b/e	c'	
5			TT				TT	d			TT	d'	
6	**Y**	BS	b/e	a"		BS	b/e			BS	b/e	a'''	
7			TT	b"			TT				TT	b'''	
8		BB	b/e	c"		BB	b/e			BB	b/e	c'''	
9			TT	d"			TT				TT	d'''	
10	**Z**	BS	b/e	a""		BS	b/e	a""		BS	b/e		
11			TT	b""			TT	b""			TT		
12		BB	b/e	c""		BB	b/e	c""		BB	b/e		
13			TT	d""			TT	d""			TT		

Notes: The complete spreadsheets related to YSB's flow-of-funds have been formatted in this manner and were uploaded to figshare (Schiltz, 2017a, 2017b, 2018).

On abbreviations: BS: 'bills sold', BB: 'bills bought', b/e: 'bills of exchange', TT: 'telegraphic transfers'

White cells contain: (1) the amounts (a, b, c, d) as can be found in the mid-term reports; the column next to the values amounts (a, b, c, d) is (a) used for the inclusion of other types of bills (e.g., interest bills), some of which were—for reasons to be discussed—not included in the flow data, but mentioned under the balance data on 'loans and bills discounted'. It is also used (b) for calculations (aggregations/subtractions; conversions).

Source: Created by the author.

As noted by Ishii (1999, pp. 245ff.; still the most authoritative source on this matter), *bills bought* is the category signifying a positive transfer of funds, as branch X, after buying a bill from an exporter in the country of X, sends it on to branch Y, which books it as a 'bill for collection' (*daikin toritate tegata* 代金取立手形). At maturity, it collects the money as 'adverse exchange' (*gyaku kawase* 逆為替 or, alternatively, *toritate kawase* 取立為替) from an importer in the country in which Y is located, and books the bill to its asset side as a 'bill collected'. In the case of export bills, *money thus follows*, or in other words, has the same direction of, *the goods*. In the case of *bills sold*, however, the direction of the transfer is reversed. Branch X sells a bill to an importer of country X (so the latter can remit his payment to an exporter in country Y), and receives an amount of domestic currency for the latter. Branch Y is in charge of the pay-out into the account of the exporter in the country of Y, and therefore deals with the bill as a 'bill payable'. Clearly, the latter operation implies a transfer of funds from branch Y to branch X, or, in other words, a 'negative transfer'.[12]

In its most rudimentary or pure form, that is, when leaving out the concerns with relative liquidity, differences in institutional set-up and other dissimilarities, the direction

---

[12] For a concise exploration hereof in accounting technical terms, see Adachi (1970).

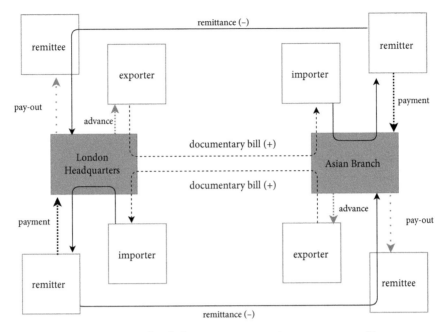

Figure App 02. International trade finance in a symmetric two-country world

Note: as the reader may realize, the inclusion of a remitter respectively remittee is strictly speaking not required. Importers and exporters can deal directly with a branch of an international bank. We do include them, however, in order to allow for a situation in which these dealings were mediated by yet another institution. Historically, this was the case in India, where the Presidency Banks played the role of middlemen. In the metropolis, one may think of the role of clearing and merchant banks, whose 'signing across' (an expression of the promise to pay the bills at maturity) raised a bill's creditworthiness, so the latter could easily be sold in the London discount market. Their 'reputability' was, in other words, integral to the smooth functioning of the mechanism of bill finance (Brunyate, 1900) (Suzuki, 2012, p. 92).

Source: illustration created by the author, after Suzuki (2005, p. 50) (Suzuki, 2012, p. 93).

of the flow-of-funds related and indication of a positive versus negative fund flow (+/−) between two countries would look as shown in Figure App 02.

This is, of course, an oversimplification and distortion of the historical reality. As explained in the Preface and further explored in Chapter 3, differences between capital markets in the core and those in the periphery were numerous. They do not warrant the assumption that the finance of export to and import from the periphery would be the perfect mirror image of the finance of export to and import from the core countries.

We refer to the other chapters for the evolution of trade finance between Europe and Asia after 1870, but it is important to note here that, when calculating the flow-of-funds between branches, *one should subtract the amount of bills sold* (both bills of exchange and telegraphic transfers) *from the amount of bills bought* (again: both bills and telegraphic transfers). Returning to Tables App 02 and App 03, calculating the flow-of-funds from will look as shown in Table App 04.

The latter is crucial, as it factually makes it possible to conceive of net 'negative' flows or transfers. Such negative transfers are obviously the case in the event a branch ledger shows an amount of bills sold that was higher than the amount of bills bought, or, in other words,

Table App 03. Interpreting the flow-of-funds in a simple banking network with 3 branches (X, Y, Z)

	X	Y	Z
X		[amount a] ↗	
Y	[amount b] ↗		
Z			

Source: Created by the author.

in the event a branch has engaged itself more in import- rather than export-finance vis-à-vis another branch.

This, in turn, endorses the ethno-historiographical problem consciousness that informs the book's findings in the first place. YSB management expressed continuous concern about the fact that certain branches (e.g., the Lyon branch for a large part of its history) were chronic net 'withdrawers', exactly because of persistent trade imbalances between such branches with other branches in the network. And consequently, this demanded ever more creative ways to provide 'matching funds' (*kawase deai* 為替出合), for example, through aggressively expanding its deposit base or else. Only in this way would the bank be able to close (*kanketsu* 完結) its exchange circle and avoid a reliance on more costly arrangements with its network of correspondent banks.

Again referring to the discussions in the chapters, the accounting surrounding the above calculations is a little bit more complicated. As we have seen in Chapter 3, the use of *interest bills* demand a yet different type of attention. Here, we simply point out that they should be added to the amounts of bills bought (i.e., they too constitute a positive transfer), because they stipulated that they were to be collected at the receiving end.

6. Fund-matching and Exchange Position

Returning to the vocabulary and thinking of social network analysis (SNA), the ultimate objective of the database has been to capture our exchange bank's network of branches in terms of each node's above-described 'fund-matching' vis-à-vis the network as a whole. Put simply, the questions are (1) whether, how, and to what degree we can define a branch's position as 'positive' or 'negative' at a point in time, and (2) how we can describe this position longitudinally, that is, over time.

As we only want to calculate the relative share of each and every node in closing the bank's exchange cycle, a very straightforward measure can suffice. We aggregate the amounts of funds a certain branch i in the network sent to *all other branches of the network* (again: taking into account the bookkeeping technicalities laid out in earlier paragraphs), and deduct from the latter the total amounts of funds sent *by all other branches of the network* to branch i. Note that the latter gives us a (positive or negative) number for any branch in any semester. This number—which is, by definition, the *inverse of a branch's exchange position* at semester $_n$—functions as the indicator of a branch's contribution to providing exchange cover on the branch network. Branches with a positive number are 'givers', that is, they enable other branches to accumulate net surpluses. Vice versa, branches with a negative number are net 'takers' or, in extreme cases, 'sinks', causing other branches

Table App 04. Calculating the flow-of-funds in a simple banking network with 3 branches (X, Y, Z)

	X	Y	Z
X		$(c+d)-(a+b)$ ↗	
Y	$(c"+d")-(a"+b")$ ↗		
Z			

Source: Created by the author.

Table App 05. Calculating the flow-of-fund index of branch X in a simple three-branch network (X, Y, Z) at semester$_n$

	X	Y	Z	
X		X→Y: (bills bought minus bills sold)	X→Z: (bills bought minus bills sold)	SUM1: $(X{\to}Y)+(X{\to}Z)$
Y	Y→X: (bills bought minus bills sold)		Y→Z: (bills bought minus bills sold)	
Z	Z→X: (bills bought minus bills sold)	Z→Y: (bills bought minus bills sold)		
	SUM2: $(Y{\to}X)+(Z{\to}X)$			

Source: Created by the author.

Table App 06. Calculating the flow-of-fund positions of branches in a simple three-branch network (X, Y, Z) at several intervals (semesters)

	semester$_n$	semester$_{n+1}$	semester$_{n+2}$
X	$(X{\to}Y+X{\to}Z)-$ $(Y{\to}X+Z{\to}X)$	...	...
Y	$(Y{\to}X+Y{\to}Z)-$ $(X{\to}Y+Z{\to}Y)$	...	...
Z	$(Z{\to}X+Z{\to}Y)-$ $(X{\to}Z+Y{\to}Z)$	...	...

Source: Created by the author.

to experience a drain on their capital. We call the ranking of every branch at any semester$_n$ the 'flow-of-fund index'.

Returning to our simple matrix of a branch network comprising three branches (see Table App 04), for node X, in Table App 05 we subtract the sum of 'total amounts received' (SUM2) from the sum of 'total amounts sent' (SUM1).

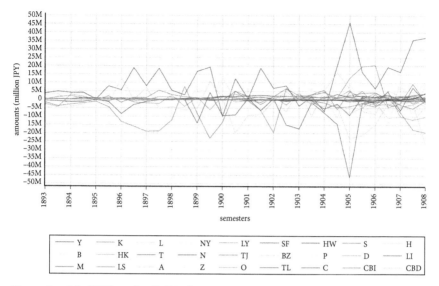

Figure App 03. YSB branches FoF-index, 01-1893 - 07-1908

Y: Yokohama Head Office; K: Kobe; L: London; NY: New York LY: Lyon; SF: San Francisco; HW: Hawai; S: Shanghai; H: Hankow; B: Mumbai (Bombay); HK: Hong Kong; T: Tokyo; N: Nagasaki; TJ: Tianjin; NZ: Niuzhang; P: Beijing (Peking); D: Dairen; LI: Liaoyang; M: Mukden; LS: Lushun; A: Andong; Z: Yantai (Chefoo); O: Osaka; TL: Tieling; C: Changchun; CBI: correspondent banks (international); CBD: correspondent banks (domestic).

Source: calculations by the author.

The methodological innovation of this book lies with the realization that this can be done *for every branch* and *for every semester*, and thus allows the construction of a time series, which describes the evolution of any branch's flow-of-fund position over time. This can be found in Table App 06.[13]

In the concrete case of the YSB, the flow-of-fund index for the period between January 1893 and July 1908 can be visualized as shown in Figure App 03.

As a descriptive statistic, the graph in Figure App 03 already contains some important clues to later findings. We note, first of all, a few instances in which the flow-of-fund position of a certain branch is the approximate mirror image of another one, as for London and Lyon for the period around 1894, or for Yokohama and Tokyo in 1905. Second, it is striking that, for the whole period of analysis, the flow-of-fund position of most branches constantly hovers around zero. For those branches, the amount of bills bought is close to the amount of bills sold, that is, their exchange position is more or less squared. Branches with values that are substantially plus or minus are a minority. However, these branches are (1) invariably located in major exchange centers, and (2) probably unsurprisingly, also mostly remain plus or minus throughout the whole period.

At the same time, however, the graph leaves important question marks. Not in the least, it is impossible to gain insights from the branch network as a whole, especially after 1897, when the Japanese branches turn their original silver unit of account into a gold one. And

---

[13] For YSB data material for longitudinal visualization, see Schiltz (2015).

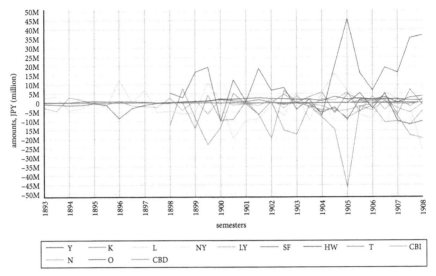

Figure App 04. YSB gold branches centrality, 01-1893 - 07-1908
Y: Yokohama Head Office; K: Kobe; L: London; NY: New York LY: Lyon; SF: San Francisco;
HW: Hawai; S: Shanghai; H: Hankow; B: Mumbai (Bombay); HK: Hong Kong; T: Tokyo;
N: Nagasaki; O: Osaka; CBI: correspondent banks (international).
Source: calculations by the author

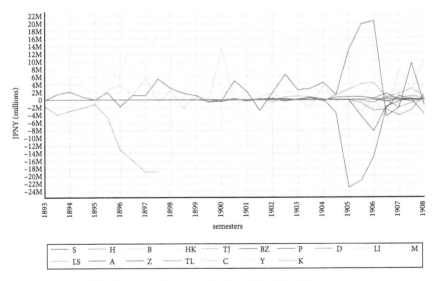

Figure App 05. YSB silver branches centrality, 01-1893 - 07-1908
S: Shanghai; H: Hankow; B: Mumbai (Bombay); HK: Hong Kong; T: Tokyo; N: Nagasaki;
TJ: Tianjin; NZ: Niuzhang; P: Beijing (Peking); D: Dairen; LI: Liaoyang; M: Mukden; LS:
Lushun; A: Andong; Z: Yantai (Chefoo); TL: Tieling; C: Changchun; Y: Yokohama Head
Office; K: Kobe.
Source: calculations by the author

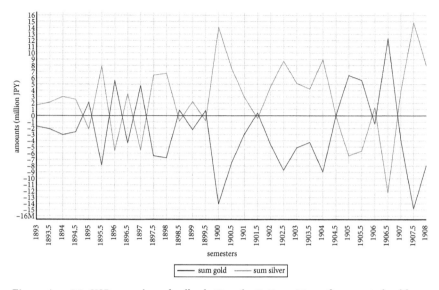

Figure App 06. YSB on an 'even keel' -plotting the FoF-position of aggregated gold branches and aggregated silver branches.

most importantly, the sharp increase of bank branches in the later period, mostly in the wake of the Russo-Japanese War of 1905 makes the graph difficult to read: the overlapping of values of branches in China and Manchuria appear as a tangled knot.

Although this clearly necessitated further analysis, it was not always obvious how to proceed. Descriptive evidence of exchange banking practice has turned out to be scarce, and what one finds as commentaries in newspapers at the time may be misleading. More often than not, the success of certain bank managers or chairmen in reading the course of the exchange has been inflated. One must only think of monikers such as 'Lucky Jackson'[14] to understand how contemporaries (just as today) were inclined to ascribe a bank's success to the *chutzpah* of its managers rather than to the dictates of management practice. As this is reflected in many of the banking histories we possess,[15] we were, out of necessity, the proverbial blind men touching the elephant in order to gain an understanding of its looks. Isolating the gold branches from the silver ones was, we believed, a legitimate and self-evident, although not very insightful, step (Figures App 04 and App 05).

Ultimately, however, the lively debate in the *North China Herald* (see Chapter 4) made it clear that a hedging strategy, if in place, would have to shield the bank's operations against exchange risk arising from bill operations resulting in the holding of silver assets/liabilities. Indeed, plotting the aggregated flow-of-fund position of branches of the gold area vs. those of the silver area raised important issues with respect to accounting practices (see Figure App 06).

The descriptive analysis of this graph, in close relationship with the accounting work-flow associated with certain types of bills, has therefore been at the heart of several

---

[14] In reference to Sir Thomas Jackson, the third Chief Manager of the HSBC.
[15] We feel that it is appropriate not to include any references here. A singular exception to this, however, is the aforementioned Muirhead (1996).

chapters. First in Chapter 3, and then in Chapter 4, we have explored how contractual specifications relate to late nineteenth-century strategies for hedging exchange risk.

7. The Visual Presentation of Branch Relationships on the Cross-sectional Level: 'Multi-dimensional Scaling' vs. 'Force-directed Drawing'

Given that we aim to discuss the flow-of-funds comprehensively, our analysis cannot be confined to the branch network level (*intra-network*), but should also take into account relationships between specific branches within the network (*inter-branch*), and this at selective points in time. As we know that these relationships were modified according to short- and medium-term needs (e.g., changes of unit of account of Japanese branches, extension of the branch network in silver-China, etc.), this also implies a shift of focus from the longitudinal to the *cross-sectional* or *synchronic* dimension.

Speaking in strict accounting terms, a discussion of how inter-branch transfers affect the balance-sheets of all branches involved could suffice; and, indeed, given the sheer complexity of calculations in cases where these cannot be automated, this is how Japanese business historians have proceeded. Typically, they aggregated the balance sheet surpluses/deficits on the national level (and mostly into yearly rather than semestrial data), in order to obtain a two-dimensional representation of the flow-of-funds that is quite straightforward in terms of interpretation; snapshots of flow-of-funds can then be compared over time, that is, by comparing them at fixed intervals, or as representative of periods in the bank's management history.

As already hinted to above, however, contemporary advances in SNA have been impossible to ignore. Or perhaps it has been the sharply enhanced computability coming with corollary software packages that has made all the difference. Whereas SNA-central notions such as 'centrality', 'connectedness', etc., have been defined decades ago, it is nowadays possible to explore their significance for networks containing several thousands, even millions, of nodes.

Of particular importance for our discussion has been the literature with respect to the visualization of proximity matrices in order to explore the structural set-up of networks at particular points in time. The number of incoming connections ('in-degree'), the amount of outgoing connections ('out-degree'), the degree to which nodes are connected to other nodes that are themselves well connected, and so on, all factor in a node's position among other nodes of the network. Designing algorithms that rank similarities have been instrumental in the visualization of how a node or 'ego' is embedded within its 'neighborhood' (the actors that are connected to ego, and their connections to one another) and to the larger graph (is ego an 'isolate', within the network, or a 'pendant'?). In the case of our bank branch network, it may reveal:

1. Which nodes were given more power than others to decide on the distribution of balance sheet imbalances in order to achieve the matching of gold and silver liabilities on the network level;

2. Concretely, which nodes were in charge of flattening out or smoothing imbalances within currency clusters; and

3. Which nodes were pendants, that is, branches at the very edges of the bank's foreign exchange operations, in that they were characterized by a very small in- and/or out-degree (called *source vertices* respective to *sink vertices*).

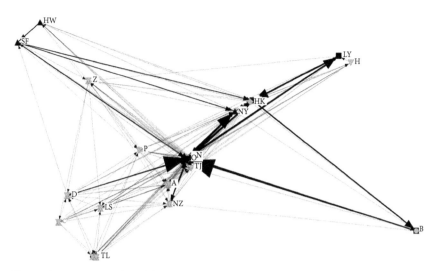

Figure App 07. MDS plot of the Yokohama Specie Bank branch network for the period July 1907 – December 1907.

Y: Yokohama Head Office; K: Kobe; L: London; NY: New York LY: Lyon; SF: San Francisco; HW: Hawai; S: Shanghai; H: Hankow; B: Mumbai (Bombay); HK: Hong Kong; T: Tokyo; N: Nagasaki; TJ: Tianjin; NZ: Niuzhang; P: Beijing (Peking); D: Dairen; LI: Liaoyang; M: Mukden; LS: Lushun; A: Andong; Z: Yantai (Chefoo); O: Osaka; TL: Tieling; C: Changchun; CBI: correspondent banks (international); CBD: correspondent banks (domestic).

Source: calculations by the author.

Traditionally, multidimensional scaling or MDS has been used for these purposes (Torgerson, 1958). Put simply, the MDS algorithm of a square item-by-item proximity matrix determines coordinates for each item in a k-dimensional (typically, two-dimensional) space such that the Euclidean distances among the points most fittingly approximates the input proximities. Input proximities are typically differentiated between similarities and dissimilarities. In the case of dissimilarities (e.g., geographic distances), the relationship between input proximities and the Euclidean distances on the MDS map are, for obvious reasons, positive: larger input proximities correspond to larger map distances; in the case of similarities, the same relationship is negative. Further specifications, for instance metric and non-metric MDS, are still possible. However, the point is that MDS representations must always be compatible with the defining characteristics of Euclidean space.

It will not come as a surprise that, when working with data that do not fit the limitations of these criteria, MDS representations suffer from considerable drawbacks. Analyses in the social and cultural domain, especially when the focus is on flows or transfers among nodes—as in the case of a flow-of-funds analysis—often pose problems defying the constraints of Euclidean order. As we analyze a bank branch network in which all nodes are reasonably similar in that they have relationships to at least a few other nodes, and in which the number of nodes is still limited, *dimensionality* and *outliers* are thereby not so much of a problem (DeJordy et al., 2007). Things that do matter, however, are issues of *transitivity* and *symmetry*. Put simply, MDS has a tendency towards obfuscating the

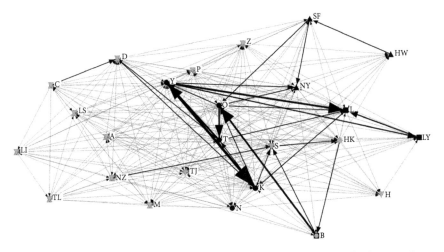

Figure App 08. FDD plot of the Yokohama Specie Bank branch network for the period July 1907 – December 1907.
Y: Yokohama Head Office; K: Kobe; L: London; NY: New York LY: Lyon; SF: San Francisco; HW: Hawai; S: Shanghai; H: Hankow; B: Mumbai (Bombay); HK: Hong Kong; T: Tokyo; N: Nagasaki; TJ: Tianjin; NZ: Niuzhang; P: Beijing (Peking); D: Dairen; LI: Liaoyang; M: Mukden; LS: Lushun; A: Andong; Z: Yantai (Chefoo); O: Osaka; TL: Tieling; C: Changchun; CBI: correspondent banks (international); CBD: correspondent banks (domestic).
Source: calculations by the author.

location of points, possibly suggesting implicit explanations for certain constellations, whereas such interpretation need not exist at all (Figure App 07).

The MDS algorithm performs very well in showing the grouping or clustering of branches in terms of currency type. Typically San Francisco (SF) and Hawaii (HW) are represented as very similar, just as the Manchurian branches (perhaps with the exception of Chefoo, which is determined by its dissimilarity from the other Manchurian branches, rather than its similarity to, say, San Francisco). Remark, however, that the MDS algorithm is particularly weak in handling triangle inequality. In order to represent the axis of central (and close or similar) branches, it compresses the triangular relationships among these branches into a flat bow-like structure, thereby obscuring the location of several crucial nodes, such as, for instance, London, Kobe, and Shanghai.

For the above reasons, our discussion does not employ MDS, but relies on force-directed drawing (FDD) algorithms, concretely the graph layout algorithms (GLA) that are built into the network visualization software as UCINET (written in Delphi), graph-tool (written in C++), NetworkX (pure python), igraph (implemented in C), and so on. FDD algorithms proceed in a way that is rather different from MDS. They do not attempt to map a network's structure (i.e., its relations of similarities respective to dissimilarities) in terms of the raw distances of the proximity matrix, yet conceive of it in terms of energy. As put in the original formulation by Eades,

> we replace the vertices by steel rings and replace each edge with a spring to form a mechanical system. The vertices are placed in some initial layout and let go so that the spring forces on the rings move the system to a minimal energy state.   (Eades, 1984)

Core to minimizing energy is strain. Typically, FDD algorithms are therefore referred to as 'spring embedders'. As the name suggests, they act as a system of springs, stretched between posts in a force field. If two posts with a spring between them are placed too close to each other, the spring is compressed and tries to push the posts apart (which we also refer to as 'node repulsion'). If, on the other hand, the posts are too far apart, the spring is stretched and tries to pull the posts together (called 'node attraction'). In essence, the algorithms are methods of locating the posts in such a way as to bring the repulsive and attractive forces throughout the entire field into a stable, balanced state. Many variations are possible (Kobourov, 2012), but the principle remains the same. Most common in network visualization software are the algorithms formulated by Kamada-Kawai (1989) and Fruchterman and Reingold (1991).

Interesting for our discussion, FDD algorithms transcend the limitations of Euclidean space by abstracting from the precise values in the proximity matrix, concretely by dichotomizing the proximities. Ideally, SNA software packages allow the user to specify filtering criteria defining (1) when lines are to be drawn between nodes in the graph and (2) at what cut-off levels the length of lines is to be fixed. Clearly, this is also where inaccuracies are going to occur. Even then, accuracy is always to be compromised, and not only because of the static nature of the (two-dimensional) printed publication. In the end, what has been sacrificed in terms of accuracy has been gained in terms of aesthetic proportions, and, more importantly, ease of interpretation (Figure App 08).

As in the case of Figure App 07, the graph makes it possible to discern the network's structure in terms of currency groups; yet it corrects the location of Chefoo, and makes it clear that, within the Manchurian currency group, Dairen (D) has the position of a 'hub'. The most central nodes are clearly indicated. Of special relevance is Shanghai (S), which has clearly come to function as the node negotiating imbalances between branches in the gold and silver currency blocs. Note furthermore the location of Bombay (B) as an outlier: the algorithm only takes into account node similarity in terms of network specific characteristics; the calculation of similarity is indifferent to the weight of the vertices connecting the nodes.

Exchange Banking

A Concise Japanese-English Glossary

boki 簿記, bookkeeping, booking

bōeki torihiki 貿易取引, visible trade (as opposed to *bōeki gai torihiki* 貿易外取引, invisible trade, that is, the body of international transactions that does not include an exchange of tangible goods)

chihōsai 地方債, local bond

chōbo 帳簿, bank book

chūkainin tesūryō 仲介人手数料, brokerage

chūshin shijō 中心市場, central market

daikin toritate kawase 代金取立為替, bills for collection (B/C)

denpyō 伝票, payment slip

denshin kawase 電信為替, telegraphic transfer (often abbreviated as TT)

Ei-Ōkurashō tanki shōken 英大蔵省短期証券, (British) treasury bill (T/B)

fukushiki-boki 複式簿記, double entry bookkeeping

funazumori shorui 船積書類, shipping documents

furidashinin 振出人, drawer

gaikoku kawase 外国為替, foreign exchange

gaikoku kawase kanjō 外国為替勘定, foreign exchange account

gaikoku kawase kanri seido 外国為替管理制度, foreign exchange control system

gaikoku kawase sōba 外国為替相場, foreign exchange rate

gaikoku kawase tegata 外国為替手形, foreign exchange bill

gaikoku shōken 外国証券, foreign securities

genkin zandaka 現金残高, cash position

ginkō-kan torihiki sōba 銀行間取引相場, interbank rate

ginkō kawase 銀行為替, banker's bill (alternatively: banker's instruction)

gyaku kawase 逆為替, 'adverse exchange' (alternatively *toritate kawase* 取立為替)

haitōkin 配当金, dividend

hakuchi uragaki 白地裏書, blank endorsement

hikiuke 引受, acceptance

hikiukewatari 引受渡, documents against acceptance (D/A)

hiraki 開き, spread

honshiten-kanjō 本支店勘定, inter-office account

hotto mane- ホットマネー, hot money

ichiran-barai 一覧払, payable 'at sight' or 'on demand'

ippōteki shūshi 一方的収支, unilateral transfer

jigane 地金, bullion

jikimono 直物, spot

jikimono sōba 直物相場, spot exchange rate

jōto kanō shin'yōjō 譲渡可能信用状, assignable (transferable) credit

junkan shin'yōjō 循環信用状, revolving credit

juyō no danryokusei 需要の弾力性, elasticity of supply

kakuteijitsu-barai 確定日払, payable at a fixed time

kai-kawase-tegata 買為替手形, bills bought

kaine 買値, buying quote

kari 借, debit

kashi 貸, credit

kashikarihyō 貸し借り表, balance sheet (alternatively *kashikari taishōhyō* 貸借対照表)

kawase chūkainin 為替仲介人, exchange bill broker

kawase-jiri 為替尻, balance of exchange

kawase mochidaka 為替持高, exchange position

kawase monku 為替文句, exchange clause

keijō torihiki 経常取引, current transactions

kigentsuki tegata 期限付手形, time bill (alternatively *yūzansu biru* ユーザンス・ビ
ル, usance bill)

kijiku tsūka 基軸通貨, key currency, 'hard currency'

kimeishiki uragaki 記名式裏書, special endorsement

kingin kinkōsaku 金銀均衡策, 'even keel'

kinjigane 金地金, gold coin or gold bullion

kōbairyoku heika 購買力平価, purchasing power parity

kogitte 小切手, 'check' or 'cheque'

kōka 硬化, hard currency (as the antonym of *nanka* 軟貨, soft currency)

kōkansei 交換性, convertibility

kokusai kashikari 国際貸し借り, international indebtedness (international debits and
credits)

kokusai kashikari-jiri 国際貸し借り尻, international balance of indebtedness

kokusai shūshi 国際収支, international balance of payments

kokusai torihiki jisseki 国債取引実績, international transactions account

kokusai tsūka 国際通貨, international currency

kurīn biru クリーンビル, clean bill

kyokutō ritsuki kawase shin'yōjō 極東利付為替信用状, Far Eastern interest bill credit

kyōkyū no danryokusei 供給の弾力性, elasticity of supply

maegashi 前貸し, advance

makkijitsu 末期日, maturity

mochidaka chōsei torihiki 持高調整取引, exchange cover (alternatively *kawase no kaba-為替のカバー*)

motochō 元帳, ledger

mutanpo uragaki 無担保裏書, qualified endorsement

na'atenin 名宛人, drawee

naikoku kawase tegata 内国為替手形, inland bill of exchange

nami kawase 並為替, remittance exchange (alternatively *sōkin kawase* 送金為替)

nikkichō 日記帳, daybook

nigawase shinyōjō 荷為替信用状, documentary letter of credit (documentary L/C) (as opposed to *niochi shinyōjō* 荷落信用状, documentary clean L/C)

niochi kawase tegata 荷落為替手形, documentary clean bill

nitsuki kawase tegata 荷付為替手形, documentary bill

norikae torihiki 乗換取引, 'swap' or change cover

oya ginkō 親銀行, bank of banks

rishi 利子, interest

ritsuki kawase tegata 利付為替手形, interest bill

ritsuki kawase tegata risoku 利付為替手形利息, interest on interest bills

rondon hikiuke shin'yōjō 倫敦引き受け信用状, London acceptance

sai-waribiki 再割引, rediscounting

sakimono 先物, forward; future

sakimono kawase 先物為替, forward exchange

sanchaku kawase sōba 参着為替相場, sight rate as opposed to *kigen kawase sōba* 期限為替相場, usance rate

sashizuninshiki 指図人式, payable to the order of a specified person

seikyūbarai hōshiki 請求払方式, pay on application (P/A)

Seitō shojinin 正当所持人, holder-in-due-course

senpō kanjō 先方勘定, your account ('vostro')

shasai 社債, debenture

shiharai chōka 支払超過, unfavorable balance

shiharai itaku monku 支払委託文句, order to pay

shiharai kijitsu 支払期日, due date

shiharaishōdaku 支払承諾, acceptances and guarantees

shiharai watari 支払渡, documents against payment (D/P)

shihon no yu'nyū/yushutsu 資本の輸入・輸出, the import/export of capital

shihon torihiki 資本取引, capital transactions

shijō shutsudō 市場出動, market intervention

shijō sōba 市場相場, market rate

shikin idō 資金移動, capital movements

shin'yōjō 信用状, letter of credit (L/C)

shin'yōjō kawase 信用状為替, credit bill

shin'yō shōken 信用証券, credit instrument

shōnin kawase 商人為替, merchant bill (alternatively: private bill)

shūnyū/shishutsu 収入・支出, receipts and payments

sōkanjō motochō 総勘定元帳, general ledger

son'eki keisansho 損益計算書, statement of profit and loss

taigai tōshi 対外投資, foreign investments

tatenkanjō 他店勘定, correspondent account (abbrev. as 'corres A/C')

teitōjō 抵当状, letter of hypothecation

tegata waribiki 手形割引, bill discounting

tenki 転記, 'posting' (transferring an item from a daybook to a ledger)

tōhō kanjō 当方勘定, our account ('nostro')

torikeshi funō shin'yōjō 取消不能信用状, irrevocable credit

toritate inin uragaki 取立委任裏書, agency endorsement

tōza kashikoshi 当座貸越, overdraft facility

tsūchibarai hōshiki 通知払方式, advice and pay (A/P)

uchibu 打歩, premium (as opposed to *waribiki* 割引, discount)

uketori chōka 受取超過, favorable balance

uragaki 裏書, endorsement

uragaki kinshi uragaki 裏書禁止裏書, non-negotiable endorsement

urikawase tegata 売為替手形, bills sold

urine 売値, selling quote

yakusoku tegata 約束手形, promissory note

yushutsu kawase maegashi 輸出為替前貸, advance for export bill

yūsō tojō 郵送途上, 'en route' (as a reference to a yet unsettled transaction)

References

1. Archives and Databases

Commercial Databases

- https://parlipapers.proquest.com/parlipapers
- https://www.gale.com/c/the-economist-historical-archive
- https://www.gale.com/intl/c/financial-times-historical-archive
- https://primarysources.brillonline.com/browse/north-china-herald-online
- https://www.gale.com/primary-sources/the-making-of-the-modern-world

The **British Parliamentary Papers** (BPP) provided the necessary documentary evidence for putting the contemporary discussions concerning silver risk into context; Brill's database of the **North China Herald** (NCH) was an indispensable source for reconstructing the debate on the so-called Even Keel.

Non-commercial, Readily Accessible Databases

- https://www.jacar.go.jp/
- http://eresources.nlb.gov.sg/newspapers/
- http://www.lib.kobe-u.ac.jp/sinbun/index.html
- http://dl.ndl.go.jp/

Items in the **Japan Center for Asian Historical Records** of the National Archives of Japan (JACAR) are marked in the text as JACAR, together with the relevant reference code (mostly A***********, as these are held within the National Archives of Japan). The **National Diet Library** maintains the excellent and extensive 'National Diet Library digital collections' (国立国会図書館デジタルコレクション), which contains the readily consultable full-text versions of many of the primary sources mentioned in the book. The Singapore government database of historical newspapers was useful when trying to understand how Western banking institutions were perceived in the East.

I have also profited from the **Morrison collection at the Tōyō Bunko Library** in Tokyo, which contained several pamphlets that turned out to be invaluable for the discussion in several chapters (http://www.toyo-bunko.or.jp/library3/shozou/morison.html). This collection was named after George Ernest Morrison, Australia-born journalist and later advisor to the Chinese government, who collected pamphlets related to 'Far Eastern Affairs'.

For the construction of the database, we have used the detailed **Semestrial reports of the Yokohama Specie Bank**. These are available on microfilm:

- Takeda Haruhito 武田晴人 and Yokohama Shōkin Ginkō 横濱正金銀行. 2003. 横濱正金銀行：マイクロフィルム版 *Yokohama Shōkin Ginkō: maikurofirumu-han* (The Yokohama Specie Bank: microfilm edition). 丸善. http://ci.nii.ac.jp/ncid/BA64916118. In particular: reels E003–E005.

Facsimiles of the original semestrial reports are also included in the appendices of primary materials to the 1976 expanded edition of the bank's official history (originally published in 1920):

- Yokohama Shōkin Ginkō 横濱正金銀行. 1976. 『横浜正金銀行史：資料』 *Yokohama Shōkin Ginkō: Shiryō* (Yokohama Specie Bank: materials). 坂本経済研究所, 日本経済評論社(発売) (http://ci.nii.ac.jp/ncid/BN02127303). Vols. 1; 2 (1/2); 3 (1/2).

2. Books and journal articles

Adachi Tadashi 足立禎. 1970. 「<論説>外国為替決済勘定： 'Nostro', 'Vostro'および 'Loro' Accountについて」 *(Ronsetsu) gaikoku kawase kessai kanjō: 'Nostro', 'Vostro' oyobi 'Loro' Account ni tsuite* (clearing accounts for foreign exchange: about 'Nostro', 'Vostro', and 'Loro' accounts). 『商學討究』 *Shōgaku tōkyū* 21 (2): 1–20. http://ci.nii.ac.jp/naid/110000231064

Adams, John. 1971. 'The Impact of the Suez Canal on India's Trade.' *Indian Economic & Social History Review* 8 (3): 229–40. doi:10.1177/001946467100800301

Akagawa Motoaki 赤川元章. 2006. 「19世紀末のドイツ銀行業と東アジア」 *Jūkyū seikimatsu no Doitsu ginkō to higashi Ajia* (The Activities of the Deutsche Bank in East Asia in the Late Nineteenth Century) 三田商学研究 *Mita shōgaku kenkyū* 49 (5): 51–65. http://ci.nii.ac.jp/naid/120000800404

Akami, Tomoko. 2012. *Japan's News Propaganda and Reuters' News Empire in Northeast Asia, 1870-1934*. Dordrecht: Republic of Letters.

Akerlof, George A. 1970. 'The Market for "Lemons": Quality Uncertainty and the Market Mechanism.' *The Quarterly Journal of Economics* 84 (3): 488–500. doi:10.2307/1879431

Amano Tameyuki 天野爲之. 1—. 『外國爲替論』 *Gaikoku kawase-ron* (A Theory of Foreign Exchange). 早稲田大學出版部 Waseda daigaku shuppankai. http://ci.nii.ac.jp/ncid/BA58498851

Andō Minoru 安藤實. 1966a. 「漢冶萍公司借款(一).」 *Kanyahyō kōshi shakkan (1)* (The Loans to the Hanyeping Concern (1)). 静岡大学法経研究 *Shizuoka Daigaku hōkei kenkyū* 15 (1): 99–130. https://ci.nii.ac.jp/naid/110007667193

Andō Minoru 安藤實. 1966b. 「漢冶萍公司借款(二).」 *Kanyahyō kōshi shakkan (2)* (The Loans to the Hanyeping Concern (2)) 静岡大学法経研究 *Shizuoka Daigaku hōkei kenkyū* 15 (2): 57–100. https://ci.nii.ac.jp/naid/110007667186

Andō Morito 安東盛人. 1957. 『外國爲替概論：その機構と機能』 *Gaikoku kawase gairon: sono kikō to kinō* (A General Theory of Foreign Exchange: Mechanisms and Functions). 有斐閣 Yūhikaku. http://ci.nii.ac.jp/ncid/BN0286978X

Andrew, A. Piatt. 1901. 'Review of a *History of the Latin Monetary Union*, by Henry Parker Willis.' *Political Science Quarterly* 16 (3): 530–34. doi:10.2307/2140273

Andrew, A. Piatt. 1904. 'The End of the Mexican Dollar.' *The Quarterly Journal of Economics* 18 (3): 321–56. doi:10.2307/1884074

Andrews, E. Benj. 1893. 'The Monetary Conference of 1892.' *Political Science Quarterly* 8 (2): 197–219. doi:10.2307/2139642

Atkinson, Fred J. 1898. 'Silver Prices in India for 1897.' *Journal of the Royal Statistical Society* 61 (2): 387–403. http://www.jstor.org/stable/2979739

Atkinson, Fred J. 1903. 'Rupee Prices in India, 1898–1901.' *Journal of the Royal Statistical Society* 66 (1): 103–18. http://www.jstor.org/stable/2339482

Atkinson, Fred J. 1909. 'Rupee Prices in India, 1870 to 1908; with an Examination of the Causes Leading to the Present High Level of Prices.' *Journal of the Royal Statistical Society* 72 (3): 496–573. doi:10.2307/2340357

Bagchi, Amiya Kumar. 1997. 'Contested Hegemonies and *Laissez Faire*: Controversies over the Monetary Standard in India at the High Noon of the British Empire.' *Review (Fernand Braudel Center)* 20 (1): 19–76. doi:s

Bak Jun Geon 朴埈健. 1992. 「産業資本成立期における横浜正金銀行の資金循環構造-利付為替手形の処理問題を中心として」*Sangyō shihon seiritsu-ki ni okeru Yokohama Shōkin Ginkō no shihon junkan kōzō—ritsuki tegata no shori mondai wo chūshin toshite* (The Structure of the Flow-of-Funds in the Yokohama Specie Bank in the Early Period of Industrial Capital—With a Special Focus on the Problem of Processing of Interest Bills) 経済論究 *Keizai ronkyū*, March, pp. 147–62. http://ci.nii.ac.jp/naid/40000909339

Balachandran, G. 1996. *John Bullion's Empire: Britain's Gold Problem and India between the Wars*. London Studies on South Asia 10. Richmond, Surrey: Curzon.

Bell, H. F. 1919. *A Record of Exchange: Bar Silver, T.T. and 4 m/s Credits from 1890-1918*. Shanghai: North-China Daily News and Herald.

Ben-Shahar, Omri, and Kyle Logue. 2012. 'Outsourcing Regulation: How Insurance Reduces Moral Hazard.' *Michigan Law Review* 111 (2): 197–248. http://repository.law.umich.edu/mlr/vol111/iss2/2

Best, Gary Dean. 1972. 'Financing a Foreign War: Jacob H. Schiff and Japan, 1904–05.' *American Jewish Historical Quarterly* 61 (4): 313–24. http://www.jstor.org/stable/23880523

Bignon, Vincent, and Marc Flandreau. 2011. 'The Economics of Badmouthing: Libel Law and the Underworld of the Financial Press in France Before World War I.' *The Journal of Economic History* 71 (03): 616–53. doi:10.1017/S0022050711001860

Blagg, Michele. 2014. '1897-1939, A New Era for the London Silver Price.' *Alchemist: London Bullion Market Association*, October: 18–21.

Bloomfield, Arthur I. 1963. *Short-Term Capital Movements under the Pre-1914 Gold Standard*. Princeton Studies in International Finance, no. 11. Princeton, NJ: International Finance Section, Dept. of Economics, Princeton University.

Bonin, Hubert, Nuno Valério, and Kazuhiko Yago, eds. 2015. *Asian Imperial Banking History*. Brookfield, VT: Ashgate Pub Co.

Bordo, Michael D., and Marc Flandreau. 2003. 'Core, Periphery, Exchange Rate Regimes, and Globalization.' *NBER*, January, 417–72. http://www.nber.org/chapters/c9595

Bordo, Michael D., and Hugh Rockoff. 1996. 'The Gold Standard as a "Good Housekeeping Seal of Approval."' *The Journal of Economic History* 56 (2): 389–428. http://www.jstor.org/stable/2123971

Bratter, Herbert Max. 1933. *Silver Market Dictionary*. New York: Commodity Exchange Inc. http://hdl.handle.net/2027/uc1.$b102112

Braudel, Fernand. 1979. *Civilisation Matérielle, Économie et Capitalisme: XVe–XVIIIe Siècle*. Vol. II. Paris: A. Colin.

Broner, Fernando A., Guido Lorenzoni, and Sergio L. Schmukler. 2013. 'Why Do Emerging Economies Borrow Short Term?' *Journal of the European Economic Association* 11 (January): 67–100. doi:10.1111/j.1542-4774.2012.01094.x

Brunero, Donna. 2006. *Britain's Imperial Cornerstone in China: The Chinese Maritime Customs Service, 1854-1949*. 1st edn. London: Routledge.

Bytheway, Simon James. 2005. 『日本経済と外国資本―1858-1939』 *Nihon keizai to gaikoku shihon―1895-1939* (The Japanese Economy and Foreign Capital: 1858-1939). 東京: 刀水書房.

Bytheway, Simon James, and Mark Metzler. 2016. *Central Banks and Gold: How Tokyo, London, and New York Shaped the Modern World*. Ithaca, NY: Cornell University Press.

Caballero, Ricardo J., Kevin Cowan, and Jonathan Kearns. 2005. 'Fear of Sudden Stops: Lessons from Australia and Chile.' *The Journal of Policy Reform* 8 (4): 313–54. doi:10.1080/13841280500387141

Cain, P. J., and A. G. Hopkins. 1993. *British Imperialism: Innovation and Expansion, 1688-1914*. London: Longman.

Calomiris, Charles W. 1993. 'Greenback Resumption and Silver Risk: The Economics and Politics of Monetary Regime Change in the United States, 1862-1900.' *Monetary Regimes in Transition*, 86–132. Studies in Macroeconomic History. Cambridge: Cambridge University Press. http://dx.doi.org/10.1017/CBO9780511664564.004

Chang, Chihyun. 2012. *Government, Imperialism and Nationalism in China: The Maritime Customs Service and Its Chinese Staff*. London: Routledge.

Chosŏn Ŭnhaeng. 1920. *Economic History of Manchuria, Compiled in Commemoration of the Decennial of the Bank of Chosen*. Seoul.

Cochrane, Sarah. 2009. *Explaining London's Dominance in International Financial Services, 1870-1913*. Department of Economics Discussion Paper Series 455. Department of Economics, University of Oxford. http://www.economics.ox.ac.uk/research/WP/pdf/paper455.pdf

Conant, Charles A. 1903. 'Putting China on the Gold Standard.' *The North American Review* 177 (564): 691–704.http://www.jstor.org/stable/25119477

Conant, Charles A. 1909. 'The Gold Exchange Standard in the Light of Experience.' *The Economic Journal* 19 (74): 190–200. doi:10.2307/2221426

Coste, Adolphe. 1889. 'The International Monetary Congress of 1889.' *Journal of the Royal Statistical Society* 52 (4): 577–95. http://www.jstor.org/stable/2979103

De Cecco, Marcello. 1975. *Money and Empire: The International Gold Standard, 1890-1914*. Totowa, NJ: Rowman and Littlefield.

DeJordy, Rich, Stephen P. Borgatti, Chris Roussin, and Daniel S. Halgin. 2007. 'Visualizing Proximity Data.' *Field Methods* 19 (3): 239–63. doi:10.1177/1525822X07302104

Devereux, Michael B., and Shouyong Shi. 2013. 'Vehicle Currency.' *International Economic Review* 54 (1): 97–133. http://www.jstor.org/stable/23352320

Devereux, Michael B., Philip R. Lane, and Juanyi Xu. 2006. 'Exchange Rates and Monetary Policy in Emerging Market Economies.' *The Economic Journal* 116 (511): 478–506. doi:10.1111/j.1468-0297.2006.01089.x

Eades, Peter. 1984. 'A Heuristics for Graph Drawing.' *Congressus Numerantium* 42: 146–60. http://ci.nii.ac.jp/naid/10000075358/

Eichengreen, Barry, and Marc Flandreau. 2009. 'The Rise and Fall of the Dollar (or When Did the Dollar Replace Sterling as the Leading Reserve Currency?).' *European Review of Economic History* 13 (3): 377–411. doi:10.1017/S1361491609990153

Eichengreen, Barry, Ricardo Hausmann, and Ugo Panizza. 2002. 'Original Sin: The Pain, the Mystery, and the Road to Redemption.' *IADB Conference 'Currency and Maturity Matchmaking: Redeeming Debt from Original Sin*. http://economika.com.ve/material/Macro3/papersma3/Hausmann-Original%20Sin.pdf

Eichengreen, Barry, Ricardo Hausmann, and Ugo Panizza. 2003. 'The Pain of Original Sin.' *Other People's Money: Debt Denomination and Financial Instability in Emerging Market*

Economies. Chicago: University of Chicago Press. http://eml.berkeley.edu/~eichengr/research/ospainaug21-03.pdf

Eichengreen, Barry, Ricardo Hausmann, and Ugo Panizza. 2007. 'Currency Mismatches, Debt Intolerance, and the Original Sin: Why They Are Not the Same and Why It Matters.' *Capital Controls and Capital Flows in Emerging Economies: Policies, Practices and Consequences*, 121–70. Chicago: University of Chicago Press. http://www.nber.org/chapters/c0150.pdf

Eichengreen, Barry, Arnaud Mehl, and Livia Chitu. 2017. *How Global Currencies Work: Past, Present, and Future*. Princeton, NJ: Princeton University Press.

Einzig, Paul. 1937. *The Theory of Forward Exchange*. London: Macmillan and Co., limited.

Ejrnæs, Mette, and Karl Gunnar Persson. 2010. 'The Gains from Improved Market Efficiency: Trade before and after the Transatlantic Telegraph.' *European Review of Economic History* 14 (3): 361–81. doi:10.1017/S1361491610000109

Engel, Alexander. 2015. 'Buying Time: Futures Trading and Telegraphy in Nineteenth-Century Global Commodity Markets.' *Journal of Global History* 10 (2): 284–306. doi:10.1017/S1740022815000078

Estevadeordal, Antoni, Brian Frantz, and Alan M. Taylor. 2003. 'The Rise and Fall of World Trade, 1870–1939.' *The Quarterly Journal of Economics* 118 (2): 359–407. doi:10.1162/003355303321675419

Evans, D. Morier, Robert Harry Inglis Palgrave, and Thomas Skinner, eds. 1800–.... *The Bankers' Almanac and Year Book*. London: Groombridge and sons.

Ferguson, Niall, and Moritz Schularick. 2012. 'The 'Thin Film of Gold': Monetary Rules and Policy Credibility.' *European Review of Economic History* 16 (4): 384–407. doi:10.1093/ereh/hes006

Ferrell, Robert H. 1955. 'The Mukden Incident: September 18-19, 1931.' *The Journal of Modern History* 27 (1): 66–72. http://www.jstor.org/stable/1877701.

Fisher, Irving. 1907. *The Rate of Interest: Its Nature, Determination and Relation to Economic Phenomena*. New York: The Macmillan company.

Flandreau, Marc. 1996a. 'The French Crime of 1873: An Essay on the Emergence of the International Gold Standard, 1870–1880.' *The Journal of Economic History* 56 (04): 862–97. doi:10.1017/S0022050700017502

Flandreau, Marc. 1996b. 'Adjusting to the Gold Rush: Endogenous Bullion Points and the French Balance of Payments 1846–1870.' *Explorations in Economic History* 33 (4): 417–39. https://doi.org/10.1006/exeh.1996.0023

Flandreau, Marc. 2000a. *L'or du monde . La France et la stabilité du système monétaire international, 1848–1873*. Paris: Editions L'Harmattan.

Flandreau, Marc. 2000b. 'The Economics and Politics of Monetary Unions: A Reassessment of the Latin Monetary Union, 1865–71.' *Financial History Review* 7 (01): 25–44.

Flandreau, Marc, ed. 2003. *Money Doctors: The Experience of International Financial Advising, 1850–2000*. Routledge International Studies in Money and Banking 26. London: Routledge.

Flandreau, Marc. 2004. *The Glitter of Gold: France, Bimetallism, and the Emergence of the International Gold Standard, 1848–1873*. Oxford: Oxford University Press.

Flandreau, Marc, and Clemens Jobst. 2005. 'The Ties That Divide: A Network Analysis of the International Monetary System, 1890–1910.' *The Journal of Economic History* 65 (04): 977–1007. doi:10.1017/S0022050705000379

Flandreau, Marc, and Clemens Jobst. 2009. 'The Empirics of International Currencies: Network Externalities, History and Persistence.' *The Economic Journal* 119 (537): 643–64. doi:10.1111/j.1468-0297.2009.02219.x

Flandreau, Marc, and Juan H. Flores. 2009. 'Bonds and Brands: Foundations of Sovereign Debt Markets, 1820–1830.' *The Journal of Economic History* 69 (03): 646–84. https://doi.org/10.1017/S0022050709001089

Flandreau, Marc, Christophe Galimard, Clemens Jobst, and Pilar Nogués-Marco. 2009. 'Monetary Geography before the Industrial Revolution.' *Cambridge Journal of Regions, Economy and Society* 2 (2): 149–71. doi:10.1093/cjres/rsp009

Flandreau, Marc, and Mathilde Maurel. 2005. 'Monetary Union, Trade Integration, and Business Cycles in 19th Century Europe.' *Open Economies Review* 16 (2): 135–52. doi:10.1007/s11079-005-5872-4

Flandreau, Marc, and Kim Oosterlinck. 2012. 'Was the Emergence of the International Gold Standard Expected? Evidence from Indian Government Securities.' *Journal of Monetary Economics* 59 (7): 649–69. doi:10.1016/j.jmoneco.2012.09.001

Flandreau, Marc, and Nathan Sussman. 2005. 'Old Sins: Exchange Clauses and European Foreign Lending In the Nineteenth Century.' In Barry Eichengreen and Ricardo Haussman (eds.). *Other People's Money: Debt Denomination and Financial Instability in Emerging Market Economies.* Chicago: University of Chicago Press. http://chicago.universitypressscholarship.com/view/10.7208/chicago/9780226194578.001.0001/upso-9780226194554-chapter-7

Flandreau, Marc, and Stefano Ugolini. 2013. 'Where It All Began: Lending of Last Resort at the Bank of England Monitoring During the Overend-Gurney Panic of 1866.' *The Origins, History, and Future of the Federal Reserve.* Studies in Macroeconomic History. Cambridge: Cambridge University Press. http://dx.doi.org/10.1017/CBO9781139005166.006

Flandreau, Marc, and Frederic Zumer. 2004. *The Making of Global Finance 1880–1913.* Organization for Economic Cooperation & Development.

Fletcher, Max E. 1958. 'The Suez Canal and World Shipping, 1869–1914.' *The Journal of Economic History* 18 (4): 556–73. http://www.jstor.org/stable/2114548

Ford, A. G. 1983. *The Gold Standard, 1880–1914: Britain and Argentina. Gold, Money, Inflation & Deflation.* New York: Garland Pub.

Foxwell, H. S. 1892. 'Mr. Goschen's Currency Proposals.' *The Economic Journal* 2 (5): 139–56. https://doi.org/10.2307/2955956

Fraser, David. 1905. *A Modern Campaign; Or, War and Wireless Telegraphy in the Far East.* London: Methuen & co. http://archive.org/details/cu31924023037231

Friedman, Milton. 1990a. 'Bimetallism Revisited.' *The Journal of Economic Perspectives* 4 (4): 85–104. http://www.jstor.org/stable/1942723

Friedman, Milton. 1990b. 'The Crime of 1873.' *Journal of Political Economy* 98 (6): 1159–94. http://www.jstor.org/stable/2937754

Fruchterman, Thomas M. J., and Edward M. Reingold. 1991. 'Graph Drawing by Force-Directed Placement.' *Software: Practice and Experience* 21 (11): 1129–64. https://doi.org/10.1002/spe.4380211102

Furuta Kazuko 古田 和子. 2000. 『上海ネットワークと近代東アジア』 *Shanhai nettowāku to kindai higashi Ajia* (The Shanghai Network and Modern East Asia). Tōkyō: 東京大学出版会.

Gallarotti, Giulio M. 1995. *The Anatomy of an International Monetary Regime: The Classical Gold Standard, 1880–1914.* New York: Oxford University Press.

Gallarotti, Giulio M. 2001. 'The Rise of the Classical Gold Standard: The Role of Focal Points and Synergistic Effects in Spontaneous Order.' *Humane Studies Review* 13.1: 1–23.

Gallego, Francisco A., and F. Leonardo Hernández. 2003. 'Microeconomic Effects of Capital Controls: The Chilean Experience during the 1990s.' *International Journal of Finance & Economics* 8 (3): 225–53. doi:10.1002/ijfe.207

Garber, Peter M. 1986. 'Nominal Contracts in a Bimetallic Standard.' *The American Economic Review* 76 (5): 1012–30. http://www.jstor.org/stable/1816466

Gerbig-Fabel, Marco. 2008. 'Photographic Artefacts of War 1904–1905: The Russo-Japanese War as Transnational Media Event.' *Revue Européenne d'Histoire* (*European Review of History*) 15 (6): 629–42. doi:10.1080/13507480802500301

Gipouloux, François. 2011. *The Asian Mediterranean: Port Cities and Trading Networks in China, Japan and South Asia, 13th–21st Century*. Cheltenham: Edward Elgar.

Gower, A. 2016. 'Jacob Schiff and the Financing of Japan.' Doctoral thesis. http://discovery.ucl.ac.uk/1522336/

Gutwein, Daniel. 1992. *The Divided Elite: Economics, Politics, and Anglo-Jewry, 1882–1917.* Leiden: Brill.

Hagino Chūzaburō 荻野仲三郎. 1926. 『園田孝吉傳』 *Sonoda Kōkichi-den* (The Biography of Sonoda Kōkichi). 荻野仲三郎. http://ci.nii.ac.jp/ncid/BN08465535

Hamashita Takeshi 浜下武志. 1980. 「中国通商銀行の設立と香港上海銀行」：一八九六年、盛宣懷の設立案をめぐって.」 *Chūgoku tsūshō ginkō no setsuritsu to Honkon Shanhai Ginkō* (The Chinese Bank of Communications and the Hongkong and Shanghai Bank—the Proposals by Sheng Xuan-huai in 1896) 『一橋論叢』 *Hitotsubashi ronsō* 84 (4): 448–64. https://doi.org/info:doi/10.15057/11490

Haupt, Ottomar. 1870. *The London Arbitrageur*. London: Trübner and co.

Haupt, Ottomar. 1871. *Der praktische Wiener Arbitrageur. Eine Zusammenstellung von kaufmännischen Usancen und Formeln für das Arbitragegeschäft in Wechseln, fonds, Münzen, Gold und Silber mit allen bedeutenden Börsenplätzen*. Wien: Beck.

Haupt, Ottomar. 1872. *Arbitrages et parités, traité pratique des opérations d'arbitrages sur lettres de change, fonds publics et matières d'or et d'argent avec les principales places de l'étranger, par Ottomar Haupt, …* Paris: Lacroix, Verboeckhoven et Cie.

Haupt, Ottomar. 1874. *Arbitrage und Paritäten. Praktische Darstellung des Arbitragegeschäftes in Wechseln, Fonds, Gold und Silber*. Wien: Verlag von Friedrich Beck.

Haupt, Ottomar. 1890. 'La hausse de l'argent et l'emprunt indien 4 1/2 % en roupies' ('Rupee-Paper'). http://www.jstor.org/stable/60221845

Hausmann, Ricardo, and Ugo Panizza. 2003. 'On the Determinants of Original Sin: An Empirical Investigation.' *Journal of International Money and Finance*, Regional and International Implications of the Financial Instability in Latin America 22 (7): 957–90. doi:10.1016/j.jimonfin.2003.09.006

Hausmann, Ricardo, and Ugo Panizza. 2011. 'Redemption or Abstinence? Original Sin, Currency Mismatches and Counter Cyclical Policies in the New Millennium.' *Journal of Globalization and Development* 2 (1). doi:10.2202/1948-1837.1127

Henry, J. A. 1963. *The First Hundred Years of the Standard Bank*. London: Oxford University Press.

Horesh, Niv. 2013. 'Money for Empire: The Yokohama Specie Bank Monetary Emissions Before and After the May Fourth (Wusi) Boycott of 1919.' *Modern Asian Studies* 47 (4): 1377–1402. https://doi.org/10.1017/S0026749X12000030

Horie Kiichi 堀江歸一. 1907. 「銀價騰貴ノ原因竝ニ其影響」 *Ginka tōki no gen'in nami ni sono eikyō* ('Reasons behind the Rise of the Silver Price and their Influence'). 經濟學商業學國民經濟雜誌 *Keizaigaku shōgyōgaku kokumin keizai zasshi* 2 (1): 33–49. http://ci.nii.ac.jp/naid/110000573590

Hyōdō Tōru 兵頭徹. 1996. 「日清戦後財政と松方正義(1)」 *Nisshin sensō-go zaisei to Matsukata Masayoshi (1)* (Public Finance in the Aftermath of the Sino-Japanese War and Matsukata Masayoshi (1)) 東洋研究 *Tōyō kenkyū*, no. 121 (November): 103–27. http://ci.nii.ac.jp/naid/40002658649

Hyōdō Tōru 兵頭徹. 1998. 「日清戦後財政と松方正義(2)」 *Nisshin sensō-go zaisei to Matsukata Masayoshi (2)* (Public Finance in the Aftermath of the Sino-Japanese War and Matsukata Masayoshi (2)) 東洋研究 *Tōyō kenkyū*, no. 130 (December): 29–52. http://ci.nii.ac.jp/naid/40002658672

Hyōdō Tōru 兵頭徹. 1999. 「日清戦後財政と松方正義(3)」 *Nisshin sensō-go zaisei to Matsukata Masayoshi (3)* (Public Finance in the Aftermath of the Sino-Japanese War and Matsukata Masayoshi (3)) 東洋研究 *Tōyō kenkyū*, no. 133 (November): 79–105. http://ci.nii.ac.jp/naid/40002658684

Imura Shigeo 井村薫雄, and Shanhai, Shuppan Kyōkai, Chōsabu, 上海出版協會調査部. 1925. 『支那の金塊投機と銀相場』 *Shina no kinkai tōki to gin-sōba* (Speculation in Bar Gold in China and the Silver Price). 上海出版協會, 大阪屋號書店(発兌). http://ci.nii.ac.jp/ncid/BA76465956

Ishii Kanji 石井寛治. 1979a. 「イギリス植民地銀行群の再編―1870・80年代の日本・中国を中心に」 *Igirisu shokuminchi ginkō-gun no saihen—1870–1880 nendai no Nihon-Chūgoku wo chūshin ni* (The Reorganization of British Colonial Banks—With a Focus on Japan and China in the 1870s and 1880s). 経済学論集 *Keizaigaku ronshū* 45 (1): 19–60. http://ci.nii.ac.jp/naid/40000858867

Ishii Kanji 石井寛治. 1979b. 「イギリス植民地銀行群の再編―1870・80年代の日本・中国を中心に-2完-.」 *Igirisu shokuminchi ginkō-gun no saihen—1870–1880 nendai no Nihon-Chūgoku wo chūshin ni (2 kan)* (The Reorganization of British Colonial Banks—With a Focus on Japan and China in the 1870s and 1880s (2-final)). 経済学論集 *Keizaigaku ronshū* 45 (3): 17–46. http://ci.nii.ac.jp/naid/40000859016

Ishii Kanji 石井寛治. 1984. 『近代日本とイギリス資本―ジャーディン=マセソン商会を中心に』 *Kindai Nihon to Igirisu shihon—Jādīn Maseson shōkai wo chūshin ni* (Modern Japan and British Capital: Focusing on the Jardine-Matheson Trading House). Tōkyō: 東京大学出版会.

Ishii Kanji. 1994. 'Japanese Foreign Trade and the Yokohama Specie Bank, 1880–1913', in Olive Checkland, Shizuya Nishimura, and Norio Tamaki (eds.). *Pacific Banking, 1859–1959: East Meets West.* New York: St. Martin's Press.

Ishii Kanji 石井寛治. 1999. 『近代日本金融史序説』 *Kindai Nihon kin'yū-shi josetsu* (An Introduction to the Financial History of Modern Japan). Tōkyō: 東京大学出版会 (Tōkyō daigaku shuppankai). http://ci.nii.ac.jp/ncid/BA41843751

Ishii Kanji 石井寛治. 2001. 『日本銀行金融政策史』 *Nihon Ginkō kin'yū seisakushi* (A Financial Policy History of the Bank of Japan). Tōkyō: 東京大学出版会 (Tōkyō daigaku shuppankai). http://ci.nii.ac.jp/ncid/BA50770808

Ishii Kanji. 2002. 'British-Japanese Rivalry in Trading and Banking.' In Janet E. Hunter and S. Sugiyama (eds.). *The History of Anglo-Japanese Relations, 1600–2000*, 110–32. *The History of Anglo-Japanese Relations, 1600–2000.* London: Palgrave Macmillan UK. https://doi.org/10.1057/9781403919526_2

Ishii Kanji. 2009. 'The Mercantile Response in the Meiji Period: Capital Accumulation by Merchants and the Government's Rejection of Foreign Capital.' *Social Science Japan Journal* 12 (2): 211–25. http://www.jstor.org/stable/40649683

Ishikawa Yoshirō 石川由郎. 1907. 『英國爲替銀行ニ關スル復命書』 *Eikoku kawase ginkō ni kan suru fukumeisho* (Report with Regard to the British Exchange Banks). 三井銀行 Mitsui ginkō. http://ci.nii.ac.jp/ncid/BN14148082

Izquierdo, Alejandro. 2002. 'Sudden Stops, the Real Exchange Rate and Fiscal Sustainability in Argentina.' *World Economy* 25 (7): 903–23. doi:10.1111/1467-9701.00471

Jarvis, Adrian. 1993. 'Alfred Holt and the Compound Engine'. In Robert Gardiner and Basil Greenhill (eds.). *The Advent of Steam—The Merchant Steamship before 1900*, ch. 9. London: Conway Maritime Press Ltd.

Kamada, Tomihisa, and Satoru Kawai. 1989. 'An Algorithm for Drawing General Undirected Graphs.' *Information Processing Letters* 31 (1): 7–15. https://doi.org/10.1016/0020-0190(89)90102-6

Kaneko Fumio 金子文夫. 1977. 「日露戦後の「満州経営」と横浜正金銀行」 *Nichiro sengo no 'Manshū keiei' to Yokohama Shōkin Ginkō* (The 'Administration of Manchuria' after the Russo-Japanese War and the Yokohama Specie Bank) 土地制度史学 *Tochi seidoshi-gaku* 19 (2): 28–52. http://ci.nii.ac.jp/naid/110007018199

Kaneko Fumio 金子文夫. 1979. 「第一次大戦期における植民地銀行体系の再編成 : 朝鮮銀行の「満洲」進出を中心に」 *Dai ichiji taisen-ki ni okeru shokuminchi ginkō taikei no saihensei: Chōsen Ginkō no 'Manshū' shinshutsu wo chūshin ni* (The Restructuring of the Colonial Banking System during the First World War: Focusing on the Bank of Chosen's Penetration of 'Manchuria') 土地制度史学 *Tochi seido shigaku* 21 (2): 1–21. http://ci.nii.ac.jp/naid/110007018250

Kaneko Fumio 金子文夫. 1981a. 「1920年代における日本帝国主義と「満州」(一) : 鉄道・金融問題を中心に」 *1920 nendai ni okeru Nihon teikokushugi to 'Manshū' (ichi): tetsudō/kin'yū mondai wo chūshin ni* (Japanese Imperialism in the 1920s and 'Manchuria' (One): Focusing on the Problems of Railroads and Finance) 社會科學研究 *Shakai kagaku kenkyū* 32 (4): 149–224. http://ci.nii.ac.jp/naid/110000464168

Kaneko Fumio 金子文夫. 1981b. 「1920年代における日本帝国主義と「満州」(二) : 鉄道・金融問題を中心に」 *1920 nendai ni okeru Nihon teikokushugi to 'Manshū' (ni): tetsudō/kin'yū mondai wo chūshin ni* (Japanese Imperialism in the 1920s and 'Manchuria' (Two): Focusing on the Problems of Railroads and Finance) 社會科學研究 *Shakai kagaku kenkyū* 32 (6): 195–286.

Kaneko Fumio 金子文夫. 1990. 「対満州投資の構成と展開(1905～1930年)」 *tai-Manshū tōshi no kōsei to tenkai (1905-1930)* (The Structure and Development of Investments in Manchuria (1905-1930)) 横浜市立大学論叢 人文科学系列 *Yokohama shiritsu daigaku ronsō Jinbunkagaku keiretsu* 41 (1): 489–543. http://ci.nii.ac.jp/naid/40003713622

Kaneko Fumio 金子文夫. 1991. 『近代日本における対満州投資の研究』 *kindai Nihon ni okeru tai-Manshū tōshi no kenkyū* (An Inquiry into Modern Japanese Investments in Manchuria). Tokyo: 近藤出版社.

Kasuya Makoto. 2012. 'The Activities of Japanese Banks in Interwar Financial Centres: The Cases of the Yokohama Specie Bank's Offices in London and New York.' In Shizuya Nishimura, Toshio Suzuki, and Ranald C. Michie (eds.), *The Origins of International Banking in Asia*, 196–212. Oxford: Oxford University Press. http://www.oxfordscholarship.com/view/10.1093/acprof:oso/9780199646326.001.0001/acprof-9780199646326-chapter-10

Kawamura, Tomotaka. 2015. 'British Exchange Banks in the International Trade of Asia from 1850 to 1890.' In Ulbe Bosma and Anthony Webster (eds.), *Commodities, Ports and Asian Maritime Trade Since 1750*, 179–97. Cambridge Imperial and Post-Colonial Studies Series. London: Palgrave Macmillan UK. http://link.springer.com/chapter/10.1057/9781137463920_10

Kemmerer, E. W. 1905. 'The Establishment of the Gold Exchange Standard in the Philippines.' *The Quarterly Journal of Economics* 19 (4): 585–609. doi:10.2307/1885290

Kemmerer, E. W. 1912. 'The Recent Rise in the Price of Silver and Some of Its Monetary Consequences.' *The Quarterly Journal of Economics* 26 (2): 215–74. doi:10.2307/1884764

Kennedy, P. M. 1971. 'Imperial Cable Communications and Strategy, 1870–1914.' *The English Historical Review* 86 (341): 728–52. http://www.jstor.org/stable/563928

Keynes, John Maynard. 1913. *Indian Currency and Finance*. London: Macmillan and Co.

Kikuchi Michio 菊池道男. 1997. 「日本資本主義の発展と横浜正金銀行の経営制度」 *Nihon shihonshugi no hatten to Yokohama Shōkin Ginkō no keiei seido* (The Development of Japanese Capitalism and the Management System of the Yokohama Specie Bank). 中央学院大学商経論叢 *Chūō Gakuin daigaku shōkei ronsō* 12 (1): 3–34. http://ci.nii. ac.jp/naid/110000490104

Kindleberger, Charles Poor. 1984. *A Financial History of Western Europe*. London: Allen & Unwin.

King, Frank H. H. 1987. *The Hongkong Bank in Late Imperial China, 1864-1902: On an Even Keel*. Vol. 1: *The History of the Hongkong and Shanghai Banking Corporation*. Cambridge: Cambridge University Press.

Kitabayashi Masashi 北林雅志. 1982. 「銀価下落期におけるイギリス植民地銀行—1870年代末—80年代初頭にかけての為替取引方法の変化を中心として」 *Ginka geraku-ki ni okeru Igirisu shokuminchi ginkō—1870 nendai matsu—80 nendai shotō ni kakete no kawase torihiki hōhō no henka wo chūshin toshite* (The British Colonial Banks in the Era of the Fall of Silver: Concentrating on Changes in Foreign Exchange Transactions in the Late 1870s and Early 1880s). 商学論纂 *Shōgaku ronsan* 24 (3): 187–229. http://ci.nii.ac.jp/naid/40001787585

Kitabayashi Masashi 北林雅志. 1987. 「十九世紀末におけるイギリス植民地銀行の為替業務とポンド利付為替手形」 *Jūkyū seikimatsu ni okeru Igirisu shokuminchi ginkō no kawase gyōmu to pondo ritsuki tegata* (Foreign Exchange Operations by the British Colonial Banks in the Late Nineteenth Century and Interest Bills). 経営史学 *Keieishi-gaku* 21 (4): 1–28. http://ci.nii.ac.jp/naid/110000180968

Kitabayashi Masashi 北林雅志. 1992. 「イギリス植民地銀行の対銀価下落政策：香港上海銀行の Even Keel Policy を中心に」 *Igirisu shokuminchi ginkō no tai-ginka geraku seisaku: Honkon Shanhai ginkō no Even Keel Policy wo chūshin ni* (British Exchange Banks' Policies at Countering the Fall of Silver: Concentrating on HSBC's 'Even Keel Policy'). 経営史学 *Keieishi-gaku* 26 (4): 42–70, iii. doi:10.5029/bhsj.26.42

Kitabayashi Masashi 北林雅志. 1999. 「詐欺と管理–イギリス植民地銀行の支店管理」 *Sagi to kanri—Igirisu shokuminchi ginkō no shiten kanri* (Fraud and Management: Bank Branch Management in British Colonial Banks). *Sapporo Gakuin University Review of Economics and Business* 16 (1): 31–60. http://ci.nii.ac.jp/naid/40004523679

Kitabayashi Masashi 北林雅志. 2001. 「19世紀後半アジアにおけるイギリス植民地銀行の支店活動」 *19 seiki kōhan Ajia ni okeru Igirisu shokuminchi ginkō no shiten katsudō* (Branch Activity of the British Colonial Banks in Late Nineteenth Century Asia). *Sapporo Gakuin University Review of Economics and Business* 18 (2): 33–62. http:// ci.nii.ac.jp/naid/40004523712

Kitabayashi Masashi 北林雅志. 2010. 「19世紀後半におけるチャータード銀行の本支店勘定」 *19 seiki kōhan ni okeru Chātādo Ginkō no hon-shiten kanjō* (Balances between the Head Office and Branches of the Chartered Bank of India, Australia and China in the Late nineteenth Century) 札幌学院大学経営論集, no. 2 (August): 87–99. https://ci.nii.ac.jp/naid/120002988413

Kittler, Friedrich. 1999. *Gramophone, Film, Typewriter*. Trans. Geoffrey Winthrop-Young and Michael Wutz. Stanford, CA: Stanford University Press.

Kiyotaki, Nobuhiro, and Randall Wright. 1993. 'A Search-Theoretic Approach to Monetary Economics.' *The American Economic Review* 83 (1): 63–77. http://www.jstor.org/stable/2117496

Kobayashi Atsushi. 2019. 'International Bimetallism and Silver Absorption in Singapore, 1840-73.' *The Economic History Review* 72 (2): 595–617. https://doi.org/10.1111/ehr.12662

Kobayashi Midori 小林緑. 1910. 『実践国際為替』 *Jissen kokusai kawase* (Foreign Exchange in Practice). 宝文館. http://ci.nii.ac.jp/ncid/BN15396727<CONT>

Kobourov, Stephen G. 2012. 'Spring Embedders and Force Directed Graph Drawing Algorithms.' *arXiv:1201.3011* [cs], January. http://arxiv.org/abs/1201.3011

Kojima Hitoshi 小島仁. 1977. 「第一次大戦前の在外正貨制度と横浜正金銀行」 *Dai ichiji taisenmae no zaigai seika seido to Yokohama Shōkin ginkō* (The Specie Held Abroad System before World War I and the Yokohama Specie Bank) 経済と経営 *Keizai to keiei* 7 (3): 1–44. http://ci.nii.ac.jp/naid/110004031326

Kojima Hitoshi 小島仁. 1978. 「第一次大戦以前 (一八九五～一九一四年) の東洋為替と植民地銀行が果たした役割:東洋の銀本位制が国際金本位制に包摂されたしくみ、特に中国について。」 *Dai-ichiji taisen izen (1895–1914) no tōyō kawase to shokuminchi ginkō ga hatashita yakuwari: tōyō no ginhon'i-sei ga kokusai kinhon'i-sei ni hōsetsu sareta shikumi, toku ni Chūgoku ni tsuite* (The Eastern Exchanges before World War I and the Role Played by the Eastern Exchange Banks—The Process by which the Silver Standard of the East Was Subsumed under the International Gold Standard, with Special Attention for China). 国際経済 *Kokusai keizai* 1978 (29): 135–44. doi:10.5652/kokusaikeizai.1978.135

Kubota Yūji 久保田裕次. 2011. 「日露戦後における対中国借款政策の展開–漢冶萍公司を中心に」 *Nichiro sengo ni okeru Chūgoku shakkan seisaku no tenkai—kanyahyō kōshi wo chūshin ni* (The Development of the China Lending Policy after the Russo-Japanese War: Focusing on the Hanyeping Concern). 日本史研究 *Nihonshi kenkyū*, no. 589 (September): 16–41. https://ci.nii.ac.jp/naid/40018992631

Kumagai Jirō 熊谷次次郎. 1992. 「19世紀末国際通貨会議と複本位制論：ルイス・マレットの議論を中心として」 *19 seikimatsu kokusai tsūka kaigi to fukuhon'isei-ron: Ruis Maretto no giron wo chūshin toshite* (International Monetary Conferences in the Late Nineteenth Century and Bimetallism: Concentrating on the Arguments of Louis Mallet). 桃山学院大学経済経営論集 *Momoyama gakuin daigaku keizai keiei ronshū* 34 (2): 61–90. http://ci.nii.ac.jp/naid/110006965493

Kuroda, Akinobu. 2008a. 'What Is the Complementarity among Monies? An Introductory Note.' *Financial History Review* 15 (1): 7–15. doi:10.1017/S0968565008000024

Kuroda, Akinobu. 2008b. 'Concurrent but Non-Integrable Currency Circuits: Complementary Relationships among Monies in Modern China and Other Regions.' *Financial History Review* 15 (1): 17–36. doi:10.1017/S0968565008000036

Laughlin, J. Laurence. 1896. *The History of Bimetallism in the United States*. 3rd edn. New York: D. Appleton and company.

Leavens, Dickson Hammond. 1939. *Silver Money*. Cowles Commission for Research in Economics. Monograph, no. 4. Bloomington, IN: Principia Press, inc.

Lew, Byron, and Bruce Cater. 2006. 'The Telegraph, Co-Ordination of Tramp Shipping, and Growth in World Trade, 1870–1910.' *European Review of Economic History* 10 (2): 147–73. doi:10.1017/S1361491606001663

Lindert, Peter H. 1969. *Key Currencies and Gold, 1900–1913*. Princeton Studies in International Finance, no. 24. Princeton, NJ: International Finance Section, Princeton University.

López-Córdova, Ernesto J., and Christopher M. Meissner. 2003. 'Exchange-Rate Regimes and International Trade: Evidence from the Classical Gold Standard Era.' *American Economic Review* 93 (1): 344–53. doi:10.1257/000282803321455331

Lucas, Robert E. 1976. 'Econometric Policy Evaluation: A Critique.' *Carnegie-Rochester Conference Series on Public Policy*, Vol. 1, 19–46. Amsterdam: Elsevier. http://www.sciencedirect.com/science/article/pii/S0167223176800036

Luhmann, Niklas. 1995. *Social Systems*. Writing Science. Stanford, CA: Stanford University Press.

Luhmann, Niklas. 2000. *The Reality of the Mass Media*. Trans. Kathleen Cross. 1st edn. Stanford, CA: Stanford University Press.

Luhmann, Niklas. 2005. 'Gesellschaftliche Komplexität und öffentliche Meinung.' *Soziologische Aufklärung*, Vol. 5, 163–75. Wiesbaden: VS Verlag für Sozialwissenschaften. https://doi.org/10.1007/978-3-663-11449-9_7

Luhmann, Niklas. 2012. *Theory of Society*, Vol. 1. Trans. Rhodes Barrett. Stanford, CA: Stanford University Press.

Luhmann, Niklas. 2013. *Theory of Society*, Vol. 2. Trans. Rhodes Barrett. Stanford, CA: Stanford University Press.

MacGregor, David R. 1983. *Tea Clippers: Their History and Development, 1833–1875*. 2nd revised and enlarged edn. Annapolis, MD: Naval Institute Press.

Mackenzie, Compton. 1954. *Realms of Silver: One Hundred Years of Banking in the East*. London: Routledge & K. Paul.

Martinho-Marques, C. A. 1908. *The International Exchange Tables: For the Conversion of Any One Currency into Another....* Shanghai: s.n.

Matsukata Masayoshi, ed. 1899. *Report of the Adoption of the Gold Standard in Japan*. Tokyo: Government Press.

Matsuoka Kōji 松岡孝児. 1936. 『金爲替本位制の研究』 *Kingawase hon'isei no kenkyū* (A Study of the Gold Exchange Standard). 日本評論社 Nihon hyōronsha. http://ci.nii.ac.jp/ncid/BN13264088

Matsuoka Kôji. 1938. *L'Etalon de change or en Extrême-Orient, par Kôji Matsuoka,....* Paris / Tôkyo: P. Geuthner /Mitsukoshi.

Matsuyama Kiminori, Nobuhiro Kiyotaki, and Akihiko Matsui. 1993. 'Toward a Theory of International Currency.' *The Review of Economic Studies* 60 (2): 283–307. doi:10.2307/2298058

McGuire, John. 2004. 'The Rise and Fall of the Oriental Bank in the Nineteenth Century: A Product of the Transformations That Occurred in the World Economy or the Result of Its Own Mismanagement.' *Asia Examined Proceedings of the 15th Biennial Conference of the Asian Studies Association of Australia*. Canberra: Asian Studies Association of Australia (ASAA) & Research School of Pacific and Asian Studies (RSPAS), The Australian National University.

McLean, D. 1973. 'The Foreign Office and the First Chinese Indemnity Loan, 1895.' *The Historical Journal* 16 (2): 303–21. http://www.jstor.org/stable/2638314

Mehl, Arnaud, and Julien P. M. Reynaud. 2005. 'The Determinants of "Domestic" Original Sin in Emerging Market Economies.' SSRN Scholarly Paper ID 863946. Rochester, NY: Social Science Research Network. http://papers.ssrn.com/abstract=863946

Meissner, C. M. 2013. 'The Limits of Bimetallism.' Cleveland Federal Reserve Bank Conference Paper.

Metzler, Mark. 2006. *Lever of Empire: The International Gold Standard and the Crisis of Liberalism in Prewar Japan*. Berkeley, CA: University of California Press.

Meuleau, Marc. 1990. *Des Pionniers en Extrême-Orient. Histoire de la Banque de l'Indochine, 1875-1975*. Paris: Fayard.

Michie, Ranald. 2012. 'City of London as a Centre for International Banking: The Asian Dimension in the Nineteenth and Twentieth Centuries.' In Shizuya Nishimura, Toshio Suzuki, and Ranald Michie (eds.). *The Origins of International Banking in Asia*. Oxford:

Oxford   University   Press.   http://www.oxfordscholarship.com/view/10.1093/acprof:
oso/9780199646326.001.0001/acprof-9780199646326-chapter-2

Miller, Edward S. 2007. *Bankrupting the Enemy: The U.S. Financial Siege of Japan before Pearl Harbor*. Annapolis, MD: Naval Institute Press.

Minami Manshū Tetsudō Kabushiki Gaisha 南満州鉄道株式会社東亜経済調査局, Remer C. F. (Charles Frederick), and Tōa keizai chōsakyoku 東亜経済調査局. 1934. 『列國の對支投資』 *Rekkoku no tai-Shi tōshi* (Investment in China by Foreign Countries). 東亞經濟調查局 Tōa Keizai Chōsakyoku. http://ci.nii.ac.jp/ncid/BN09149519

Mitchell, Wesley C. 1911. 'The Publications of the National Monetary Commission.' *The Quarterly Journal of Economics* 25 (3): 563–93. doi:10.2307/1883616

Mitchener, Kris James, and Hans-Joachim Voth. 2011. 'Trading Silver for Gold: Nineteenth-Century Asian Exports and the Political Economy of Currency Unions.' In Robert J. Barro and Jong-Wha Lee (eds.), *Costs and Benefits of Economic Integration in Asia*, 126–56. Oxford: Oxford University Press. http://www.oxfordscholarship.com/view/10.1093/acprof:oso/9780199753987.001.0001/acprof-9780199753987-chapter-005

Mitchener, Kris James, and Marc D. Weidenmier. 2015. 'Was the Classical Gold Standard Credible on the Periphery? Evidence from Currency Risk.' *The Journal of Economic History* 75 (2): 479–511. https://doi.org/10.1017/S0022050715000686

Mitchener, Kris James, Masato Shizume, and Marc D. Weidenmier. 2010. 'Why Did Countries Adopt the Gold Standard? Lessons from Japan.' *The Journal of Economic History* 70 (01): 27–56. doi:10.1017/S0022050710000045

Mizuno Shigenari 水野重也. 1908. 『最新外國爲替』 *Saishin gaikoku kawase* (Recent Foreign Exchange). 宝文館. http://ci.nii.ac.jp/ncid/BA33745542

Motono, Eiichi. 1994. 'Bonded Warehouses And The Indent System, 1886–95.' In Heita Kawakatsu and A. J. H. Latham (eds.). *Japanese Industrialization and the Asian Economy*, 108–28. London: Routledge. doi:10.4324/9780203024959.ch5

Muirhead, Stuart. 1996. *Crisis Banking in the East: The History of the Chartered Mercantile Bank of India, London, and China, 1853–93*. Aldershot / Brookfield, VT: Scolar Press / Ashgate Pub. Co.

Naikoku Kirokukyoku 内閣記録局. 1891. 『制度雜款7：貨幣第5：紙幣第3』 *Seido zatsukan7: kahei dai-go: shihei dai-san* (Various Articles Related to Regime: Money Part 5; Paper Money Part 3). 内閣記録局. http://ci.nii.ac.jp/ncid/BA35555526

Nish, Ian. 2000. *Japan's Struggle with Internationalism*. 1st edn. London: Routledge.

Nishimaki Isaburō 西巻畏三郎, and Yokohama Shōkin Ginkō 橫濱正金銀行. 1910. 『孟買爲換問答』 *Bonbei kawase mondō* (Problems of the Bombay Exchange). 橫濱正金銀行總務部行報係. http://ci.nii.ac.jp/ncid/BA63556050

Nishimura Shizuya. 1971. *The Decline of Inland Bills of Exchange in the London Money Market, 1855–1913*. Cambridge: Cambridge University Press.

Nishimura Shizuya 西村閑也. 1993. 「香港上海銀行の行内資金循環，1913年」 *Honkon Shanhai ginkō no kōnai shikin junkan, 1913 nen* (Internal Flow-of-Funds of the Hongkong and Shanghai Banking Corporation, 1913). 経営志林 *Keieishirin* 30 (1): 1–26. http://ci.nii.ac.jp/naid/110000062908

Nishimura Shizuya. 1994. 'The Flow of Funds within the Hongkong and Shanghai Banking Corporation in 1913.' In Olive Checkland, Shizuya Nishimura and Norio Tamaki (eds.). *Pacific Banking, 1859–1959: East Meets West*. New York: St. Martin's Press.

Nishimura Shizuya 西村閑也. 1998. 「在上海外国銀行と現地銀行(銭荘), 1890–1913: チョップ・ローンのメカニズム」 *zai Shanhai gaikoku ginkō to genchi ginkō,*

1890–1913: choppu rōn no mekanizumu (The Foreign Banks in Shanghai and the Local Banks (qianzhuang), 1890-1913: The Chop Loan Mechanism) 経営志林 *Keiei shirin* 35 (3): 1–19. http://ci.nii.ac.jp/naid/110000063075

Nishimura Shizuya. 2005. 'The Foreign and Native Banks in China: Chop Loans in Shanghai and Hankow before 1914.' *Modern Asian Studies* 39 (01): 109–32. doi:10.1017/S0026749X04001404

Nishimura Shizuya 西村閑也. 2007.「香港上海銀行、1870–1913」 *Honkon Shanhai ginkō, 1870–1913* (The Hongkong and Shanghai Banking Corporation, 1870–1913). 金融構造研究 *Kin'yū kōzō kenkyū* no. 29 (May).

Nishimura Shizuya. 2012. 'British International Banks in Asia, 1870–1914: An Introductory Essay.' In Shizuya Nishimura, Toshio Suzuki, and Ranald C. Michie (eds.). *The Origins of International Banking in Asia*, 55–79. Oxford: Oxford University Press. http://www.oxfordscholarship.com/view/10.1093/acprof:oso/9780199646326.001.0001/acprof-9780199646326-chapter-3

Nishimura Shizuya, Toshio Suzuki, and Ranald C. Michie. 2012. *The Origins of International Banking in Asia: The Nineteenth and Twentieth Centuries*. Oxford: Oxford University Press.

Nishimura Shizuya 西村閑也, Suzuki Toshio 鈴木俊夫, and Akagawa Motoaki 赤川元章. 2014. 『国際銀行とアジア：1870～1913』 *Kokusai ginkō to Ajia: 1870-1913* (The International Banks and Asia: 1870-1913). 慶應義塾大学出版会 Keiō gijuku daigaku shuppankai. http://ci.nii.ac.jp/ncid/BB15855309

Nishimura Takeshi. 2012. 'The Activities of the Yokohama Specie Bank in the Foreign Trade Financing Operations for Raw Cotton before the First World War.' In Shizuya Nishimura, Toshio Suzuki, and Ranald C. Michie (eds.). *The Origins of International Banking in Asia*, 174–89. Oxford: Oxford University Press. http://www.oxfordscholarship.com/view/10.1093/acprof:oso/9780199646326.001.0001/acprof-9780199646326-chapter-9

Nishimura Takeshi 西村雄志. 2014. 「横浜正金銀行　1880－1913年」 *Yokohama shōkin ginkō 1880-1913 nen* (The Yokohama Specie Bank, 1880-1913). In 『国際銀行とアジア　1870～1913』 *Kokusai ginkō to Ajia 1870-1913* (The International Banks and Asia, 1870-1913), by 西村閑也 Nishimura Shizuya, 鈴木俊夫 Suzuki Toshio, and 赤川元彰 Akagawa Motoaki, 1271–330. 東京: 慶応大学出版会.

Noguchi Takehiko 野口建彦. 2005. 「19世紀の国際通貨会議の歴史的意義」 *19-seiki no kokusai tsūka kaigi no rekishiteki igi* (The Historical Significance of the International Monetary Conferences of the Nineteenth Century). 経科研レポート *Keikaken repōto*, no. 29 (November): 37–43. http://ci.nii.ac.jp/naid/40007297235

Noguchi Takehiko 野口建彦. 2006. 「19世紀国際通貨会議の歴史的意義」 *19-seiki no kokusai tsūka kaigi no rekishiteki igi* (The Historical Significance of the International Monetary Conferences of the Nineteenth Century). 日本大学経済学部経済科学研究所紀要 *Nihon daigaku keizaigakubu keizaika kenkyūjo kiyō*, no. 36 (March): 59–111. http://ci.nii.ac.jp/naid/40015150738

Nōchi Kiyoshi 能地清. 1981. 「日清・日露戦後経営と対外財政 1896～1913：在外政府資金を中心に」 *Nisshin-nichiro sengo keiei to taigai zaisei 1896–1913: zaigai seifu shikin wo chūshin ni* (The Administrations in the Wake of the Sino-Japanese and Russo-Japanese Wars and Fiscal Policy, 1896–1913: Concentrating on Government Funds Held Abroad). 土地制度史学 *Tochi seidoshi gaku* 23 (4): 19–40. http://ci.nii.ac.jp/naid/110007018410

Ofem, Brandon, Theresa M. Floyd, and Stephen P. Borgatti 2012. 'Social Networks and Organizations.' *A Companion to Organizational Anthropology*, Wiley Online Books, October. https://doi.org/10.1002/9781118325513.ch6

Ohkawa, Masazo. 1965. 'The Armaments Expansion Budgets and the Japanese Economy after the Russo-Japanese War.' *Hitotsubashi Journal of Economics* 5 (2): 68–83. http://www.jstor.org/stable/43295443

Ono Kazuichirō 小野一一郎. 1959. 「東亜におけるメキシコドルをめぐる角逐とその本質」 *Tōa ni okeru Mekishiko doru wo meguru kakuchiku to sono honshitsu* (Competition Surrounding the Mexican Dollar in East Asia and Its Essence). 経済論叢 *Keizai ronsō* 83 (1): 18–44. http://ci.nii.ac.jp/naid/120002690744

Ono Kazuichirō 小野一一郎. 1962. 「東亜におけるメキシコドル終焉の過程」 *Tōa ni okeru Mekishiko doru shūen no katei* (The Process of the Demise of the Mexican Dollar in East Asia). 経済論叢 *Keizai ronsō* 89 (4): 347–67 http://ci.nii.ac.jp/naid/12000

Ono Kazuichirō 小野一一郎. 1963. 「東亜におけるメキシコドル終焉の論理」 *Tōa ni okeru Mekishiko doru shūen no ronri* (A Theory Regarding the Demise of the Mexican Dollar in East Asia). 経済論叢 *Keizai ronsō* 90 (3): 167–84 http://ci.nii.ac.jp/naid/120002690951

Ono Kazuichirō 小野一一郎. 2001. 『近代日本幣制と東アジア銀貨圏―円とメキシコドル』 *Kindai Nihon heisei to higashi Ajia ginkaken—en to Mekishiko doru* (Modern Japan's Monetary System and the East Asian Silver Sphere—The Yen and the Mexican Dollar). ミネルヴァ書 Minerva shobō.

Ono Keishi 小野圭司. 2008. 「明治末期の軍事支出と財政・金融–戦時・戦後財政と転位効果の考察」 *Meiji makki no gunji shishutsu to zaisei-kin'yū/sengo zaisei to ten'i kōka no kōsatsu* (Military Expenditure in the Late Meiji Period and Public Finance—An Appraisal of Postwar Public Finance and Its Displacement Effect). 戦史研究年報 *Senshi kenkyū nenpō*, no. 11 (March): 41–63. http://ci.nii.ac.jp/naid/40016054419

Ōkurashō. 1900. *Report on the Post-Bellum Financial Administration in Japan, 1896–1900*. Tokyo: Printed at the Government Press.

Ōkurashō Rizaikyoku 大蔵省理財局. 1994. 『金融事項参考書』 *Kin'yū jikō sankōsho* (Reference Book of Financial Matters). 復刻版. 雄松堂. http://ci.nii.ac.jp/ncid/BN11415499

Oppers, Stefan Erik. 1996. 'Was the Worldwide Shift to Gold Inevitable? An Analysis of the End of Bimetallism.' *Journal of Monetary Economics* 37 (1): 143–62. doi:10.1016/0304-3932(95)01238-9

Oppers, Stefan Erik. 2000. 'A Model of the Bimetallic System.' *Journal of Monetary Economics* 46 (2): 517–33. doi:10.1016/S0304-3932(00)00032-5

Ōtsuki Tamehachi 大槻爲八. 1909. 『外國爲替實務誌』 *Gaikoku kawase jitsumu-shi* (A Practical Journal of Foreign Exchange). 同文館. http://ci.nii.ac.jp/ncid/BA34071138

Panizza, Ugo. 2006. ' "Original Sin" and Monetary Cooperation.' In Barbara Fritz and Martina Metzger (eds.). *New Issues in Regional Monetary Coordination*, 26–41. London: Palgrave Macmillan UK. http://link.springer.com/chapter/10.1057/9780230502444_2

Peck, Anne E. 2001. 'The Development of Commodity Exchanges in the Former Soviet Union, Eastern Europe, and China.' *Australian Economic Papers* 40 (4): 437–60. doi:10.1111/1467-8454.00136

Redish, Angela. 1995. 'The Persistence of Bimetallism in Nineteenth-Century France.' *The Economic History Review* 48 (4): 717–36. doi:10.1111/j.1468-0289.1995.tb01441.x

Remer, C. F. 1933. *Foreign Investments in China*. New York: The Macmillan Company.

Reti, Steven. 1998. *Silver and Gold: The Political Economy of International Monetary Conferences, 1867–1892*. Westport, CN: Praeger.

Rogers, James Steven. 2004. *The Early History of the Law of Bills and Notes: A Study of the Origins of Anglo-American Commercial Law*. 1st pbk. edn. Cambridge Studies in English Legal History. Cambridge: Cambridge University Press.

Rosenberg, Emily S. 1985. 'Foundations of United States International Financial Power: Gold Standard Diplomacy, 1900–1905.' *The Business History Review* 59 (2): 169–202. doi:10.2307/3114929

Rosenberg, Emily S. 2003. *Financial Missionaries to the World: The Politics and Culture of Dollar Diplomacy, 1900–1930*. American Encounters/Global Interactions. Durham: Duke University Press.

Saitō Hisahiko 斎藤寿彦. 1973. 「第一次世界大戦期の正貨獲得政策：日本正貨政策史研究(一).」 *Dai ichiji taisenki no seika kakutoku seisaku: Nihon seika seisaku-shi kenkyū (1)* (The Policy of Obtaining Specie During World War I: Studies in the History of Japanese Specie Policy (1)) 三田商学研究 *Mita shōgaku kenkyū* 16 (3): 112–45. http://ci.nii.ac.jp/naid/110002555360

Saitō Hisahiko 斎藤寿彦. 1976. 「第一次世界大戦期における「正貨の産業資金化」政策(小竹豊治教授退任記念号)」 *Dai ichiji taisenki ni okeru 'seika no sangyō shikinka' seisaku* (The Policy of the 'Industrial Financialization' of Specie during World War I). 三田商学研究 *Mita shōgaku kenkyū* 19 (4): 148–216. http://ci.nii.ac.jp/naid/110002555445

Saitō Hisahiko 斉藤寿彦. 1978a. 「大正期の日本正貨政策史研究 (1)」 *Taishōki no Nihon seika seisaku kenkyū (1)* (A Study of the Specie Collection Policy in the Taishō Period (1)). 千葉商大論叢 *Chiba shōdai ronsō* 16 (2): 39–66. http://ci.nii.ac.jp/naid/40004128698

Saitō Hisahiko 斉藤寿彦. 1978b. 「大正期の日本正貨政策史研究 (2)」 *Taishōki no Nihon seika seisaku kenkyū (2)* (A Study of the Specie Collection Policy in the Taishō Period (2)). 千葉商大論叢 *Chiba shōdai ronsō* 16 (3): 65–96. http://ci.nii.ac.jp/naid/40004128694

Saitō Hisahiko 斉藤寿彦. 1985. 「横浜正金銀行の本来の外国為替銀行化過程」 *Yokohama Shōkin Ginkō no honrai no gaikoku kawase ginkōka katei* (The Process of Turning the Yokohama Specie Bank in a True Exchange Bank) 三田商学研究 *Mita shōgaku kenkyū* 28 (5): 66–83. http://ci.nii.ac.jp/naid/110004059224

Saitō Hisahiko 斉藤寿彦. 1986. 「日清戦争以後における横浜正金銀行の資金調達：準備的考察」 *Nisshin sensō ikō ni okeru Yokohama Shōkin Ginkō no shikin chōtatsu: junbiteki kōsatsu* (Capital Raising by the Yokohama Specie Bank after the Sino-Japanese War: A Provisional Inquiry). 金融経済 *Kin'yū keizai* 218: 71. http://ci.nii.ac.jp/naid/110000174471

Saitō Hisahiko 齊藤壽彦. 2002. 「外国為替・貿易金融機関としての横浜正金銀行の発展過程」 *gaikoku kawase—bōeiki kin'yū kikan toshite no Yokohama Shōkin Ginkō no hatten katei* (The Process through which the Yokohama Specie Bank Developed into an Institution Handling Foreign Exchange and Trade Finance) 千葉商大紀要 *Chiba shōdai kiyō* 39 (4): 69–95. https://ci.nii.ac.jp/naid/40005493358

Saitō Hisahiko 齊藤壽彦. 2015. 『近代日本の金・外貨政策』 *Kindai Nihon no kin-gaika seisaku* (Gold and Foreign Exchange Policy in Modern Japan). Tōkyō: 慶應義塾大学出版会.

Saitō Toshisaburō 齋藤利三郎. 1940. 『國際貨幣制度の研究・ラテン貨幣同盟を中心として』 *Kokusai kahei seido no kenkyū—raten kahei dōmei wo chūshin toshite* (A Study of the International Monetary System—Concentrating on the Latin Monetary Union). Tokyo: Nihon Hyōronsha.

Sakamoto Masako 坂本雅子. 2003. 『財閥と帝国主義—三井物産と中国』 *Zaibatsu to teikokushugi—Mitsui bussan to Chūgoku* (The Zaibatsu and Imperialism: Mitsui Bussan and China). Kyōto: ミネルヴァ書房.

Sano Zensaku 佐野善作. 1905. 『清國貨幣問題・滬漢金融機關調查報告』 *Shinkoku kahei mondai—kōkan kin'yū kikan chōsa hōkoku* (The Monetary Problem of Qing China—A Report of the Financial Institutions in Greater Shanghai). 東京高等商業學校 Tōkyō kōtō shōgakkō. http://ci.nii.ac.jp/ncid/BN15641897

Schiltz, Michael. 2012a. 'Money on the Road to Empire: Japan's Adoption of Gold Monometallism, 1873–97.' *The Economic History Review* 65 (3): 1147–68. doi:10.1111/j.1468-0289.2011.00619.x

Schiltz, Michael. 2012b. *The Money Doctors from Japan: Finance, Imperialism, and the Building of the Yen Bloc, 1895–1937.* Cambridge, MA: Harvard University Asia Center.

Schiltz, Michael. 2015. Centrality Tests YSB 1893-1908.xlsx. Figshare. Dataset. https://doi.org/10.6084/m9.figshare.1309394.v1

Schiltz, Michael. 2016c. 'YSB Bookkeeping Workflow Illustrations' 横濱正金銀行計表・帳簿・記帳模本 *Yokohama Shōkin Ginkō keihyō-chōbo-kichō mohon* (Internal Accounting Manual of the Yokohama Specie Bank, Japan). Figshare. Fileset. https://doi.org/10.6084/m9.figshare.2074609.v3

Schiltz, Michael. 2016d. 山川勇木, 「清国出張復命書」 *Yamakawa Yūki 'Shinkoku shucchō fukumeisho* (Yamakawa Yūki—Report of My Dispatch to Qing China) [the report that would mark the beginning of the Yokohama Specie Bank's venturing into China]. 山川勇木. 1904. Figshare. Fileset. https://doi.org/10.6084/m9.figshare.4028301.v1

Schiltz, Michael. 2017a. 'Yokohama Specie Bank Flow-of-Funds Data, 1893-1908 II (Originals)' [multiple file formats, including .xslx, .csv, and .pdf. These matrices contain calculations of the amount of funds transferred]. Figshare. https://doi.org/10.6084/m9.figshare.4059807.v3

Schiltz, Michael. 2017b. 'Yokohama Specie Bank Flow-of-Funds Data, 1893–1908 III (originals)' [multiple file formats, including .xslx, .csv, and .pdf. These matrices contain calculations of the amounts of funds transferred, and their conversions into Japanese yen]. Figshare. https://doi.org/10.6084/m9.figshare.4059843.v3

Schiltz, Michael. 2018. 'Yokohama Specie Bank Flow-of-funds Data, 1893–1908.' III (originals) [multiple file formats including: .xslx, .csv, and .pdf; these matrices contain calculations of the amounts of funds transferred, and their conversions into Japanese yen]. Figshare. Dataset: https://doi.org/10.6084/m9.figshare.4059843.v4

Schiltz, Michael. 2019a. 'The Daily Exchange Quotations'—An Address Delivered by C. S. Addis before the Foreign Y.M.C.A at Shanghai on Feb. 4th, 1903. Courtesy of the Toyo Bunko 東洋文庫 (http://www.toyo-bunko.or.jp/). Figshare. Online resource. https://doi.org/10.6084/m9.figshare.3799305.v3

Schiltz, Michael. 2019b. 'The Shanghai Tael and the Currency of Shanghai.' https://doi.org/10.6084/m9.figshare.7813577.v1

Schottenhammer, Angela, ed. 2005. *Trade and Transfer across the East Asian 'Mediterranean.'* East Asian Economic and Socio-Cultural Studies. East Asian Maritime History 1. Wiesbaden: Harrassowitz.

Schottenhammer, Angela, ed. 2008. *The East Asian Mediterranean: Maritime Crossroads of Culture, Commerce and Human Migration.* Vol. 6: *East Asian Maritime History.* East Asian Economic and Socio-Cultural Studies. Wiesbaden: Harrassowitz Verlag.

Seyd, Ernest. 1868. *Bullion and Foreign Exchanges Theoretically and Practically Considered; Followed by a Defence of the Double Valuation, with Special Reference to the Proposed System of Universal Coinage.* London: Wilson.

「上海ニ於ケル金ノ投機取引」 *Shanhai ni okeru kin no torihiki* (gold transactions in Shanghai). 19—. S.l. [出版者不明]. http://ci.nii.ac.jp/ncid/BA74940210

Sheehan, Paul. 2019. 'Did the Bankruptcy of Hu Kwang-Yung and the Shanghai Crisis of 1883 Cause the 1884 Failure of the Oriental Bank?' (Master's dissertation). October. https://dash.harvard.edu/handle/1/42004018

Sherman, A. J. 1983. 'German-Jewish Bankers in World Politics: The Financing of the Russo-Japanese War.' *The Leo Baeck Institute Year Book* 28 (1): 59–73. https://doi.org/10.1093/leobaeck/28.1.59

Shibata Yoshimasa 柴田善雅. 1977. 「日本の対「満州」通貨金融政策の形成とその機能の実態：第一次大戦から二〇年代中頃にかけて」 *Nihon no tai-'Manshū' tsūka kin'yū seisaku no keisei to sono kinō no jittai: dai ichiji taisen kara nijū nendai nakagoro ni kakete'* (The Formation of Japan's Monetary and Financial Policies towards Manchuria and the Nature of its Functions: From the First World War to the Mid-Twenties), 社會經濟史學 *Shakai keizaishi gaku* 43 (2): 145–73. http://ci.nii.ac.jp/naid/110001212636

Shiratori Keishi 白鳥圭志. 2008. 「産業革命期の横浜正金銀行：中国大陸におけるビジネスの拡大と経営管理体制の変容」 *sangyō kakumeiki no Yokohama shōkin ginkō: Chūgoku tairiku ni okeru bijinesu no kakudai to keiei kanri taisei seido* ('The Yokohama Specie Bank in the Period of the Industrial Revolution: The Expansion of Business Activity on China's Mainland and the Management System'), February [working paper]. https://hermes-ir.lib.hit-u.ac.jp/rs/handle/10086/16081

Shiratori Keishi 白鳥圭志. 2012. 「創業期の横浜正金銀行：貿易金融業務の開始と経営管理体制の構築」 *sōgyōki no Yokohama shōkin ginkō: bōeki kin'yū gyōmu no kaishi to keiei kanri taisei no kōchiku* ('The Yokohama Specie Bank at its Inception: The Start of the Business of Trade Finance and the Structure of its Management System'). 社会経済史学 *shakai keizaishi gaku* 78 (2): 223–45. https://doi.org/10.20624/sehs.78.2_223

Smethurst, Richard. 2006. 'Takahashi Korekiyo, the Rothschilds and the Russo-Japanese War, 1904–1907.' *The Rothschild Archive Review of the Year*, 20–5.

Smith, Grant H. 1998. *The History of the Comstock Lode*. 1st edn. Reno: University of Nevada Press.

Soetbeer, Adolf. 1877. *Bulletin de statistique et de législation comparée*, April, pp. 235–8.

Soto, Hernando de. 2000. *The Mystery of Capital: Why Capitalism Triumphs in the West and Fails Everywhere Else*. New York: Basic Books.

Spalding, William Frederick. 1915. *Foreign Exchange and Foreign Bills in Theory and in Practice*. 2nd impression. London: Sir Isaac Pitman & Sons, Ltd.

Spalding, William Frederick. 1917. *Eastern Exchange, Currency and Finance*. London: Sir I. Pitman & Sons, Ltd.

Spalding, William Frederick. 1922. *The London Money Market: A Practical Guide to What It Is, Where It Is, and the Operations Conducted in It*. London: Sir I. Pitman & sons, ltd.

Starkey, Samuel Cross. 1849. *A Dictionary, English and Punjabee, Outlines of Grammar, Also Dialogues, English and Punjabee*. Calcutta: D'Rozario.

Steinberg, John W. 2008. 'Was the Russo-Japanese War World War Zero?' *The Russian Review* 67 (1): 1–7. http://www.jstor.org/stable/20620667

Steinberg, John W., and David Wolff, eds. 2006. *The Russo-Japanese War in Global Perspective: World War Zero*. Vols. 29 and 40: *History of Warfare*. Leiden: Brill, 2005–7.

Sugihara Kaoru 杉原薫. 1985. 「アジア間貿易の形成と構造 (近代アジア貿易圏の形成と構造：19世紀後半～第一次大戦前を中心に)」 *Ajia-kan bōeki no keisei to kōzō (kindai Ajia bōekiken no keisei to kōzō: 19 seiki kōhan—dai ichiji taisenmae wo chūshin ni)* (The Formation and Structure of Intra-Asian Trade: With a Focus on the Second Half of the Nineteenth Century and the Period before World War I). 社會經濟史學 *Shakai keizaishigaku* 51 (1): 17–53. http://ci.nii.ac.jp/naid/110001213535

Sugihara Kaoru 杉原薫. 1996. 『アジア間貿易の形成と構造』 *Ajia-kan bōeki no keisei to kōzō* (The Formation and Structure of Intra-Asian Trade). ミネルヴァ書房 Minerva shobō.

Suizu Yakichi 水津彌吉. 1911. 『上海ニ於ケル金ニ就テ』 *Shanhai ni okeru kin ni tsuite* (About Gold in Shanghai). 横濱正金銀行. http://ci.nii.ac.jp/ncid/BA65550306

Sussman, Nathan, and Yishay Yafeh. 2000. 'Institutions, Reforms, and Country Risk: Lessons from Japanese Government Debt in the Meiji Era.' *The Journal of Economic History* 60 (02): 442–67. https://doi.org/10.1017/S0022050700025171

Suzuki, Toshio. 1994. *Japanese Government Loan Issues on the London Capital Market 1870–1913*. 1st edn. London: Athlone Press.

Suzuki Toshio 鈴木俊夫. 1998. 『金融恐慌とイギリス銀行業—ガーニィ商会の経営破綻』 *Kin'yū kyōkō to Igirisu ginkō gyō—Gānī shōkai no keiei hatan* (Financial Crisis and British Capital: The Business Failure of the Gurney Merchant House). 東京: 日本経済評論社 Tokyo: Nihon keizai hyōronsha.

Suzuki, Toshio. 2002. 'Japanese Government Loan Issues on the London Capital Market During the Interwar Period.' In Janet E. Hunter and S. Sugiyama (eds.), *The History of Anglo-Japanese Relations, 1600–2000: The History of Anglo-Japanese Relations, 1600–2000*, 183–218. London: Palgrave Macmillan UK.

Suzuki Toshio 鈴木俊夫. 2005. 「オリエンタル銀行設立の一齣」 *Orientaru Ginkō setsuritsu no hitokoma* (A Depiction of the Establishment of the Oriental Bank Corporation). 三田商学研究 *Mita shōgaku kenkyū* 48 (5): 41–61. http://ci.nii.ac.jp/naid/120000800144

Suzuki Toshio. 2012. 'The Rise and Decline of the Oriental Bank Corporation, 1842–84.' In Shizuya Nishimura, Toshio Suzuki, and Ranald C. Michie (eds.), *The Origins of International Banking in Asia*, 86–106. Oxford: Oxford University Press. http://www.oxfordscholarship.com/view/10.1093/acprof:oso/9780199646326.001.0001/acprof-9780199646326-chapter-4

Suzuki, Toshio 鈴木俊夫. 2014. 「東洋銀行　1842〜1884年」 *Tōyō ginkō 1842–1884nen* (The Oriental Bank, 1842–1884). In 『国際銀行とアジア　1870〜1913』, by 西村閑也, 鈴木俊夫, and 赤川元彰, 433–538. 東京: 慶応大学出版会.

Taira Tomoyuki 平智之. 1984a. 「第1次大戦前の国際金本位制下における横浜正金銀行−日銀の兌換制維持政策との関連において-上-」 *Dai ichiji taisen-mae no kokusai hon'iseika ni okeru Yokohama shōkin ginkō—nichigin no dakansei iji seisaku to no kanren ni oite* (jō) (The Yokohama Specie Bank under the Pre-World War I Gold Standard System—Related to the Policy of Defending Convertibility of Bank of Japan [notes] (part 1)). 金融経済 *Kin'yū keizai*, no. 208 (October): 41–81. http://ci.nii.ac.jp/naid/40000792001

Taira Tomoyuki 平智之. 1984b. 「第1次大戦前の国際金本位制下における横浜正金銀行−日銀の兌換制維持政策との関連において-下-」 *Dai ichiji taisen-mae no kokusai hon'iseika ni okeru Yokohama shōkin ginkō—nichigin no dakansei iji seisaku to no kanren ni oite (ge)* (The Yokohama Specie Bank under the Pre-World War I Gold Standard System—Related to the Policy of Defending Convertibility of Bank of Japan [notes] (part 2)). 金融経済 *Kin'yū keizai*, no. 209 (December): 1–27. http://ci.nii.ac.jp/naid/40000792007

Taira Tomoyuki 平智之. 1986. 「第一次大戦以前の対中国借款の投資主体」 *Dai ichiji taisen izen no tai-Chūgoku shakkan to tōshi shutai* (The Loans to and Investments in China before World War I). In Kokka shihon yushutsu kenkyūkai 国家資本輸出研究会, ed. 『日本の資本輸出・対中国借款の研究』 *Nihon no shihon yushutsu: tai-Chūgoku shakkan no kenkyū* (Japanese Capital Exports: A Study of the China Loans). Tokyo: Taga shuppan, 13–49.

Taira Tomoyuki 平智之. 1990. 「再建金本位制下の横浜正金銀行」 *Saiken kinhon'isei ka no Yokohama Shōkin Ginkō* (the Yokohama Specie Bank in the period of the restored gold standard). 経済と貿易 *Keizai to bōeki*, no. 152 (March): 30–60. http://ci.nii.ac.jp/naid/40000896831

Taira Tomoyuki 平智之. 1993. 「経済制裁下の横浜正金銀行−ニューヨーク支店を中心として」 *Keizai seisaika no Yokohama shōkin ginkō—nyūyōku shiten wo chūshin toshite* (The Yokohama Specie Bank Facing Economic Sanctions—With a Focus on the New York Office). 横浜市立大学論叢 社会科学系列 *Yokohama shiritsu daigaku ronsō shakai kagaku keiretsu* 44 (1): 117–46. http://ci.nii.ac.jp/naid/40003713128

Taira Tomoyuki 平智之. 1994. 「太平洋戦争下の横浜正金銀行(1)」 *Taiheiyō sensō-ka no Yokohama shōkin ginkō (1)* (The Yokohama Specie Bank during the Pacific War (1)). 横浜市立大学論叢 社会科学系列 *Yokohama shiritsu daigaku ronsō shakai kagaku keiretsu* 45 (3): 163–207. http://ci.nii.ac.jp/naid/40003713145

Taira Tomoyuki 平智之. 1995a. 「日中戦争期の日英経済関係と横浜正金銀行ロンドン支店」 *Nicchū sensōki no nichiei kankei to Yokohama shōkin ginkō* (Anglo-Japanese Relations during the Second Sino-Japanese War and the Yokohama Specie Bank). 横浜市立大学論叢 社会科学系列 *Yokohama shiritsu daigaku ronsō shakai kagaku keiretsu* 46 (2): 95–141. http://ci.nii.ac.jp/naid/40003712668

Taira Tomoyuki 平智之. 1995b. 「太平洋戦争下の横浜正金銀行(2)」 *Taiheiyō sensō-ka no Yokohama shōkin ginkō (2)* (The Yokohama Specie Bank during the Pacific War (2)). 横浜市立大学論叢 社会科学系列 *Yokohama shiritsu daigaku ronsō shakai kagaku keiretsu* 46 (1): 101–41. http://ci.nii.ac.jp/naid/40003713151

Takamura Naosuke 高村直助. 1968. 「日本紡績業の確立と構造(一)：1890～1900」 *Nihon bōsekigyō no kakuritsu to kōzō (1): 1890–1900* (The Establishment and Structure of the Japanese Spinning Industry (1): 1890–1900). 社會科學研究 *shakai kagaku kenkyū* 19 (4): 1–76. https://ci.nii.ac.jp/naid/110000463801

Tamaki Norio. 1990. 'The Yokohama Specie Bank: A Multinational in the Japanese Interest 1897–1931.' In Geoffrey Jones (ed.). *Banks as Multinationals*, 191–216. London: Routledge.

Tamura Hidemi 田村秀實. 1908. 『銀行實務誌』 *Ginkō jitsumu-shi* (The Journal of Banking Practice). 同文館 Dōbunkan. http://ci.nii.ac.jp/ncid/BA34286892

Tang, Ke, and Haoxiang Zhu. 2015. 'Commodities as Collateral.' SSRN Scholarly Paper ID 2355674. Rochester, NY: Social Science Research Network. http://papers.ssrn.com/abstract=2355674

Tashiro Meguru 田代循. 1902. 『銀行及外国為替論』 *Ginkō oyobi gaikoku kawase-ron* (A Theory of Banking and Foreign Exchange). 実業之日本社 Jitsugyō no Nihon-sha. http://ci.nii.ac.jp/ncid/BA60448153

Tate, William [from old catalog]. 1842. *The Modern Cambist, Forming a Manual of Foreign Exchanges*. 4th edn. London: E. Wilson.

Thiemeyer, Guido. 2007. *Internationalismus und Diplomatie. Währungspolitische Kooperation im europäischen Staatensystem 1865-1900*. München: Oldenbourg Wissenschaftsverlag.

Thierry, François. 2017. *Les monnaies de la Chine ancienne. Des origines à la fin de l'Empire*. 1st edn. Paris: Les Belles Lettres.

Tōkyō Ginkō 東京銀行. 19—. 『正金為替資金の史的発展』 *Shōkin kawase shikin no shiteki kenkyū* (Historical Studies in the Exchange Fund of the Specie Bank). 4 vols. 東京.

Tomita Gentarō 富田源太郎. 1894. 『外国為替の説明』 *Gaikoku kawase no setsumei* (An Explanation of Foreign Exchange). 東京: 富田源太郎.

Torgerson, Warren S. 1958. *Theory and Methods of Scaling*. New York: Wiley.

Tsuchiko Kinshirō 土子金四郎. 1895. 『外国為替詳解』 *Gaikoku kawase shōkai* (A Detailed Explanation of Foreign Exchange). 哲学書院 Tetsugaku shoin, 有斐閣 Yūhikaku (發賣). http://ci.nii.ac.jp/ncid/BN15396567

United States. 1903. *Stability of International Exchange: Report on the Introduction of the Gold-Exchange Standard into China and Other Silver-Using Countries.* Washington, DC: Government Printing Office.

United States. 1904. *Gold Standard in International Trade: Report on the Introduction of the Gold-Exchange Standard into China, the Philippine Islands, Panama, and Other Silver-Using Countries, and on the Stability of Exchange.* Washington, DC: Government Printing Office.

Vissering, Willem. 1877. *On Chinese Currency: Coin and Paper Money.* Leiden: E. J. Brill. http://archive.org/details/cu31924023306875

Vries, Jan de. 2008. *The Industrious Revolution: Consumer Behavior and the Household Economy, 1650 to the Present.* Cambridge: Cambridge University Press.

Wagel, Srinivas Ram. 1915. *Chinese Currency and Banking.* Shanghai: North-China Daily News & Herald. http://archive.org/details/chinesecurrencyb00wageuoft

Webster, Anthony. 2006. 'The Strategies and Limits of Gentlemanly Capitalism: The London East India Agency Houses, Provincial Commercial Interests, and the Evolution of British Economic Policy in South and South-East Asia 1800–50.' *The Economic History Review* 59 (4): 743–64. doi:10.1111/j.1468-0289.2006.00366.x

Webster, Anthony, Ulbe Bosma, and Jaime de Melo, eds. 2015. *Commodities, Ports and Asian Maritime Trade Since 1750.* 1st edn. London: Palgrave Macmillan.

Wenzlhuemer, Roland. 2012. *Connecting the Nineteenth-Century World: The Telegraph and Globalization.* Cambridge: Cambridge University Press.

White, Harry Owen, and Henry R Kinnear. 1903. *Exchange Calculations with Tables of Equivalents.* Shanghai: Oriental Press.

Williams, Talcott. 1897. 'Silver in China: And Its Relation to Chinese Copper Coinage.' *The Annals of the American Academy of Political and Social Science* 9: 43–63. https://www.jstor.org/stable/1009669

Willis, Henry Parker. 1968 [1901]. *A History of the Latin Monetary Union: A Study of International Monetary Action.* New York: Greenwood Press.

Winseck, Dwayne R., and Robert M. Pike. 2007. *Communication and Empire: Media, Markets, and Globalization, 1860-1930.* Durham: Duke University Press Books.

Yamaguchi Kazuo 山口和雄 and Katō Toshihiko 加藤俊彦. 1988. 『両大戦間の横浜正金銀行』 *Ryōtaisenkan no Yokohama shōkin ginkō* (The Yokohama Specie Bank in the Interbellum). 日本経営史研究所. http://ci.nii.ac.jp/ncid/BN03449032

Yasutomi Ayumu 安冨歩. 2003. 「香港上海銀行の資金構造, 1913年〜1941年」 *Honkon Shanhai ginkō no shikin kōzō, 1913-1941* (Flow-of-Funds within the Hongkong & Shanghai Banking Corporation, 1913–1941). アジア経済 *Ajia keizai* 44, no. 10 (October): 27–54.

Yasutomi Ayumu 安冨歩. 1997. 『「満洲国」の金融』 *'Manshūkoku' no kin'yū* (The Finances of 'Manchukuo'). Tōkyō: 創文社.

Yokohama-shi 横浜市. 1958-. 横浜市史 *Yokohama-shishi* (A History of the City of Yokohama). 横浜市. http://ci.nii.ac.jp/ncid/BN01627322

Yokohama Shōkin Ginkō 横浜正金銀行. 1898. 『第三拾七回半季報告』 *Dai-sanjū-nanakai hanki hōkokusho* (The 37th Semestrial Report). Yokohama (?).

Yokohama Shōkin Ginkō 横濱正金銀行. 1908. 『第壹東洋支店長会議録』 *Dai-ichi tōyō shitenchō kaigiroku* (The Transcripts of the First Meeting of the Eastern Branch Directors). [横浜正金銀行]. http://ci.nii.ac.jp/ncid/BN04887997

Yokohama Shōkin Ginkō 横濱正金銀行. 1909. 『東洋支店長会議録 第二回第一巻』. *Tōyō shitenchō kaigiroku dai-nikai dai-ikkan* (The Transcripts of the Meetings of the Eastern Branch Directors). [横浜正金銀行] (2nd meeting, Vol. 1). http://ci.nii.ac.jp/ncid/BN04887997

Yokohama Shōkin Ginkō 横濱正金銀行. 1920. 『横濱正金銀行史』 *Yokohama Shōkin Ginkōshi* (A History of the Yokohama Specie Bank). [横濱正金銀行]. Vol. 1-5. http://ci.nii.ac.jp/ncid/BA7808165X

Yokohama Shōkin Ginkō 横濱正金銀行. 1923. 『横濱正金銀行外國爲替実務見學報告書』 *Yokohama Shōkin Ginkō gaikoku kawase jitsumu kengaku hōkokusho* (A Report of the First-hand Observation of Foreign Exchange in the Yokohama Specie Bank). Yokohama (?). http://ci.nii.ac.jp/ncid/BA84845781

Yokohama Shōkin Ginkō 横濱正金銀行調査課. 1924. 『發行銀行引受手形信用状取引ノ法律關係』 *hakkō ginkō hikiuke tegata shin'yōjō torihiki no hōritsu kankei* (Legal Matters Concerning the Underwriting of Bills and the Handling of Letters of Credit in Banks of Issue). 横濱正金銀行調査課. Yokohama (?). http://ci.nii.ac.jp/ncid/BN14786464

Yokohama Shōkin Ginkō 横濱正金銀行調査課. 1931. 『銀行實務より見たる英國手形法解説』 *Ginkō jitsumu yori mitaru Eikoku tegata-hō kaisetsu* (An Explanation of British Law Concerning Negotiable Instruments from the Viewpoint of Banking Practice). 横浜正金銀行調査課. Yokohama (?). http://ci.nii.ac.jp/ncid/BA43172668

Yokouchi Masao 横内正雄. 1996. 「<論文>第一次大戦前のインドと東南アジアにおけるマーカンタイル銀行 (1)」 *[ronbun] dai-ichiji sensō-mae no Indo to tōnan Ajia ni okeru mākantairu ginkō* (Pre-World War I India and the Mercantile Bank in Southeast Asia). 経営志林 *Keiei shirin* 32 (4): 125-44. http://ci.nii.ac.jp/naid/110000063002

Yoshida Tsutomu 吉田勉. 2014. 「船舶技術に対するスエズ運河開通のインパクト」 *Senpaku gijutsu ni tai suru Suezu unga kaitsū no inpakuto* (The Impact of the Opening of the Suez Canal on Naval Technology). 技術と文明：日本産業技術史学会会誌 *Gijutsu to bunmei: Nihon sangyō gijutsu shigakukai kaishi* (*Journal of the Japan Society for the History of Industrial Technology*) 19 (1): 21-33. http://ci.nii.ac.jp/naid/40020250771

Yoshino Toshihiko 吉野俊彦. 1974. 『忘れられた元日銀総裁：富田鉄之助伝』 *Wasurerareta moto nichigin sōsai: Tomita Tetsunosuke-den* (A Forgotten Former Governor of the Bank of Japan: The Biography of Tomita Tetsunosuke). 東洋経済新報社 Tōyō keizai shinpōsha. http://ci.nii.ac.jp/ncid/BN10133210

Yoshihara Tatsuyuki 蔭原達之. 1979. 「横浜正金銀行における「連合的営業法」の創設と展開」 *Yokohama shōkin ginkō ni okeru 'rengōteki eigyōhō' no sōsetsu to tenkai* (The Origins and Development of the 'Combinatory Management Style' in the Yokohama Specie Bank). 経営史学 *Keieishi-gaku* 13 (3): 41-60. http://ci.nii.ac.jp/naid/40000827988

Yoshihara Tatsuyuki 蔭原達之. 1995. 「明治前・中期の横浜正金銀行」 *Meiji zen-chūki no Yokohama Shōkin Ginkō* ('The Yokohama Specie Bank in the Early- and Mid-Meiji-period'). In Masada Ken'ichirō (ed.). 正田健一郎 『日本における近代社会の形成』 *Nihon ni okeru kindai shakai no keisei* (The Formation of Modern Society in Japan), 261-86. Tokyo: 三嶺書房.

Index

Note: Tables and figures are indicated by an italic "*t*" and "*f*", respectively, following the page number.